A Race Against Time

A RACE AGAINST TIME

The Crisis in Urban Schooling

▣　　▣　　▣

edited by
JAMES G. CIBULKA
WILLIAM LOWE BOYD

CONTEMPORARY STUDIES IN SOCIAL AND POLICY ISSUES IN EDUCATION:
THE DAVID C. ANCHIN CENTER SERIES

Kathryn M. Borman, *Series Editor*

Westport, Connecticut
London

Library of Congress Cataloging-in-Publication Data

A race against time : the crisis in urban schooling / edited by James G. Cibulka and
William Lowe Boyd.
      p.   cm. — (Contemporary studies in social and policy issues in education)
      Includes bibliographical references (p.) and index.
      ISBN 1-56750-640-2 (alk. paper)
      1. Education, Urban—United States. 2. School improvement programs—
United States. I. Cibulka, James G. II. Boyd, William Lowe, 1935– III. Series.
      LC5131 .R33   2003
      370′.9173′2—dc21   2002026964

British Library Cataloguing in Publication Data is available.

Library of Congress Catalog Card Number: 2002026964
ISBN: 1-56750-640-2

First published in 2003

Praeger Publishers, 88 Post Road West, Westport, CT 06881
An imprint of Greenwood Publishing Group, Inc.
www.praeger.com

Printed in the United States of America

◻   ◻   ◻

contents

Introduction

urban education reform: competing approaches

JAMES G. CIBULKA

WILLIAM LOWE BOYD

The social and economic transformation of large American cities after World War II laid the seeds for the crisis in urban education that has festered and grown since the 1950s. The migration of poor, disadvantaged minorities into the cities and the exodus of businesses, industry, and the middle class to the suburbs set the stage for today's growing crisis. Decades of appalling test scores and failure rates, and of unsuccessful piecemeal efforts to improve urban education, have led to acute cynicism and despair. What is new today is a growing willingness, on the part of the public and policy-makers, to embrace radical solutions to reform or, indeed, even replace urban school systems (Boyd 2000). Thus, we truly are in a "race against time," both to save urban children from educational failure and to rescue and reform large urban school systems before people give up on them.

The growing support for radical solutions is exemplified by the increasing African-American support in urban areas for charter schools and voucher plans. Indeed, younger African Americans are increasingly viewing school choice and vouchers as a "civil rights" issue (Wilgoren 2000), a position articulately championed by the burgeoning Black Alliance for Educational Options (BAEO). Support for radical solutions is also seen in the mounting calls for states to "breakup" or "takeover" failing urban school systems. Pennsylvania's takeover of the Philadelphia school system, in December 2001, added "privatization" to these impulses. Governor Schweiker directed the School Reform Commission imposed by the state to "contract out" the management of at least 60 schools in Philadelphia, and to hire the for-profit Edison Schools firm to direct or assist with the overall management of the school system.

These radical developments come after two decades of sustained reform efforts that have not produced dramatic improvements, particularly in the large urban school systems, which are considered to be the weakest units in American education. Commentators generally agree about three "waves" of school reform that followed the release of the famous *A Nation at Risk* report in 1983. The first wave to respond to the report's warning of a "rising tide of mediocrity" in American education was characterized as an "intensification" effort. But steps to increase the intensity and effectiveness of the existing educational system were quickly deemed inadequate. Instead, it was argued that a second wave of reform devoted to a fundamental "restructuring" of American schools was needed to make them more effective. By 1990, however, this piecemeal effort to restructure our schools, one by one, began to be replaced by a third wave's call for a comprehensive strategy of "systemic reform."

Systemic reformers are trying to maintain the momentum of their wave via the vast accountability movement harnessed to state academic standards and high-stakes testing. But a fourth wave of reform—controversial especially among public educators and their unions—is increasingly growing around the school choice and privatization movement. As long ago as 1988, it was possible to see that a "politics of excellence and choice" was emerging and beginning to transform the American education policy debate (Boyd and Kerchner 1988). Recent developments suggest that, for better or worse, the politics of American education will increasingly revolve around a "politics of reforming or replacing public schools." The latter strategy, likely to be especially evident in our large cities, reflects the growing desire for quality education and school choice in a less bureaucratized, more diversified, and competitive delivery system for education (Boyd 2000; Hill and Celio 1998; Hill, Campbell, and Harvey 2000).

This book presents case studies and analysis of reform efforts in seven large cities (Baltimore, Boston, Chicago, Los Angeles, Philadelphia, Washington, D.C., and New York), plus Michael Kirst and Katrina Bulkley's discussion of mayoral takeovers and Heinrich Mintrop's assessment of the role of sanctions in Maryland's accountability system. The focus here is on three leading approaches to "rescuing" urban school systems: *systems reform, increased mayoral influence*, and *external intervention*. Before turning to the organizing framework for this book, in which we describe these approaches and outline their strengths and weaknesses, we should address some of the concerns that may spring to readers' minds about a book focused on seven case studies and three reform approaches. First, while generalizations are not possible from seven case studies, these are major cities whose reform efforts both reflect and influence the leading trends in American urban education. Second, we acknowledge that two of the three approaches are *governance* reforms more than *educational* reforms, and that all three may fail to adequately increase the *institutional, educational*, and *civic capacities* needed for fundamental improvement. This is a central theme that we explore in our final chapter, where we analyze what can be learned from the cases presented here and conclude that the strengths and weaknesses of the three reform approaches suggest what will be required to achieve the necessary *capacities*.

Beyond the concerns noted above about the three governance reforms, another objection is that they fail to address the frequently, and sometimes disgracefully, inadequate funding of our urban school systems, especially in view of their great needs (Kozol 1991). Consequently, there are those who claim that our urban school systems would be doing much better, if only we spent what was deserved on them. We agree that adequate funding must be part of any comprehensive solution. Yet, ample funding by itself is far from a complete answer, as demonstrated by Kansas City (Ciotti 1998; Gewertz 2000). As a result of an extraordinary court-ordered desegregation plan, Kansas City was able to spend $2 billion over 12 years, beginning in 1985, to improve its school system:

> Kansas City spent as much as $11,700 per pupil—more money per pupil, on a cost of living adjusted basis, than any other of the 280 largest districts in the country. The money bought higher teachers' salaries, 15 new schools, and such amenities as an Olympic-sized swimming pool with an underwater viewing room, television and animation studios, a robotics lab, a 25-acre wildlife sanctuary, a zoo, a model United Nations with simultaneous translation capability, and field trips to Mexico and Senegal. The student–teacher ratio was 12 or 13 to 1, the lowest of any major school district in the country. The results were dismal. Test scores did not rise; the black–white gap did not diminish; and there was less, not greater, integration. (Ciotti 1998, 1)

Both Ciotti (1998) and Gewertz (2000) indicate that much of the money in Kansas City was spent unwisely, with insufficient attention to professional development and improved teaching and learning. But that again supports the view that big urban districts generally lack the capacity to overcome their problems and improve performance, perhaps even when allowed, as in this rare case, to "throw money" at their problems. Consequently, we conclude—along with many others who have researched school improvement—that reforms must focus heavily on fundamental capacity building (O'Day, Goertz, and Floden 1995).

The seven case studies in this book are grouped and presented in sections corresponding to each of the three governance approaches, which we discuss below in some detail.

ORGANIZING FRAMEWORK:
THREE APPROACHES TO GOVERNANCE REFORM

The three approaches to reforming the governance of urban school systems discussed here are not mutually exclusive; they can be combined and in practice have been in many cities. Yet each approach—*systems reform, increased mayoral influence,* and *external intervention*—has a separate logic. That is, each makes somewhat different assumptions about what aspects of the education governance system need to be reformed, which solution(s) will accomplish this reform, and how the solution(s) will lead to improved performance of urban school systems. Moreover, the coalitions that support each reform idea, while sometimes overlapping, are in some respects different. Each reform approach has had particular periods of popularity and, in some cases, disenchantment with one has promoted growing interest in other governance approaches. In that sense, these reform approaches are competing.

Systems Reform

Perhaps the first clearly articulated advocacy of a systems approach to education reform came from Smith and O'Day (1991). They argued that the restructuring movement was not an adequate response to the first wave of education reform following publication of *A Nation at Risk* (1983). By the late 1980s, it became apparent that improving educational inputs such as expanding graduate requirements, extending the school year, and so on had not led to fundamental alterations in either the nature of classroom practices or student achievement outcomes. Yet Smith and O'Day quarreled with the assumptions of the "second-wave" reforms intended to remedy these policy shortcomings. "Bottom-up" reform focused on restructuring at the school level was not an adequate antidote to earlier "top-down" reform. Instead, they said, there was a need for a coherent systemic strategy to assure that second-wave reforms at the school level could be generalized to all schools within a state.

Smith and O'Day (1991) believed that the way to spur reform in classrooms and schools was to improve the centralized elements of the system, particularly the states. This systemic approach touched on "the administrative, governance, resource, and policy barriers to effective schooling in the USA" (p. 235). They identified the fragmented nature of the formal and informal policy system as an impediment. Among the elements requiring improved alignment, they argued, are curriculum, professional development, accountability assessment systems, and support services.

Systemic reform had the effect of shifting policy reformers' attention to the interaction of different components of the policy system. While Smith and O'Day saw its application primarily at the state level, they argued that the strategy could transform the education system at all levels. Thus, the idea of systems reform was applied within local school systems. For example, the National Science Foundation launched a funding program, the Urban Systems Initiative, to assist urban school systems in this effort. In addition, the linkage between state and local policies has been a preoccupation of state education policy-makers. Similarly, federal policy-makers have been concerned that state and federal policies should be aligned.

As the concept of systems reform has evolved, however, it has become less a tight theoretical framework and more a loose collection of ideas about aligning the different elements of the education policy system. Therefore, the specific components of the policy system vary, as do the strategies for strengthening and aligning them. Certainly the emphasis on accountability became a more dominant feature of the model as the 1990s progressed, largely in response to external pressure on the educational system from business, political leaders, and the public. Standards, high-stakes assessments, performance-based contracts, and a number of other strategies are part of this accountability emphasis. Some reformers are convinced that external accountability must be the primary driver of systemic change. However, others who work from a systems perspective focus more on aspects of the systems model that enhance the capacity of the educational system, such as professional development. In other words, within the systems-reform perspective, genuine tensions can be found.

Initially, Smith and O'Day called for curricular frameworks as a central strategy for creating "a coherent system of instructional guidance" (p. 247). Over time, the call for rigorous content and performance standards for students supplanted the focus on curricular frameworks, although in various states and localities these linguistic labels mean different things. Nonetheless, the role of standards has become a central feature of the systems approach—both standards for students and for professionals (Fuhrman 2001). Virtually all states have adopted some form of standards, and many local school systems have added their own. The development of standards also has encouraged many states to try to align their assessments with the standards. There is a vast and growing literature on standards and their role in high-stakes assessments (Heubert and Hauser 1999). This is not the place to review that literature, except to point out that standards-based reform fits within a broader theory of systemic change. For systems theorists, standards are important not only in and of themselves. Equally important, they can guide the redesign of curriculum, guide professional development, and inform efforts to assess student outcomes.

The interlocking causal connections among these components places a heavy burden on the systems approach, because of its complexity and the resultant difficulty in implementing such reforms, even if one succeeds in getting them adopted. Not only are there many elements of the policy system to change, but also the sequence and timing of the changes can be important to the success of the outcome.

Some core assumptions of the systems approach transcend its various emphases and applications. First, systems reform is built upon rationalistic assumptions about the policy system. The premise is that the fragmentation in the policy system represents a failure to design a tightly interlocking policy system. Systems reformers tend to approach the redesign as a technical planning problem of organization and coordination. The "model" assumes that those in authority at the top of the system must redesign it to provide the appropriate balance between "top-down" and "bottom-up" approaches. This technical orientation is not surprising, because systems reform is professional in its orientation, reflecting the concerns and priorities of educators; the variables given attention focus on the internal dimensions of the educational policy system. For example, the need for additional resources as a means of building the capacity of the educational system often is an expected but unstated assumption of this approach.

Political dimensions of the policy system are downplayed—the legal and political realities of the intergovernmental system, differences of political interests and ideologies among stakeholders, and the issue of whether there is the political will to redesign the educational system, given the array of vested interests in the educational institution. In fact, political variables are exogenous to the systems model. They arise only insofar as they affect the adoption and implementation of systems reform. Smith and O'Day (1991) reflect this policy orientation over a political one with this comment:

> Perhaps the most important single change in the educational governance system in many states would be to move the policy debate to a point where it is considering the substantive—and to a lesser extent the political—aspects of alternative, well-formed and long-term policies and strategies. (p. 257)

Systems reform also assumes that the basic features of the institutional framework for public schooling in the United States that were installed by progressives and their allies roughly a century ago should remain intact. These are tacit assumptions, for some things are never mentioned. For instance, it is assumed that publicly supported schools should continue to be government operated. Also, the governance arrangements concerning political and fiscal control are not questioned. In most places, progressive reformers were successful in insulating educational systems from direct political oversight, hoping to stem patronage and political pressures on schools from elected political officials. Ideally, this meant independent elections for school boards, nonpartisanship, elimination of district or ward representation, separate taxing powers for school districts, and a variety of related institutional features to assure that school systems would be administered by qualified professionals and governed by civic elites. Of course, the model did not get implemented fully in all jurisdictions. Even though many of the reforms were targeted at perceived abuses in central cities, it was here that implementation of the progressive model was most uneven. A small number of mayors such as those in Baltimore continued to have control over the public school system. The mayor still appoints school boards in some cities. Mayors and city councils often have the right to review or approve school-system budgets, to retain taxing authority, or both. Significantly, none of these arrangements have been given attention by systems reformers because such governance arrangements are not viewed as the impediments to effective institutional performance. The challenge, as they see it, is to create a coherent set of policies that act together as a "system," impelling reform.

Strong Mayoral Roles

Other reformers, however, do question the institutional arrangements in which urban school systems are embedded. Urban mayors have been among the most vocal advocates of returning more authority to them. They argue that public school systems are one of the major institutions of the city, consuming vast resources and helping to determine the city's economic and social viability. Yet they have been closed off from the ability to influence the priorities and performance of public schools through institutional arrangements that they view as ill-suited to contemporary needs. They favor restoring greater accountability to them through governance reform.

The political machines that once dominated many American cities have disappeared or are in significant decline. Thus, the reunification of public schools with other city institutions, under political control, would not necessarily lead to the political abuses that prevailed at the turn of the last century. Citizens enjoy a higher level of education and are now less dependent on politicians to meet basic needs or to intervene on their behalf with government. It is a truism to say that people today have access to a broader range of information than people did before the advent of radio and television, not to mention the Internet. Political parties also have weakened, while interest groups have gained importance in shaping governmental decision-making. All of these changes have undermined political machines. Moreover, mayors are themselves better educated than their predecessors. Many hold college degrees and even advanced degrees. They are conversant with managerial principles, economics, and other requirements for running a modern city. They are articulate spokespersons for the long-term needs of their cities.

Mayors, by virtue of their role as the chief spokesperson for the city, also have direct access to business, labor, civic, and community leaders of the city. Many of these political constituencies help to elect the mayor and may be dependent on the mayor to support something they value. Mayors have the potential to unify the diverse concerns of these stakeholders around a common direction for the city.

Of course, not everyone agrees with these arguments for reintegrating schools with other political institutions. Despite the societal changes that reduce the potential for problems, some of the same issues arise. When schools are integrated into city government, they may be in more direct competition with other city services for budget support. Mayoral interest may wane, or the election of a new mayor may introduce the same kind of instability in school policy-making that comes with frequent superintendent turnover. Arguably, the principle of mayoral control also weakens representativeness, by reducing the voice of school boards. This may prove unpopular with groups that have acquired strong voices on school boards, such as advocacy groups, minority groups, and unions.

Here we see at play a long-standing tension at the local level between the principle of executive leadership and representative democracy. The tension is built into the very fabric of municipal governments, because some cities favor strong executive controls for mayors or city managers, while others invest greater authority in city councils as the legislative branch responsive to the people. Giving mayors greater influence and control over school affairs raises the same arguments, even though mayoral power is just as much an assault on the established power of educational bureaucracies.

However, there is very little evidence on the effects of mayoral influence over public school systems or on their potential to accelerate their reform. Educational historians have concluded that the preoccupation with governance in American education reform may be misplaced (Tyack 1974). Until recently, most political scientists gave little credence to differences in governance structures as a predictor of governmental performance. Working from a behaviorist perspective, they assumed that political culture is a more powerful predictor of institutional performance than formal governance arrangements. But in recent decades the importance of institutions as a factor that can affect governmental performance has received renewed emphasis (March and Olsen 1989). The "new institutionalism" has focused on not merely the formal structures of government, but the interlocking regulatory, normative, and cognitive features of institutions that give them such pervasive power and stability. In the case of urban school systems, it has been noted that their institutional features make them highly resistant to change (Cibulka 1996). Hess (1999) uses the analogy of a "spinning wheel" to convey how such institutions are adept at generating a succession of new programs and initiatives without really changing or reforming in significant, durable ways. Working from a broadly institutional perspective, Wong and colleagues (herein) observe the growing fragmentation in urban school systems, for which "integrated governance" is an antidote.

Not all political scientists, however, are convinced of the merits of institutional approaches to reform. Rich's (1996) research in Detroit, Gary, Indiana, and Newark portrays a "public school cartel" controlled by professional educators, school-board members, and community activists for which mayoral influence is not a sufficient counterweight. While Stone, Henig, Jones, and Pierannunzi (2001) give qualified endorsement to an increased role for mayors in the governance of urban schools, they do not see its benefits in managerial or accountability terms. Rather, they prefer to focus on the need for building a substantial civic coalition, for which mayoral influence can be an asset. If the research evidence is not clear, the support for giving mayors influence over public schools nevertheless comes from a political movement launched by mayors and their allies, such as business leaders.

External Intervention

If mayors may need to intervene, what about higher levels of government? One of the checks and balances designed into our federal system is shared authority among units of government, as well as division of power among branches of government. The idea that no branch of government, nor any unit, should have plenary power is inherent in federalism. This division generally was defended as preventing the tyranny of the majority, analogous to the abuses of unbridled monarchial power.

A special circumstance arising out of this principle of checks and balances occurs when a lower level of government, such as a municipality or a special-purpose government, appears to require intervention by a higher level because of one or another failure of public performance. Any number of circumstances may arise. For example, public officials may be expropriating public money for private purposes or the unit of government may be unable to meet its financial obligations to creditors. Since in most states these local units are administrative contrivances of the state, created to carry out the state's purposes, the state ordinarily has statutory authority to intervene to correct the problem. Sometimes this intervention involves judicial oversight, if laws have been broken and legal challenges or charges have been brought against the government or its officials.

The remedy ordinarily involves the creation of some temporary external oversight body such as a board, or in the case of the courts, a special master. After the problem has been rectified, the original governance arrangements are restored. When New York City experienced a fiscal crisis in 1975 and nearly went bankrupt, the U.S. Congress provided a temporary line of credit to the state of New York, not New York City. In addition, the state legislature created the Municipal Assistance Corporation and the Emergency Financial Control Board, which sharply curtailed the policy-making authority of the mayor, the Board of Estimate, and other elected officials (David and Kantor 1979; Peterson 1981). Eventually, full authority was restored to the city to manage its own affairs. The Illinois state legislature created a School Finance Authority in 1979 with final budgetary authority when the Chicago Public School System came close to defaulting on its financial obligations. Again, this entity eventually was eliminated. In 1988, New Jersey utilized its authority to take over the management and governance of Newark (and other city school systems in the state) due to alleged fraud by public officials. They replaced the board of education and superintendent and actually assumed oversight of operations. However, this takeover was not envisioned as a permanent assumption of local responsibilities, but rather an intervention designed to restore local government to proper functioning.

On occasion, external oversight leads to an entirely new set of permanent governance arrangements, because of actions taken by a state legislature, after which the external oversight is reduced or removed altogether. An example of this, in Baltimore, is discussed in this book. In 1997,
Maryland officials insisted on restructuring the governance and management of the entire Baltimore school system, and retained some long-term
oversight.

State identification and intervention in low-performing schools represents a more recent variation of the oversight approach. Here the focus is
on failure to perform at minimally satisfactory levels, rather than financial
mismanagement or personal dishonesty. Because states have the constitutional responsibility for public education, they have a legitimate interest
in assuring that these constitutional obligations are met.

The use of high-stakes tests to impose sanctions takes the systems approach to reform a step farther. In that model, as laid out originally by
Smith and O'Day, there were no consequences attached to the use of student assessments. Their role was informational, and the assumption was
that such information on student performance would lead school officials
to improve their performance. As applied within the oversight-and-inter-
vention approach, accountability carries consequences, in this case sanctions for poor performance. These sanctions, as the change theory goes,
will create incentives for school officials to improve their performance.

A growing number of states now have some program to intervene
when they identify schools that perform poorly on state measures. Typically, there are a number of levels of intervention. Failure to improve as
specified under targets set by the state triggers a more serious level of
oversight. Eventually, the state can close or take over schools that do not
improve. This has happened in Maryland, where four Baltimore City
schools moved from "reconstitution eligibility" to actual "reconstitution"
and now are being run by private contractors. The Maryland program is
discussed later in this book, in the chapter by Heinrich Mintrop.

External oversight from a higher unit of government generally bears a
heavy burden of proof as to its legitimacy, because it upsets the normal
functioning of democratic institutions and arguably disrupts local democratic processes. Rarely do local officials accept the intervention as legitimate, and often it is unpopular with the citizenry. However, state officials
can justify their actions in terms of a larger state purpose and can call
upon support from broader coalitions than those within the local jurisdiction. This having been said, the political support for external intervention
is bound to be fragile. Often it involves the imposition of an undemocrati-
cally selected oversight body. In the case of state intervention in failing
schools, a related problem arises in establishing an oversight approach
that appears to bring superior expertise to help failing schools improve.
States have taken different approaches to this problem, including the cre-

ation of panels of peers, use of state monitors, and assignment of a "distinguished educator" to work within the poorly performing school until it improves.

Like the mayoral approach, external oversight and intervention does not directly posit what should be done to improve school or system performance. This is left to the mayor or the state interveners. Such an approach moves away from specific attention as to which elements of the policy system need reforming—curriculum, professional development, and so on. These decisions come only after authority is relinquished to the mayor or interveners. This void in the theory of change raises a certain risk. If the mayor makes the wrong assumptions about how to improve system performance, or is inept in pursuing the reforms, the mayoral strategy may fail. Similarly, if state interveners have no specific ideas as to how to bring about improved performance, the legitimacy of their intervention is likely to plummet. In both cases, the second-level concerns are outside the parameters of the required governance changes. Yet their execution is essential to achievement of the reforms sought by mayors and state officials. Just as systems reform tends to ignore the important role that politics can play in governance reform, leaving it out of its zone of attention, these last two approaches are incomplete as well. Combining the strategies may be one answer, as many cities have tried to do, but only to the degree that they prove compatible with one another.

In 2002, the U.S. Congress passed new federal legislation in response to George W. Bush's program "No Child Left Behind" (2000). This landmark legislation requires states to intervene in low-performing schools that fail to improve, based on state assessments of student performance in reading and mathematics. Moreover, states that fail to follow the federal requirements are subject to sanctions in the form of a loss of federal aid, which itself constitutes a form of external intervention.

Like mayoral reform strategies, external intervention has its critics. The limits of the courts in enforcing change from outside have been widely noted (e.g., Kirp 1982). Stone, Henig, Jones, and Pierannunzi (2001) also note that external interventions tend to lose steam, generate backlashes, and erode indigenous forces for systemic reform. Despite such criticisms, external intervention is a powerful political impulse in our body politic when the legitimacy of governmental performance is questioned. It allows elected officials to make necessary changes, but with the appearance of external accountability.

Table I.1 summarizes the essential similarities and differences we observe among these three approaches to governance reform. It is important to note that the table lists the assumptions concerning the efficacy of these three approaches. How the reforms work in practice is the task of this book. Readers interested in our assessment of how the reforms worked in the seven cities, and the implications we draw from this, can

TABLE I.1

KEY ASSUMPTIONS AMONG THREE APPROACHES TO GOVERNANCE REFORM: ESSENTIAL SIMILARITIES AND DIFFERENCES

	THREE GOVERNANCE APPROACHES		
Key questions	*Systems reform*	*Increased mayoral influence*	*External intervention*
What aspects of the education governance system need to be reformed?	Fragmentation of policy system	Lack of accountability to mayors	System requires outside intervention to restore performance
Which solution(s) will accomplish this reform?	Alignment of separate policy strands and subsystems	Authority over governance and decision-making	New authorities and/or structures to provide oversight, often imposed temporarily
How will the solution(s) lead to improved performance of urban school systems?	Will make the system more rational and improve capacity for goal achievement	Mayoral responsibility will raise institutional performance	Intervention will restore accountability and raise institutional performance

jump to our concluding chapter and then go back and read the intervening chapters. Or they can read the interesting cases first and then see if they agree with our assessment.

■ ■ ■

PART ONE

Systems Reforms of
Urban School Systems

◨   ◨   ◨

CHAPTER ONE

Accountability at the Improv

brief sketches of school reform in Los Angeles

CHARLES TAYLOR KERCHNER
DAVID MENEFEE-LIBEY

F ROM THE JESTER IN THE COURT of Henry VIII to Robin Williams in a night-club, entertainers have turned situational spontaneity into an art form. Reacting to a simple prop or a line hurled from the audience creates exciting cabaret. Improvisation also makes exciting school politics, and it is currently continuing a long-running engagement in Los Angeles, site of the nation's second-largest school system. Improvisation has been turned from simple situational responsiveness to a decades-long series of events that raised interest group and due-process accountability to high consciousness. However, improvisation does not produce durable institutional reform or create a system of schools capable of sustainable improvement. Although improvisation as a managerial form is recognizable to any seasoned school administrator and to students of policy familiar with "muddling through" or "street-level bureaucrat" concepts of leadership, it is at best an incomplete solution. In this chapter we follow the course of improvisational politics in Los Angeles over two decades, note its accomplishments and failings, and in the conclusion point to important amendments in political and institutional theory suggested by this case history.

Nominally and officially, the Los Angeles Unified School District (LAUSD) is a monument to Progressive Era rational design. Driven by the politics of water, the city annexed its suburbs and the school district took on a similar configuration: 54 miles long with a mountain range in the middle. Its 711,187 students attend 663 schools. It employs about 35,000 teachers and has a total staff of over 75,000. Its operation and governance are separate from the surrounding municipal government and the five-person school board runs by geographic area, but not under party label. The district's operating budget approaches $7.5 billion and it is the city's second largest employer. LAUSD possesses a massive bureaucracy and in many respects it is highly insular, but to stop with such a common description of large public organizations is to miss the effects of two decades of improvisation in which the district has lost control of many of its core functions.

Within the improvisational sketches in Los Angeles we find many of the themes recognized by modern organizationalists: disjointed incrementalism, bureaucratic entrepreneurship, and nascent network forms of organizations. Thus LAUSD is both a shadow of its former bureaucratic self and a vision of what we might view as a *system of schools* rather than a *school system*. Of singular interest is the ways in which accountability appears to have changed in reaction to external stimuli.

IMPROVISATIONAL REFORM: THE DOMINANT GENRE

Just as improvisational theater traces its lineage to vaudeville and far older traditions, improvisational school reform has a relatively long history in America. David Tyack traces the full flowering of the practice to the 1940s and '50s, when the NAACP and other African-American civil rights organizations began to achieve success in their long campaign for equal justice under the law. Other groups seeking changes in the nation's schools followed their example, particularly imitating their strategy of simultaneously taking many avenues to the same goal. "When local officials were deaf to their demands, activists pursued a variety of tactics. They took to the streets to protest, sought media coverage, lobbied Congress and state legislatures for new laws, and litigated in federal and state courts" (Tyack 1993, 18). To this inventory we could add ballot initiatives, labor–management collective bargaining, electing sympathetic representatives to school boards and other offices, conducting and publicizing public-interest research, and so on. As the sketches below suggest, the list is as limitless as the American political imagination.

John Chubb and Terry Moe argue that such diverse activism only makes sense, given the way we govern our schools. They note that federal, state, and a variety of local governments in the United States all share legitimate constitutional authority over school policy-making. In our responsive democratic political system, these governments "all inevitably come under pressure from organized groups and constituents to put their authority to use" (Chubb and Moe 1990, 39). As policy-makers have responded to such pressure, education policy has come to involve more levels of government involved in more ways than almost any other policy type (rivaled perhaps only by health care). Those governments use policy instruments ranging from mandates to rights to entitlements and beyond.

As activists press such programs in whatever arena they find most congenial, they face few incentives to reconcile their reform proposals either with existing institutions or with other reform proposals (Menefee-Libey, Diehl, Lipsitz, and Rahimtoola 1997; Tyack and Cuban 1995). With so many opportunities for policy initiative and veto, their activism for change tends to be ad hoc and constant. Thus, the drama of improvisational politics has become the dominant genre of school reform.

It is easy to be cynical about this politics. Its constant and improvisational form means that few reforms have an opportunity to be fully implemented before the next reform comes along to modify it. Any given reform stands only a small chance of reaching into the classroom and changing the way teaching and learning take place (Elmore 1993). Frederick Hess has recently joined a long line of scholars demonstrating that the constant "policy churn" of shallow, symbolic initiatives is difficult even for the most experienced and best-intentioned of school reformers to avoid (Hess 1999).

Yet David Tyack and Larry Cuban insistently remind us that such reforms have a cumulative effect. Though no single reform is implemented thoroughly, the system *has* changed dramatically since the dominant Progressive template was established early last century (Tyack and Cuban 1995). There are also indications in the sketches that follow that the *politics* of school reform has been affected as well. Each successive group of reform activists must compete not only with simultaneous proposals from other groups, but also with the accumulation of established programs and a growing public skepticism about the latest educational fad. (For a related analysis of administrative reform in the federal government, see Light [1997].) Activists may still lack incentives to reconcile their reforms with one another, but they face growing incentives to propose initiatives that can genuinely improve schools in some concrete ways. The run of improvisational school-reform politics may not end soon, but the act is growing stale.

IMPROVISATIONAL SKETCH 1: POROUS BOUNDARIES, CHALLENGED AUTHORITY, AND CATEGORICAL ACCOUNTABILITY

Beginning with a 1970 desegregation case, LAUSD has become increasingly controlled or influenced from outside its organizational boundaries (*Mary Ellen Crawford et al.* [on behalf of all Negro and Mexican-American pupils] *v. Los Angeles City Board of Education* 17 Cal. 3rd 280 [1976]). Desegregation, court monitoring, and the rise of critical school-watching groups such as the ACLU effectively stripped independent rule-making authority from the central office and had the effect of legitimating race- and ethnic-based interest groups. From the Black and Hispanic caucuses formed by the district itself to the San Fernando Valley organization, BUSTOP—designed to halt mandatory student busing—school politics became increasingly racialized. Passage of collective-bargaining legislation in 1976 transformed the United Teachers of Los Angeles (UTLA) from a sometimes-effective gadfly union to a powerful political organization. The combination of the *Serrano v. Priest* (487 Pacific 2d 1241 [1971]) tax-equity decision and Proposition 13, a property-tax-limitation measure passed in 1978, created the fiscal crisis that forced the state to centralize school finance. The state contributes only 61 percent of the district's operating revenue (local, 23.5 percent; federal, 12.5 percent), but tax-limitation measures make raising local revenues extremely difficult. Changes in operating revenue are almost all dependent on "the one big school board" in Sacramento.

Ironically, having lost control of its personnel, its rule-making capacity, and its finances, the district entered a period where school board members became highly visible. Some used the board as a stepping-stone to higher political office. Three are particularly memorable. Kathleen Brown, daughter of one governor and sister of a soon-to-be one, was elected to the board in 1972. She went on to become state treasurer and run unsuccessfully for the governorship. Diane Watson, a former teacher in the district, became the lightning rod for integration and the symbol of a generation of activist Black politicians. She is now in her third term as a state senator. Bobbie Fiedler, a San Fernando Valley activist in BUSTOP, became Watson's sparring partner over integration issues. Fiedler rode the wave of conservatism into the U.S. House of Representatives for two terms.

The public face of the school district during this era became one of lawsuits, sound bites, and increasingly well-defined interest-group and racial politics. Accountability was attached to categories, and the management of the category system created its own, tightly coupled compliance system (Meyer and Rowan 1978; Weick 1976). This was true for the streams of resources that went into the federal and state categorical programs, desegregation orders, and the collective-bargaining contracts of teachers and other employees. Categorical rules were reinforced by increasingly apparent political advocacy that evaluated school leadership by its responsiveness to equity concerns and challenges, and accountability was expressed in equity terms: the racial balance of a student body, the balance between students and staff, procedural openness and access, representation on committees, staff, and the central administration.

However, by the mid-1980s Los Angeles was swept into the new politics of excellence that emerged in the wake of *A Nation at Risk* (National Commission on Excellence in Education 1983). As with the turn to equity politics, the precipitating leadership did not come from within the school district.

IMPROVISATIONAL SKETCH 2: THE POLITICS OF EXCELLENCE AND TEST-SCORE ACCOUNTABILITY

In 1982 Bill Honig, a wealthy former advertising executive turned teacher and school administrator, was elected state school superintendent. He introduced curriculum frameworks, pushed for school restructuring, and promised incentive rewards for achievement gains. S.B. 813, the state's educational-reform legislation, was a 200-page monster that included curriculum reforms, incentives for lengthening the school day and year, augmented counseling for tenth graders, a mentor-teacher program, a "Golden State" examination for high schools, and incentives for increasing test scores, quickly dubbed "cash for CAPs." None of it created radical reform, but the curriculum frameworks are credited with substantial changes in instruction, probably the state's most effective reform. Comparative test scores—first by district and then by school—were released to the newspapers. There was a ground swell of interest in achievement within the city. The emerging politics of excellence created a new constituency that was not directly oppositional to the politics of equity. But it placed reform accountability at the center of public discussions about the schools (Boyd and Kerchner 1988).

Although test-score accountability temporarily lost its edge, attention to what might be broadly considered the excellence agenda attracted the attention of the city's business elite. During the previous decades there had been relatively low levels of civic attention to the public schools. Most of the corporate and business leadership either lived outside the city or had sent their children to private schools. However, by the mid-1980s, the Los Angeles Educational Partnership (LAEP) was founded with strong business-community support. LAEP's small staff brokered ideas between private funders and LAUSD, beginning with a small faculty-development grant. By 1986 they had won a $500,000 grant from the Rockefeller Foundation to begin an interdisciplinary humanities program, named Humanitas.

Humanitas, which now operates in more than a hundred schools, has been extremely successful. It modeled instruction that made the humanities both exciting and accessible to students from many performance levels. The program thrives because of four vital inputs: teacher and student ownership and dedication, time and flexibility in the school schedule, unobtrusive administrators, and relatively small amounts of money. In many ways Humanitas was able to persist, because while it had powerful friends, the program itself was low profile and not dependent on the district's central office.

Humanitas became organizationally important because it symbolized the movement of pedagogical and academic reforms away from the school district's central office to persons and locations outside the bureaucratic control. Peggy Funkhouser, the highly visible president of LAEP who retired in 2000, was a consummate diplomat who never openly challenged the superintendent, staff, or school board. Yet, by the 1990s it became clear that LAEP was an important private center for innovation and advocacy directed at the district. Reformist administrators and teachers found ways to work through LAEP to accomplish that which they could not through the school district directly. LAEP became the structural prototype for lodging reform efforts in external private organizations.

In the late 1980s the district tried and failed to create a cogent reform program similar to that practiced in Dade County, Florida. Leonard Britton was brought in from Miami to serve as Los Angeles superintendent with the expectation that the district would undergo decentralization and restructuring similar to that which Britton and his charismatic deputy, Joseph Fernandez, fostered in Florida. It didn't turn out that way.

Britton's arrival turned into an almost immediate era of bad feeling with the UTLA. In 1989 its president, Wayne Johnson, took the teachers into their first strike in 20 years. The settlement gave the teachers a 24 percent wage increase over three years and a site-based management plan viewed by the district administrators as a union power-grab rather than a reform effort. Structurally, the LAUSD version of site-based management had many of the elements of teacher professional development and growth present in other urban district reforms such as in Miami, Rochester, and Pittsburgh. However, it contained none of the collegiality or sense of shared mission. The bitter strike poisoned the well of cooperation at school sites, and after two years only 84 of the district's 600-plus schools ever established school decision-making councils or developed a school-improvement plan.

Meanwhile, the 1990s' recession flooded the district with deficit—an occurrence widely attributed to the teacher wage settlement. Superintendent Britton resigned following a UTLA campaign of denigration and funding for reform efforts was slashed to the bone. However, even during this time, it became apparent that strong external forces were demanding reform of the school district, or at least the appearance of reform. Although many in the district were leery of reform and contemptuous of outsiders meddling in the district, they were increasingly quiet about their beliefs. Reform and educational excellence became the new "right answer" to political questions.

IMPROVISATIONAL SKETCH 3: CORPORATIST POLITICS, RADICAL ALTERNATIVES, REFORM ACCOUNTABILITY

The Los Angeles Educational Alliance for Reform Now (LEARN) was born in the poststrike era of the early 1990s. William Anton, a LAUSD veteran, became the district's first Hispanic superintendent. What became a school-reform coalition pressured Anton to accept a reform plan. Part of LEARN's logic was to create an unbeatable political coalition, such as that found in other urban reforms and recommended by the school-reform literature (Hill 1992; Hill, Foster, and Gendler 1990). In its founding, LEARN was able to combine the forces of three streams of reform activism. The first was comprised of business and foundation activists, led by the Los Angeles Educational Partnership. The second came from the remains of the site-based management program. While some United Teachers of Los Angeles leaders remained skeptical about LEARN, its president, Helen Bernstein, who succeeded to the presidency after the strike, strongly supported the program. The third stream of reform activism emerged from four Alinsky-style community organizations joined together to launch "Kids 1st" at large rallies in 1990. These included the Industrial Areas Foundation–affiliated organizations: UNO (United Neighborhood Organizing Committee based in East Los Angeles), SCOC (South Central Organizing Committee based in South Central Los Angeles and Compton), EVO (East Valley's Organization based in the San Gabriel and Pomona Valleys), and VOICE ([San Fernando] Valley Organized in Community Efforts). Although the coalition was largely grass roots, Kids 1st was co-chaired by Los Angeles businessmen Joe Alibrandi and Richard Riordan, who was subsequently elected mayor. It was endorsed by UTLA President Bernstein. The leaders reached out to form a coalition from the various reform streams, and LEARN emerged.

By the time the LEARN coalition went public it had an astonishingly broad coalition.[1] Its principal leaders were part of what was called the "LEARN Working Group," an informal organization that acted in many ways as a shadow school board. The operational leadership of LEARN was taken over by Mike Roos, former Speaker Pro Tem of the California Assembly and a close political ally of its powerful former Speaker and later San Francisco Mayor Willie Brown.

Essentially, the LEARN program bundled the conventional wisdom of school reform into a package designed to give it political protection and sustainability.[2] Budget and governance were to be shifted to school sites. Parent involvement would increase. Social services were to be brought onto the campuses. Schools adopted LEARN though election. Seventy-five percent of the teaching staff was required to approve it, and there must have been evidence of parent involvement in the application. If selected, the school's principal and a "lead teacher" attended an intensive training program provided by the UCLA Advanced Management Program. By the fall of 1996 four cohorts, totaling about 40 percent of the district's schools, had entered the program.

LEARN training consisted of residential programs held in the summers—three weeks the first summer, and two the second—along with several weekends. The training rested heavily on the shoulders of a tiny staff and small group of "master practitioners": teachers, principals, school staff-development personnel. They conducted the summer workshops and worked with each school during the year. But ultimately the school had to wrestle with creating a reform document called a "site action plan" and bringing it to realization.

LEARN's intent was to tie reforms to student-outcome accountability. But its training program was focused less on measurable student achievement than it was on the process skills necessary for adults in the schools to successfully collaborate, plant, and put into place the conditions thought necessary for achievement. Focusing on achievement proved difficult. The master practitioners reported extreme nervousness among teachers and administrators about using achievement diagnostics that would compare teachers within a school. School district administrators said that there was substantial disagreement among the master practitioners about what should be a school's outcome measures, and as a result the entire topic was down-played. Evaluating student achievement was certainly not the highlight of LEARN training (Matsui 1998).

LEARN's designers had hoped to create instructional and pedagogical coherence by linking accountability, student testing, and the curriculum. The primary vehicle for this effort was to have been the California Learning Assessment System (CLAS). CLAS was developed in 1991 to replace the existing California Assessment Program. In addition to tightly linking to curriculum frameworks, CLAS was designed to be a more thorough performance examination. It had longer writing assignments, presented problem-solving situations, and holistic scoring as opposed to right or wrong answers. CLAS was an almost-perfect example of professionally driven reform. Test creating involved some of the best-known subject-matter specialists and testing-and-measurement experts in the country. It would be fair to characterize CLAS as containing much of the leading-edge thinking among educators about what children should know and how schools can tell whether they know it.

CLAS was administered once—in 1993, and then its budgetary reauthorization was vetoed by Governor Pete Wilson (SB 1273). What had started as an example of professional competence and design ended as an example of the tension between technical precision and political common sense. CLAS had always been controversial. Religious groups complained that the writing prompts asked students to reflect on their home lives and upon moral dilemmas that should not be the province of the public schools. Others objected to the holistic scoring techniques and the lack of "objective" scores. The controversy intensified after the first round of test administration in 1993. Some schools that had fared well on previous assessments did poorly on the new tests, including some from the wealthiest areas in the state. The *Los Angeles Times* published an investigation critical of the sampling procedures, one that claimed that some 11,000 sampling errors produced results that invalidated any cross-school or cross-district comparisons (Wilgoren and O'Reilly 1994). Conservative foundations filed suit against the test. And finally, the California Teachers'

Association denounced the test and particularly its administration by the California Department of Education. The department's advocacy function was also somewhat weakened during this period. Superintendent Honig, a powerful reform advocate, had been convicted of a felony and required to resign from office, leaving the superintendency in the hands of an acting administrator.

Regardless of the politics, the effect of the CLAS test veto was to leave the school-reform effort in Los Angeles (as well as in the rest of the state) without an anchor assessment, particularly one that worked at the individual level. To be sure, there are still other indicators available, but neither LEARN nor the school district had invested in a comprehensive indicator system that would connect changes in classroom practice and school organization with measured cognitive assessment or any other forms of student output. Some LEARN schools became proficient at tracking their progress, but this characteristic did not become widespread.

The swirl of external politics also deflected attention from outcome accountability. While LEARN sought a broad political base and succeeded in creating one, it failed to create a monopoly on reform efforts in the district or a political umbrella large enough to cover all, and it has not eliminated more radical reform efforts outside of it. Two radical reforms reappear periodically: efforts to pass a voucher plan, and efforts to break up the Los Angeles Unified School District. Both efforts have long histories; neither has achieved electoral success or captured the mainstream of professional reform as has LEARN. But neither has gone away, and, given the nature of improvisation, the possibility remains of one or the other capturing the public attention long enough to win a populist victory or form an elite policy coalition.

In 1993 Joe Alibrandi, the businessman who had co-chaired Kids 1st, broke ranks with those advocating internal reforms to spearhead a voucher initiative. Proposition 174 would have provided a $2,500 state payment for nearly any student attending a private school in the state. There were some, but few, restrictions. The open-ended free-market approach narrowed the coalition favoring the initiative, and some long-standing advocates, such as U.C. Berkeley law professors Jack Coons and Steven Sugermann, disassociated themselves. More importantly, the state's large businesses did not join in support. The California Business Roundtable, which had been a mainstay of support for Ronald Reagan, declared neutrality over the measure. Governor Wilson ultimately opposed the measure. In the end, after a lackluster campaign, the voucher initiative was badly defeated. Voucher advocates raised about $3.5 million for their campaign; opponents raised $16 million, about 70 percent from the California Teachers' Association.

The voucher challenge emerged again in 2000. This time it was backed by Silicon Valley venture-capitalist Timothy Draper, who announced his willingness to spend $20 million of his own money on the initiative. He had few allies. In addition to predictable opposition from the teachers' union and school administrators, both the governor and lieutenant governor strongly opposed the measure. Even the arch-conservative Howard Jarvis's Taxpayers Association announced its opposition (Vogel 2000). It was soundly defeated.

There have been periodic unsuccessful efforts to break up the Los Angeles Unified School District dating back to the 1950s. In the late 1990s these efforts have become more pronounced and less singly identified with conservative forces in the San Fernando Valley, although those forces remain. Organizations have been formed to explore withdrawal in South Central Los Angeles, the Carson area on the far southside, and in the San Fernando Valley. Recent legislation allows a part of a school district's territory to withdraw without approval of the school board, and it reduces the number of petition signatures required to initiate a withdrawal. Prior legislation required 25 percent of registered voters. Current legislation requires 8 percent of the voters in the last gubernatorial election. Based on the 1994 election, this would mean that the signatures of only 3.6 percent of registered voters would be required to initiate the withdrawal process. In 2002 a city succession referendum failed, but efforts to withdraw from the school system continue.

IMPROVISATIONAL SKETCH 4: CHAOTIC INNOVATION, IMMIGRANTS, AND ACCOUNTABILITY POLITICS

While LEARN continued to grow, several other reform measures began. First, the district reorganized itself administratively. In 1993, following a board-commissioned organizational audit by the accounting firm Arthur Andersen, the district moved to abolish its six administrative regions and reorganize around much smaller clusters of schools. Each cluster was made up of one-to-three high school "complexes" with between 23,000 and 50,000 students in each. Each cluster office was led by a newly hired "cluster coordinator," most of whom were former administrators from the elementary schools' regional offices or the middle schools' or high schools' divisional offices. Extensive hearings were held about the cluster process, some involving thousands of parents and citizens. Yet few LEARN leaders and activists participated in the development of these cluster plans, in part because they had not been specifically invited to the Hamilton High School event. LEARN leaders and cluster-reform leaders have remained in awkward tension ever since. A second major component of the Andersen audit recommendations was the restructuring of the central office to make it more efficient and a realignment of its culture to make it more client-service and less -compliance oriented. Some realignment has taken place, but substantive change awaits resolution of the superintendent succession question.

Meanwhile, the courts intervened in a school-finance equity case. On August 19, 1992 retired Superior Court Judge Ralph Nutter completed negotiations on a consent decree ending the *Rodriquez v. LAUSD* lawsuit after six years of debate and litigation. The premise of the suit was that the district spent less per pupil at low-status schools than at high-status ones because of personnel costs. Experienced, high-seniority and thus high-salary teachers bid out of low-status schools when they can, leaving those schools' students to be taught by low-seniority and low-salary teachers.

Under the consent decree, LAUSD agreed to equalize per-pupil spending on instruction across 90 percent of the district's schools within $100 per pupil by 1997–1998. The strategies involved to equalize resources are inherently centralizing, thus cutting against the grain of the school-site financial devolution anticipated in LEARN. As the new funding formulae were put in place, it became apparent that not all schools would benefit financially from the LEARN reforms. For some, autonomy came with less money rather than more. The decisional freedom promised by LEARN was cut back.

Third, in 1993 the state passed legislation requiring open enrollment between districts (AB 19) and within districts (AB 1114), providing that openings exist for students. LAUSD implemented the policy in June 1994, allowing applications for 22,000 open seats at 382 of the district's schools. Schools advertised for applications on local-access television and through various other outlets. While the impact is not yet clear, open enrollment clearly brings parental choice into play along with other reform forces.

In 1995 California's Proposition 187, a highly inflammatory ballot measure, denied a variety of publicly funded services to illegal immigrants and their children. Although the courts overturned the educational-services provisions, the initiative ushered in an era of bad feeling in California politics and gave rise to much more active Latino voter registration, political activity, and citizenship applications.

In 1996 the state began a new testing scheme based on the Stanford 9 (SAT-9), which is only marginally related to the state's curriculum standards. It was first administered in 1997.

By this time, the California economy, which had been in deep recession early in the decade, was booming. Faced with the prospect of budget surpluses, Governor Wilson earmarked funds to reduce class sizes to 20 students in grades K–3. In addition to smaller classes, the program had two other consequences: first, large numbers of teachers with little training or experience were placed in classrooms. As of 1999, about 10 percent of the teaching force—approximately 30,000 teachers—lacked full state certification. And second, schools and districts found themselves scrambling for space and adequate classrooms.

In 1994 a $50 million challenge grant from the Annenberg Foundation established the Los Angeles Annenberg Metropolitan Project (LAAMP). Originally, LAAMP was thought of as a way to continue LEARN's work, and indeed LEARN was badly in need of money. The school district itself had never made the monetary commitments originally anticipated and sources of private funding were on the wane. But LAAMP turned out differently. It was metropolitan in scope, with half its projects in districts outside of Los Angeles, and it was focused around groups of schools, called families, rather than individual schools. But more importantly, LAAMP was to create a different civic and political organization. Its board included many of the members who had participated in LEARN, but it pointedly excluded both the Los Angeles school administration and UTLA, the teachers' union. It saw itself as the re-creation of a civic elite, a bit of a watchdog, as well as the overseers of the Annenberg Challenge.

LAAMP continued its operations until 2001. It had been highly successful in raising matching money, and program budgets totaled over $103 million. In addition to the LAAMP families, it has funded parent initiatives, technology in the schools, and a major intervention in teacher education. But, as we shall see, the enduring legacy of the organization may well be the change in education politics it brought about.

Improvisational Sketch 5: A Hostile Takeover, Accountability at the Ballot Box, and Maybe a Playwright after All

By the summer of 1998 it became clear that LEARN had run its course. After 104 schools embraced LEARN in 1996–1997, extending the program to nearly half the schools in the district, Superintendent Sid Thompson announced that he would retire in June 1997. That summer, Helen Bernstein, who had stepped down from the teachers' union presidency after completing her second term, died tragically in a traffic accident. The departures of Thompson and Bernstein, both strong and long-term LEARN-insider advocates, left little high-profile support for the program within the LAUSD establishment. Judy Burton, the assistant superintendent in charge of LEARN, was isolated from the rest of the district's structure, as were the LEARN schools.

The school board undercut LEARN even further when it promoted Deputy Superintendent Ruben Zacarias—never a strong LEARN supporter—to replace Thompson as superintendent. Zacarias began his term in the summer of 1997 with his own initiatives for reform. Called "Hundred Low-Performing Schools," it combined publicly "naming and shaming" the schools thought to be the least productive with a revitalization of technical assistance. During that school year only 29 new schools entered the LEARN program, and the school board cut the LEARN budget by millions of dollars the following year.

At the same time, relations between Los Angeles Mayor (and LEARN participant) Richard Riordan and the seven-member school board reached a nadir. Though he lacked any formal authority over the district, the recently reelected Riordan continued to use the mayor's office as a bully pulpit to challenge district officials and advocate reform. He openly sought tougher accountability, fired bad principals, and took responsibility for reconstituting low-performing schools. "We need a revolution," he was quoted as saying. Board members resented his intrusions and mutual public recriminations grew increasingly common and ugly. Riordan publicly ridiculed board members and questioned their competence to pursue any coherent agenda (Boyarsky 1997).

The growing dissatisfaction bubbled to the surface in the 1999 school board election, but dissatisfaction was not the only thing bubbling up. Methane and other toxic gases were rising to the surface of the Belmont Learning Complex, a $200 million combined high school and retail complex near downtown. Belmont became the symbol of the board's ineptitude. It was big, it was bad, and it was unfinished. The criticism may well have been overdrawn. Much of Los Angeles sits on a pool of oil and gas, and in Beverly Hills the school district pumps and profits from oil on its high school site. Still, the symbolism of an exploding high school was headlined for months.

In 1999 four of the seven school board seats were up for election. All the incumbents ran for reelection. Riordan and others openly recruited a slate of challengers, in effect creating an opposition or reform party in this nonpartisan election. The election was punctuated by a combination of a reform vision and the political clout of a civic coalition with roots in Riordan's 1980s' Kids 1st effort. While the mayor and his friends raised and distributed cash for the campaign, some of the same individuals formed the Committee on Effective School Governance.

Twenty-one of the 26 committee members had been associated with LAAMP, LEARN, or LAEP. As the election campaign was beginning in 1999, the committee issued a stinging indictment of the school board and, in effect, a code of conduct for board members to which it challenged candidates to subscribe. Its report (CESG 1999) attacked both the board's micromanagement of the district and its lack of a coherent strategy: "Board members tend to see their primary role as satisfying the day-to-day requests of individual constituents rather than representing the community's long-term needs" it noted (p. 5). Noting that the district had set over 20 priorities in recent years, the report countered, "but having so many priorities really means having none" (p. 7).

In a series of recommendations that would have been welcomed by the administrative progressives of the early twentieth century, the committee endorsed a strong, independent superintendent ("the superintendent as chief executive officer" [p. 5]), a clearly defined set of priorities, measurable pathways to student achievement, and accountability. With a $147,000 grant from LAAMP, the committee set up four candidates' forums during the campaign and conducted mass mailings, urging substantial reform in the way the district was run (Smith and Sahagun 1999). Attendance at the forums was light, the largest being about 150 persons—this in a district of 230,000 registered voters. But the press and cable television attention to the reform agenda was substantial and so, too, was the attachment of the reform label to the three challengers and one incumbent who had won the electoral support of Riordan and his friends. All the candidates pledged independence of the mayor but fealty to reform.

The committee's activities raised the school board election's profile and gave all candidates name recognition. The reform slate and Riordan succeeded to a substantial degree in turning the election into a vote of no confidence in the school board. The difference between the challengers and the reformers was crystallized in *Los Angeles Times* candidate interviews, in which the first question was: "Do you consider the Los Angeles Unified School District to be in crises?" (*Los Angeles Times* 1999). The general public did. A *Times* poll found that 63 percent of respondents rated their local schools as being fair or poor. In the same poll, the mayor received a 57 percent approval rating and the school board a 27 percent approval rating (Sahagun 1999). It was a very ugly campaign. The contest between incumbent Barbara Boudreaux and Genethia Hayes, who is the executive director of the Southern Christian Leadership Conference, was particularly bitter. Boudreaux repeatedly attacked Riordan's support for Hayes as "plantation politics," and her supporters punctuated candidates' forums by waving pictures of the mayor and $20 bills.

In the end, all four of the reform-slate candidates won, Boudreaux losing to Hayes by 1,350 votes in a runoff election. Riordan and his allies had raised more than $2 million for the reform slate. Hayes was elected president of the new board when it was installed in June 1999, and in her installation speech she pledged to make Superintendent Zacarias "soar and to fly and to, unfettered, lead this district into the next millennium" (Hayes 1999). But within weeks there was talk of the superintendent's ouster. Riordan openly began discussions about a new superintendent (Colvin and Sahagun 1999) and, after negotiations as ugly as the school board election, Zacarias resigned. His flight into the new millennium would last only two months!

Meanwhile, other reform elements continued to pull and tug at the district. Gray Davis, a Democrat, had succeeded to the governorship in 1999 with education as a prime goal. He called the legislature into special session with a package of bills, all aimed at increasing accountability and focusing reform. Through an Academic Performance Index, based largely on the SAT-9, schools would be ranked, and those that scored poorly or failed to improve would be subject to intervention. Those that increased test scores would be eligible for monetary rewards. Social promotion was also eliminated. Schools were forbidden to pass students to the next grade unless they had demonstrated proficiency. One of the immediate results was an upturn in summer school enrollments for makeup or remedial work. The legislature also authorized a high school exit exam. Becoming effective in 2003, California students will be required to pass an exam as well as amass credits before they can graduate from high school. Students will be able to take the exam in the ninth grade and continue to take sections until they are successful.

At about the same time, transitions occurred in the reform organizations. LEARN came to an end. Mike Roos resigned, and the LEARN and LAAMP board began negotiations for a successor organization provisionally called "L2" (Smith 1999a). Early working papers from the transition team suggest that the new organization will take on a watchdog function as a continuation of the Committee on Effective School Governance and less of LAAMP's or LEARN's expensive and direct assistance to schools. At the time of this writing, the new organization is seeking an executive director. The Los Angeles Educational Partnership, which continued to provide a home for curriculum- and school-development projects, continues in existence, but its president, Peggy Funkhouser, retired in the spring of 2000. The Annenberg Challenge closed operations in 2002. Its staff has disbursed, finding new jobs and challenges.

With the advent of no-social-promotion rules and consequences attached to the Academic Performance Index, school districts throughout the state became keenly interested in measured cognitive achievement. It mattered relatively little that the SAT-9 was not well-aligned to the state's official standards or that there was a host of other measurement problems—test-score accountability was to have its day. The focus on outcome measures, which had always been urged by the LAAMP and LEARN boards, was beginning to take tangible expression. Data-driven reform became the watchword of LAAMP assistance to school families.

The new board understood well its mandate to "kill the culture of the district," as one Committee on Effective School Governance member put it. It first hobbled Zacarias by placing real estate attorney and former school board member Howard Miller in charge of all day-to-day operations (Smith 1999b). Then, with Zacarias leaving, it brought in Ramon Cortines, recently resigned chancellor of the New York City school system, as interim superintendent. Cortines, who said that he would only serve six months and was as good as his word, pledged reorganization. Within two months he and Miller had produced a plan to divide the district into 11 subunits, each with a semi-autonomous superintendent. Each of these districts would be sizable in itself—about the size of the Boston or San Francisco public school system. The plan was notable for what it did not say. There was virtually no detail about how much fiscal autonomy each district would have or how fiscal or operating autonomy would be made possible. The district would continue to have a single labor contract, all its schools would be owned and maintained by the central district, and it was apparent that at least some curricular decisions would be made centrally. (Shortly after the decentralization, the school board voted to require a single, highly prescriptive phonics-based reading program, Open Court, for all schools.)

The 11 district superintendents were named in June 2000 (Sahagun and Sauerwein 2000). As the announcement was made, Cortines promised that the new superintendents would have autonomy: "The only responsibilities that will be directed by the central core will be those things required of us by the state and federal government, and things like the busing system," he said (Sahagun and Sauerwein 2000, B1). Although promising a new broom's sweep, Cortines picked nine district veterans, with an average of 26 years experience in the district, and only two outsiders. The appointments drew both praise and more than a little skepticism. "How many times have we heard that it is going to be different?" asked Paula Boland, a legislator and leader of a group trying to break up the district (Sahagun and Sauerwein 2000, B1).

While the district was trying to reorganize itself, it was also searching for a new, permanent superintendent. Following a pattern in other large cities, the board hired a noneducator, former Colorado Governor Roy Romer. Romer, who had also been chair of the Democratic National Committee and head of the National Goals Panel, brought a reputation for settling fights and building coalitions. He had no experience in running an educational organization. His initial reception could best be described as "rough." Although business and civic leaders praised his leadership, the Latino community was still smarting from Zacarias's dismissal. The day after the appointment, the *Los Angeles Times* (2000, B10) called him a "bad fit for LAUSD . . . a well-intentioned but limited Democratic Party boss."

MOVING FROM SKETCHES TO A PLAY?

These sketches demonstrate that improvisational politics has substantially ruled school policy-making in the Los Angeles Unified School District, just as it has in virtually every large school district in the United States since the 1960s. The question we want to raise here is whether improvisational politics will continue into the foreseeable future? The analysis presented earlier in this chapter suggests that the institutional patterns and incentive systems that encourage improvisational policy-making are permanent and unchanging. Though state governments across the country are taking an increasing role in driving school reform through various accountability initiatives, in general, authority over school policy-making remains shared among many governments. And the fragmentation of school activity into multiple missions that was recognized a generation ago continues unabated today (Meyer, Scott, Strang, and Creighton 1985). School politics may permanently be a business of disjointed incrementalism and muddling through, bouncing from reform to reform, from improvisational sketch to improvisational sketch (Lindblom 1959).

There are many possible alternative paths into the future, however. And there are signs that some of the writers and actors in these sketches have begin to search for a whole new play. The leaders first of LEARN, in particular, demonstrated a belief that they faced two simultaneous tasks. They worked to develop reform programs that could reach beyond narrow initiatives focusing on one level of schooling or one aspect of curriculum or one target population, and begin to reorient the entire school district to a different way of running schools, a different way of teaching. But, more importantly for the focus of this chapter, they also worked to crowd out competing reform initiatives, to become *the* school reform for LAUSD and perhaps even the metropolitan region. They wanted to deprive competing reforms of legitimacy and public attention.

This raises the possibility that improvisational politics may not be self-sustaining, that the practice of improvisation itself has begun to alter the incentives within the system activists seek to change. As was noted at the outset of this chapter, in the improvisational system each successive group of reform activists must compete not only with simultaneous proposals from other groups, but also with the accumulation of established programs and a growing public skepticism about the entire business of improvisational reform. At some point, those accumulated programs might make it unlikely that *any* improvisational reform will have *any* impact on the system. Or the accumulated public skepticism might dramatically reduce the available channels of improvisation.

Such developments could alter the incentives of the entire improvisational system to the point where it wouldn't be worth the effort to put on the sketch, and on the contrary activists would have incentives to develop another style of activism. The apparently stable and permanent institutional and political system described by Chubb, Moe, and others would become unstable. The improvisational genre could go into decline.

At least two alternatives to improvisation appear possible. First, a school district board superintendent regime becomes powerful enough to impose coherence on the system, appear to make progress, and to crowd out competing reforms. External reformers would then take on a support role rather than being potential system changers, such as were LAAMP and LEARN. Or as a second alternative, those who are dissatisfied with the system will give up on reforms that work with the district and successfully organize around vouchers, unlimited charter schools, or a radical breakup of the district. It is possible that either of these two reforms could take place or that *both* of them could play one after the other.

Roy Romer has weighed in on the side of coherence, and he has proven a much tougher and more resilient superintendent than his critics thought. At the time of this writing, he is in his second three-year term, which he has announced he will complete. He continues to rule with great energy, oblivious to the conventional wisdom that people in their 70s are supposed to slow down. Largely, he has brought coherence to the school district by recentralizing it. The district's recent reforms tend to recreate the organizational structure David Tyack described in *The One Best System* (1974). It is not that the 11 subdistrict superintendents brought in by the Cortines plan have no power, but many important educational and resource decisions are centralized. For example, the Cortines plan embraced the Open Court reading program to force the lowest-performing schools to adopt a coherent strategy. Schools that made good progress or that scored well on state and district mandated tests were to be freed to make their own curricular choices. Under Romer, Open Court has become the district's literacy curriculum with few if any deviations allowed. Collective bargaining and the work rules it creates, the testing system, and most financial decisions also remain centralized.

The school district's test scores have risen for four years in a row, an achievement the district attributes to Open Court. Forty-four percent of the district's second graders performed above national averages on the SAT-9, the state's standardized reading test (Heflen 2002). (Even with these gains, only about 16 percent of LAUSD sixth-grade students would have passed the state's proficiency standards in reading and math.) In November 2002 Los Angeles voters approved a large construction bond measure designed to take schools off multitrack year-round schedules, which parents dislike, and to repair or replace aging structures. "If the schools were not showing progress—were not being responsible—there would not be the public support," said Kerry Mazzoni, state secretary of education (Moore and Hefland 2002, B1). At the same time, initiatives for large parts of Los Angeles to succeed and form separate cities were defeated.

No external organization continues large-scale reform efforts designed to change school-district operations in the tradition of LAAMP and LEARN. LAEP continues with teacher-development work and seeks a broader policy role, but so far to little effect. As it concluded its work, LAAMP created two new organizations that are just establishing their agendas. Families in Schools conducts a popular reading initiative, "Read with Me/Lea Conmigo," and has a number of other small programs. The Los Angeles County Alliance for Student Achievement was formed by members of the LAAMP and LEARN boards primarily to be a policy advocacy organization. It has conducted several studies, some of which hint at radical alternatives to the present school district, but at the time of this writing there is no announced policy position.

Meanwhile, Families in Schools has brought a second Annenberg-sponsored school-reform project under its wing. The Boyle Heights Learning Collaborative is an attempt to link school reform, community development, and grass-roots political organizing together. Boyle Heights, located just east of downtown Los Angeles, is a historic port of immigration and is now heavily a Latino neighborhood of the working poor. The Collaborative's design is somewhat unusual. It has established a steering committee that seeks to bring together all the influential parties in the community, not just those who receive grant funds. In addition, its parent-involvement activities are based on political activism rather than traditional school boosterism. There are several parent-involvement efforts in the community. Most prominently, LA Metro/IAF is attempting to adapt the success they have had with the Industrial Areas Foundation–organized Alliance schools in Texas to the political and social realities of Los Angeles (Shirley 1997). The Boyle Heights Learning Collaborative and LA Metro/IAF efforts could be a model for a changed educational politics in Los Angeles, one in which parents rather than the civic elite drove school change, but it will take several more years before the efficacy of this model can be known.

A second, more radical scenario—one we might call the "last improvisation"—could also emerge from the decline of improvisational politics. If a large-enough share of the public finally loses patience with efforts to reform the existing institutional and educational arrangements of American schools, they may be willing to turn to more radical measures (Hentschke 1997). Creative destruction may have its day (Romer 1989). In that case, any number of things would happen:

- key members of the current reform coalition in Los Angeles would defect and "give up" on the idea of reforming LAUSD;
- major leaders in the business and foundation community would join grass-roots activists in calling for breaking up LAUSD;
- working-class parents would join the professional middle class in fleeing the district's schools;
- voters would approve a ballot initiative creating a voucher system or unrestricted charter-school law for California; and/or
- more "revolutionary" governance models would be openly discussed among school-reform activists and politicians.

Such developments would mark a clear break with the past and would make it possible for the nation's second-largest school district to lead the nation into some uncharted path toward urban school reform.

We make no prescriptions or predictions here. As we write, education- and school-reform politics command national attention from the local school board all the way up to the White House. This is a time of tremendous controversy, but it is also a moment of great creative ferment in school politics and policy. In other words, the sketches may continue and generations hence historians may tell us that they added up to a great turning point, just as Shakespeare's Henry V found majesty in the blood of Agincourt. Or people may tire of the sketches as with over-tired television and turn to other recreations. Or then, they might just burn the theater.

NOTES

1. The leadership included: Riordan (the mayor); Anton (the superintendent); Bernstein (UTLA president); Robert Wycoff, president and CEO of ARCO; Phillip Williams, vice-president of Times Mirror, which publishes the *Los Angeles Times*; Roy Anderson, retired Lockheed CEO; John Mack, Urban League; Virgil Roberts, LAEP chair; Rosalinda Lugo of UNO; John Singleton, vice-president of Security Pacific Bank; Joe Alibrandi, CAO Whitacker Corp. and co-chair of Kids 1st; and William Ouchi, UCLA management professor (later deputy mayor). The names have changed, but not the breadth of representation.

2. The group's program combines aspects of virtually every major current approach to school reform in the United States. The April 1993 version of LEARN's own 30-page platform, "For All Our Children," is built around eight principles:

1) "Student learning and assessment": improved student learning; improved school effectiveness; and improved accountability.

2) "Governance and accountability": re-norming each school to an entrepreneurial and innovative school culture; shifting responsibility for budget, staff selection, and teaching methods to the local school; involving a broader array of "stakeholders" in the school; establishing a collaborative planning and decision-making process at the school level; and establishing clear performance standards for schools, principals, teachers, and other personnel.

3) "Educator development": instituting standards of professional practice; involving teachers in school decision-making; and improving teacher training at all career stages.

4) "Parent involvement": organizing schools around high school communities ("clusters"); creating improved opportunities for parent participation in all dimensions of the school; and actively engaging parents in that practice.

5) "Social services": reorganizing child and family health and social services to coincide with high school communities; and integrating those services into the educational programs of schools.

6) "School-to-work transition": enabling students to prepare themselves for careers in the context of a nontracked curriculum; and making career awareness and preparation part of the public school curriculum.

7) "School facilities": improving facilities use and maintenance; and advocating new construction.

8) "Finance": providing discretionary resources at every school; improving the state-funding process; and basing funding on the number of students and the intensity of services.

◧   ◧   ◧

CHAPTER TWO

Philadelphia's Children Achieving Initiative

the promise and challenge of systemic reform in an urban school district

JOLLEY BRUCE CHRISTMAN, TOM CORCORAN,

ELLEN FOLEY, THERESA LUHM

OVER THE PAST THREE DECADES, numerous efforts have been made to improve the performance of public schools serving urban children. A variety of approaches has been tried, including expanded instructional supports for students, decentralization of authority to schools, curricular and pedagogical changes, expanded professional development, whole school-reform models, expanded family and community services, and stronger accountability systems. None of these reforms has produced significant and sustained improvements at scale. Whether they have fallen short of expectations because of poor design, inadequate resources, or flawed implementation has not always been clear, but the pattern of high hopes, initial claims of success, and failure to produce widespread gains has been repeated many times.

Recently some have argued that these previous attempts at reforms have largely failed because they were too incremental, too narrowly framed, and did not attempt to alter the "system" itself. These reforms did not institutionalize high expectations for students and teachers. They did not alter governance and management structures that so often seem unable to remain focused on reforms long enough to implement them effectively. These critics of piecemeal reform, known as "systemic reformers," argue that a more comprehensive strategy that addresses standards, supports, accountability, and coheres policy is necessary. They contend

that if districts and states set academic standards for student performance, align curriculum, instruction, and assessment with these standards,
provide adequate resources and supports for schools, measure students'
progress, and offer rewards or sanctions to educators based on performance, then school staffs will make the changes in their practice necessary
to ensure that students achieve at high levels. This is the essence of the
theory of systemic reform.

Philadelphia was among the first urban school districts to take a systemic approach to school reform and to test this new theory of school
improvement. The architects of Philadelphia's ambitious reform effort
launched in 1995, and optimistically named "Children Achieving," sought
to demonstrate that every student could achieve proficiency in three core
subject areas—math, reading and science—by 2008. With the support of
$150 million from the Annenberg Challenge,[1] the business community, and
local foundations, the School District of Philadelphia set out to design and
implement major reforms in all aspects of its work, and in the words of its
fervent superintendent, David Hornbeck, to do it "all at once."

In this chapter we describe what happened during the first five years of
Children Achieving. Drawing on both quantitative and qualitative research
conducted as part of the evaluation of the Annenberg Challenge and research conducted by other groups, we examine its theory of action, its
implementation, and its key successes and major challenges.[2] We argue that
in spite of some promising early gains in achievement, serious flaws in
design and implementation and inadequate attention to the Philadelphia
context are likely to limit Children Achieving's progress in the future. In particular, we conclude that the policy dictum that "everything had to be done
at the same time," as well as poor sequencing of actions, failure to win
teacher support for the reforms, and the emphasis placed on raising standardized test scores have so far led to uneven, often superficial implementation and a culture of compliance rather than the deep changes in curriculum and instruction and the culture of continuous improvement envisioned
by the reformers.

THE CHILDREN ACHIEVING PLAN FOR TRANSFORMING PHILADELPHIA SCHOOLS

In 1995, with the support of the Annenberg Challenge, the newly appointed superintendent, David Hornbeck, launched Children Achieving, a
ten-point reform agenda that promised to do what "no city with any significant number and diversity of students" had ever done before: help "a
large proportion of its young people achieve at high levels" (School District of Philadelphia 1995, i). The task was daunting. A special section of
the *Philadelphia Inquirer* (1994) published just a few months earlier had
painted a dismal portrait of the conditions in the school system. According
to the *Inquirer*:

- Half the district's 220,000 students were from families on welfare.
- One hundred and thirty-six of 238 schools were severely segregated.
- Over half of the city's public school students were failing to master basic skills. Fifty-one percent had failed the state reading test as compared to 13 percent state-wide, and 50 percent failed the state math test as compared to 14 percent state-wide. Seventy percent of African Americans and 75 percent of Latinos failed one or both parts of the state test.
- Forty-nine percent of ninth graders failed to earn promotion to the tenth grade.
- On any given day one in four students was absent from class, and in the average year, nearly one in four students was suspended from school.

This was the system that Superintendent Hornbeck proposed to transform into an exemplar of urban education.

The Theory of Action Underlying Children Achieving

To change these conditions and raise achievement, Hornbeck offered an ambitious plan modeled after the reforms he had helped design for the state of Kentucky only a few years earlier. The following are excerpts of the plan's ten components:

- We must behave as if we believe that all students will learn at high levels.
- Standards-based reform will drive the system. . . . We must set standards, have new assessment strategies, and develop new incentive systems for both adults and students.
- Decisions will be made at the school level. . . . Authority for decisions about personnel, budget, professional development, instructional strategies and curriculum, scheduling, student and teacher assignments inside of a school, and, perhaps, discipline, should be made at the school level. . . . In addition to school employees, parents must also be partners in making those decisions.
- Staff development is critical to improved performance.
- Early childhood support is less expensive and more effective. . . . There are at least three areas of focus important to school readiness: family support; health and social services; and full-day kindergarten, pre-kindergarten, and childcare.
- Community services and supports can make the difference between success and failure. Children who are unhealthy, hungry, abused, ill-housed, ill-clothed, or otherwise face the kinds of problems outside of the school that are born of poverty cannot achieve at high levels.

- Adequate technology, instructional materials, and facilities are necessary to learning.
- Strong public engagement is required. Unless parents, civic leaders, elected officials, the business community, postsecondary educators, and the wider citizenry understand and support radical change, we cannot sustain it.
- We must have adequate resources and use them effectively.
- We must do all of these nine components. The agenda is not a pick-and-choose menu. We must approach the challenge of education reform in a comprehensive and integrated way. If one or more features of the whole agenda is not implemented, its power to yield high performance by all students will be significantly diminished (School District of Philadelphia 1995).

The theory of action—the chain of logic about how these ten propositions would lead to improvements in teaching and learning and hence improved student performance—underlying this vision was not explicit in the description of the ten components. Plans developed by work teams made up of central office staff, school staff, and community members laid out the details for implementing the ten components of the reform. Based on the examination of these plans, on other statements made by Superintendent Hornbeck and other district officials, and the actions taken by the district after the plan's adoption, we have described the plan's theory of action as follows:

> If the district works with the schools and the community to set high academic standards for student achievement; aligns assessment with those standards, establishes an accountability system that offers strong incentives; delegates more authority over school resources, organization, policies, and programs to the schools; monitors equity throughout the organization; and builds public understanding and support for reform; and if central office and the clusters provide guidance and high-quality support to schools and small learning communities, then the teachers and administrators of the Philadelphia schools, in consultation with their communities, will be motivated to develop, adopt, or adapt instructional technologies and patterns of behavior that will help all children reach the district's high standards.

The Critical Drivers of the Reform

The critical drivers in the theory were the *standards*, the *accountability system*, and *decentralization*.

STANDARDS. Content standards were a cornerstone of Children Achieving.[3] Beginning in early 1996, teams of teachers were assembled to write standards in all subject areas. By late August 1996 draft standards for

Reading/English, Language Arts, Mathematics, Science, and the Arts had been distributed to teachers. Content standards in the Social Studies, Health/Physical Education, and World Languages followed soon thereafter.

Each set of content standards outlined the knowledge and skills that Philadelphia students should acquire, with benchmarks defined at the fourth, eighth, and eleventh grades. In addition to requiring significant curriculum changes, the standards also asked teachers to address "cross-cutting competencies"—skills and values such as technology, multicultural competence, and communication—that were not part of specific content areas but were to be infused in all of them. It is important to note that Philadelphia's content standards did not specify a curriculum for Philadelphia schools. Though they superseded the previous administration's "Standardized Curriculum," which prescribed a scope and sequence by grade level, the content standards simply defined the parameters within which teachers and principals were expected to design their own curriculum.

ACCOUNTABILITY. Philadelphia's accountability system, the Professional Responsibility Index (PRI), was designed to assess schools' performance annually, and to reward progress or sanction decline every two years. The PRI was made up of five indicators: student performance in reading, mathematics, and science as measured by the Stanford Achievement Test, 9th edition (SAT-9); a combined measure of teacher and student attendance; and the promotion rate for elementary and middle schools and the persistence rate for secondary schools. These indicators were combined mathematically into an index, the PRI, which provided each school with an annual score.

The baseline year for the PRI was 1995–1996. Biennial targets that assumed consistent, linear progress were set for every school based on their baseline. New baselines were calculated every two years. The ultimate goal was for all schools to achieve or exceed a score of 95 on the PRI (out of a possible 120 points) by 2008. Schools that met or exceeded their biennial targets were to be rewarded with a cash allotment; schools that did not meet their targets would be identified for intervention. If interventions failed to bring improvement, the ultimate sanction was reconstitution. Although two high schools were identified for reconstitution in 1997, this sanction was not employed in the first five years of Children Achieving.[4]

The accountability plan included the development of promotion standards for students at grades 4 and 8 and end-of-course examinations for core high school courses, but these were to be phased in beginning in 2000. They depended on the development of curriculum-related assessments, and the superintendent and board of education made their implementation contingent on securing additional funding for the provision of supports such as an extended school day and summer school. The development of the new assessments began in 1999 and they field-tested in the spring of 2000. Thus, in its first five years, the accountability provisions in

Philadelphia were unbalanced, falling on teachers and school administrators but not on the students whose work effort was required to improve
achievement.

DECENTRALIZATION. Along with standards and accountability, the other
primary strategy was decentralization. As conceived in Philadelphia,
decentralization had four major components: small learning communities,
local school councils, clusters, and a streamlined central office.

- *Small learning communities:* Small learning communities were
  intended to improve the conditions of teaching and learning, to
  strengthen relations between teachers and students, and to be the
  primary vehicle for improving instruction. They were subunits of
  schools and typically included 400 or fewer students across several
  grade levels as well as the teachers responsible for their instruction. Many of Philadelphia's high schools and middle schools had
  voluntarily experimented with similar strategies prior to David
  Hornbeck's arrival, but small learning communities did not spread
  rapidly across the district until being mandated as part of the
  Children Achieving reforms in 1998.

- *Local school councils:* Each school was expected to establish a
  local school council (LSC) comprised of teachers, parents, the
  principal, and at the secondary level, two students. The councils
  were to be given broad responsibility for overseeing school-wide
  policies. They were also charged with reviewing the budgets
  of small learning communities and developing action plans to
  involve parents and their communities in their schools to help
  improve student achievement.

- *Clusters:* In Philadelphia, 22 cluster offices were formed to work
  directly with schools in support of reform. Cluster offices consisted
  of small staffs who worked with a comprehensive neighborhood
  high school and the middle and elementary schools in its feeder
  pattern. The first six clusters were established during the spring
  of 1995, and the remaining 16 in the fall of 1996. Clusters were
  expected to play a catalytic role in school improvement, guide and
  monitor the implementation of the reform agenda, provide focus
  for improvement initiatives, supervise principals, energize the
  schools, and mobilize resources to support improvement. They
  also were expected to provide professional development, coordinate social services for schools, and strengthen K–12 articulation.

- *A streamlined central office:* The blueprint for the Children
  Achieving initiative clearly stated that the functions of the central
  office would be limited; it would "set standards, assess progress,
  monitor for equity, and act as a guide and provider of resources
  and support" (School District of Philadelphia 1995, iv). This new

streamlined version of a central office would give schools and clusters the freedom to make instructional decisions and put in place an infrastructure to ensure that their decisions were good ones. Asserting that "[t]hose who sit closest to the action are in the best position to decide what mix of resources . . . will most effectively accomplish the goal of raising student achievement," the framers of the Strategic Action Design made a significant commitment to school autonomy (p. III-10).

Through these actions the architects of Children Achieving hoped to increase the commitment and motivation of various stakeholders and raise the productivity of the system by radically re-allocating power and resources in the school system and by reducing the isolation of teachers and school administrators.

Supports for Reform

The district also devised new supports and organizational arrangements to help schools implement the standards and meet their performance targets. These included expanded *professional development* for teachers, *curriculum frameworks*, *district-wide curriculum and instruction initiatives*, and *family and community supports* for students.

PROFESSIONAL DEVELOPMENT. The Office of Leadership and Learning (OLL) was charged with developing and implementing an overall plan for professional development for administrators and teachers. It also had responsibility for identifying and disseminating "best practices," research-based reforms that were aligned with Philadelphia's new content standards.

The Teaching and Learning Network (TLN) was part of the OLL and served as the professional development arm of the district. TLN coordinators and facilitators were based in the cluster offices and provided direct support services to schools and teachers. They offered workshops to help teachers understand and implement the reforms and coaching in the classrooms of new teachers and others who needed or requested assistance.

Summer content institutes—week-long professional-development sessions in each core discipline linked closely to the district's new content standards—were developed and first offered in the summer of 1997. They were well-received by teachers and participation in them increased dramatically over the course of the reform.

CURRICULUM FRAMEWORKS. Developed in the spring of 1998 in response to teachers' requests for more guidance on how to implement the district's standards, the curriculum frameworks offered examples of instructional activities, units of study, and assessment tools for the standards in each subject area for every grade. They did not mandate a specific curriculum, however, nor did they provide a specific scope and sequence.

DISTRICT-WIDE CURRICULUM AND INSTRUCTION INITIATIVES. Two other district-wide initiatives provided materials and sustained professional development to Philadelphia teachers. The Philadelphia Urban Systemic Initiative was a five-year (1995–2000) systemic change effort funded by the National Science Foundation (NSF) with the goal of raising high levels of mathematics and science achievement for all students in the district. Its strategies for change included providing standards-based materials and effective programs approved by NSF and creating and supporting a network of teacher leaders. The second initiative, Early Balanced Literacy (EBL), was undertaken by the district in 1998 to ensure that children would leave the primary grades with a strong foundation in reading and writing. In the early years of Children Achieving, a number of elementary schools adopted or developed early literacy programs using a balanced phonics/whole-language approach. Based on the success of these schools, the central administration made early literacy a district-wide focus and provided participating schools with materials and professional development as well as literacy interns to reduce class size in many primary-grade classrooms. The Annenberg Challenge also provided the district with additional funds to support the implementation of early literacy programs in several clusters.

FAMILY AND COMMUNITY SUPPORTS. The Family Resource Network (FRN) was led by cluster staff but also included school personnel such as nurses, guidance counselors, and teachers. It sought to strengthen student-support services by mobilizing and coordinating community-based agencies and direct-service providers. Together with school personnel, they were expected to provide the "safety nets" that so many poor children need. The superintendent also proposed that city and private agencies work together to ensure that all students entered school ready to learn by expanding early childhood opportunities. Although the district successfully implemented full-day kindergartens system-wide, the envisioned early childhood initiative never got off the ground.

IMPROVEMENT AND CHANGE OVER THE COURSE OF THE REFORM

In this section we describe the impact of these reforms on curriculum, instruction, and student performance. In the first four years of Children Achieving, student test scores in Philadelphia as reported by the district rose significantly, although unevenly.[5] Gains were greatest in the first two years of the reform; they began to level off somewhat in the third and fourth years. In the initial baseline administration of the SAT-9 tests in 1996, averaging across all subjects and grades, 29.9 percent of the students tested scored at the basic level or above. The percentage scoring at this level rose to 41.9 on the 1999 tests. Table 2.1 presents the test results by subject and grade level. While gains were made in all subjects and at all levels, the improvement was most consistent in the elementary and K–8 schools.

The improvements displayed in the table are especially noteworthy, as

TABLE 2.1

PERCENT OF STUDENTS SCORING AT OR ABOVE BASIC ON THE SAT-9, BY SUBJECT AREA AND SCHOOL LEVEL, PHILADELPHIA, 1995–96 THROUGH 1998–99

School level	Reading				Math				Science			
	1995–96	1996–97	1997–98	1998–99	1995–96	1996–97	1997–98	1998–99	1995–96	1996–97	1997–98	1998–99
Elementary school	40.4	48.7	54.4	55.1	32.2	41.9	45.3	47.8	37.1	46.4	52.5	52.2
Kindergarten through 8th grade	59.9	65.1	70.4	71.3	40.4	48.5	53.7	54.5	42.1	51.9	57.6	59.3i
Middle school	43.3	50.5	55.0	58.5	15.7	18.5	25.2	24.4	18.1	23.7	31.4	30.2
High school	25.6	34.0	33.6	37.0	11.5	13.8	15.9	15.2	4.9	8.0	8.4	12.0

Philadelphia also aggressively promoted the testing of all students. In comparison to other urban school districts, Philadelphia has one of the nation's most inclusive testing policies. From 1996 to 1999 the proportion of eligible students tested increased by 16 percent.[6] Since the students who were untested in the initial year of Children Achieving were likely to be lower achievers on average than those who were tested, the increased participation in the testing program undoubtedly acted as a drag on improving district-wide performance. Yet test scores rose significantly in spite of the inclusion of increased numbers of lower performing students.[7]

However, when normal curve-equivalent scores are examined, the gains, while still statistically significant, are not quite as dramatic. This phenomenon is due to the inclusion of untested students in the district's reporting of scores on the SAT-9. By including the percentage of untested students, the district made it possible for schools to increase both the percentage of students scoring at or above basic *and* the percentage of students scoring below basic. That happened in many schools, especially in middle and high schools, where the proportions of untested students were largest. Figure 2.1 illustrates this phenomenon, indicating that the most robust gains were made in elementary schools, followed by middle schools. The average performance of eleventh graders was flat over the course of the reform.

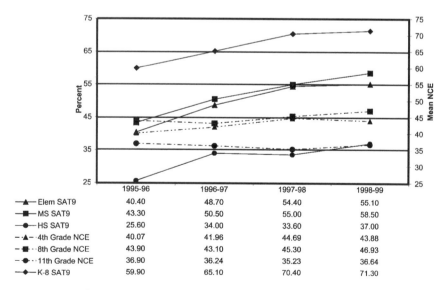

	1995-96	1996-97	1997-98	1998-99
Elem SAT9	40.40	48.70	54.40	55.10
MS SAT9	43.30	50.50	55.00	58.50
HS SAT9	25.60	34.00	33.60	37.00
4th Grade NCE	40.07	41.96	44.69	43.88
8th Grade NCE	43.90	43.10	45.30	46.93
11th Grade NCE	36.90	36.24	35.23	36.64
K-8 SAT9	59.90	65.10	70.40	71.30

FIGURE 2.1 Percentage of students scoring at or above basic by school level, compared with mean normal-curve equivalent score by grade, SAT-9 Reading, Philadelphia, 1996–1999.

Attendance, Promotion, and Persistence

Statistically significant gains were also made on all of the other indicators of school performance. The percentage of students in attendance for 90 percent or more of school days increased by three percentage points from 1996 to 1999; and the percentage of staff attending 95 percent or more of school days increased by over 6 percentage points. Persistence (on-time graduation) and promotion rates also increased significantly, but less rapidly.

Relationship of Achievement Gains to Reforms

How can we account for these changes in performance? To what degree are they related to the implementation of the reforms? What aspects of the Children Achieving reforms seem to account for the achievement gains? This section uses both qualitative and quantitative evidence to address those questions.

As we have seen, Philadelphia elementary students made the most consistent gains on the SAT-9. Our quantitative[8] and qualitative research suggests that three factors contributed to these gains in elementary schools:

- test preparation,
- focus on literacy programs in the primary grades, and
- a strong professional community.

TEST PREPARATION. Our qualitative data indicate that, in all likelihood, improvement in student achievement at all levels is linked to intensive test preparation and increasing familiarity with the content and format of the test.[9] While inadequate curriculum guidance was initially seen as a problem by teachers (leading to the development of curriculum frameworks), the preeminent role of the SAT-9 shifted the attention of many teachers from the standards to the content of the test. Various forms of test preparation were observed at all levels and were the most common instructional response to the reforms.

Not all of this test preparation was bad. Some of it entailed thoughtful improvements in curriculum such as demanding more writing and raising standards for student writing. However, much of the test preparation observed in Philadelphia was of the drill-and-kill variety. Teachers used published materials such as Harcourt-Brace Company's Key Links workbooks to develop students' test-taking skills and familiarize them with the test.

INSTRUCTIONAL FOCUS. Our qualitative data indicate that Philadelphia's focus on early literacy paid off in the primary grades. Classroom observations showed teachers in the early grades increasingly using a balanced approach to teaching reading and writing, more frequent use of cooperative groups, and more emphasis on drafting and revising. This was a result of the early literacy program.

In contrast, Children Achieving did not offer middle and high schools equally specified or effective approaches to instruction. For the most part, middle and high schools were unable to focus on one or two robust and substantive strategies for improvement in student achievement. At both levels, staff tinkered with the structural arrangements of small learning communities, interdisciplinary curricula, project learning, and experiential learning. In middle schools, teachers created curriculum tied to their small learning community themes. After five years, we judged that most of this thematic curriculum work was still at an early stage of development. It seldom involved students in rich intellectual work nor was it typically informed by multiple disciplinary perspectives. High school faculties expanded opportunities for students to participate in internships and service-learning projects, but were less successful at making classrooms more challenging learning environments or stimulating deep changes in instructional practice.

STRONG PROFESSIONAL COMMUNITY. While our analysis found no direct relationship between the degree of implementation of the Children Achieving reforms and growth in student achievement, we did find that well-implemented small learning communities were connected with higher levels of professional community. Findings from both our qualitative and quantitative data indicated a relationship among professional community, positive school conditions, and improved student achievement in elementary schools. That is, our analysis suggests that the implementation of small learning communities was associated with higher levels of professional community, and that higher levels of professional community were linked to improved student achievement (controlling for significant factors, such as poverty). Given the limitations of our data no causal relationship can be inferred, but the findings *do* suggest possible directions for future work in the district.

The data also suggests that, in some schools, strong professional communities and positive school climates preceded Children Achieving and offered fertile ground for the creation of small learning communities and for substantive pedagogical change. This was the case in two elementary schools and one middle school of the 21 schools[10] where we conducted intensive, multiyear qualitative fieldwork.

FACTORS LIMITING THE EFFECTIVENESS OF THE REFORM

Performance improved during the first four years of Children Achieving and we have described some of the primary factors contributing to the gains that were achieved, drawing on both qualitative and quantitative evidence. Are these gains likely to be sustained? What steps would be likely to bring continued improvement? In this section, we look more deeply at the context of the reform and at its implementation, and reflect on what will be needed to continue the improvements in performance.

Contextual Issues

The future of school reform in Philadelphia depends on how fundamental questions about school funding are resolved. To fully implement the ten components of Children Achieving would require significant additional funding from either the city or the state, and its initial design was based on the *assumption* that more funding would be forthcoming. The entire initiative can be viewed as a calculated risk taken by Superintendent Hornbeck. In this view, he was betting that the Annenberg Challenge grant and its match could be used to improve performance, and that improved performance would generate the political will to obtain increased state funding either through the courts or the legislature, thus allowing the reforms to be institutionalized and continued.

The funds Pennsylvania provides to each school district are currently based on a funding formula that takes into account the number of pupils, the special needs of the district, its ability to raise local taxes, and other factors. However, the state froze the formula in 1993, which meant that state aid to the district after that date did not rise in response to increases in enrollment and poverty. On a per-pupil basis adjusted for inflation, the real value of state education funds coming to Philadelphia between 1993 and 1998 actually decreased by 5.9 percent (Century 1998).

When Hornbeck became superintendent in August 1994 he had reason to believe that he had the political support needed to win more funding from the state. He began his tenure with a Democratic governor holding office, Democratic majorities in the state legislature, and a Democratic mayor, and he had strong backing from business and civic leaders in Philadelphia. However, just three months into his administration, the political landscape in Pennsylvania and Philadelphia changed dramatically. The state elected a Republican governor and Republican majorities in the state legislature who were committed to reducing government spending. Relationships between the state and the district were strained by the new governor's advocacy of vouchers and by the superintendent's allegations of racist state policies. And, midway through Hornbeck's tenure as superintendent, the leadership of Greater Philadelphia First, a coalition of business leaders, disappointed that district officials had not won major concessions from the teachers' union during contract negotiations in 1998 and sympathetic to its pro-business governor, began to withdraw its support of the district's reform agenda.

With inadequate political support and personal antagonisms between state representatives and the superintendent, the school district was unable to persuade Pennsylvania state officials to significantly increase funding. Despite two court cases and threats by the superintendent to close schools early in 1999, the governor and legislative leadership were unwilling to alter the school-funding formula or provide the money requested. They believed that funds were being used inefficiently in Philadelphia and that the district's teacher contract was a major obstacle to improvement.

In their view, better management and a better contract were prerequisites for additional state funds. The state *did* provide Philadelphia with some one-time grants, but these were small in comparison to what the school district said was required to continue with the Children Achieving reform agenda.

In addition to refusing to provide significant additional school funds for Philadelphia, the state granted itself greater power and authority over public education in the city. In response to Hornbeck's threat to close schools early during the 1998–1999 school year, the state passed a take-over law, Act 46, aimed directly at Philadelphia. It gave the state the power to appoint new governing authorities in urban districts for a range of reasons, including fiscal distress.

Meanwhile, the citizens of Philadelphia were also busy. In the spring of 2000 they elected a new mayor, who supported the superintendent's reforms during his campaign. They also approved a change to the city charter that allowed the new mayor to appoint all of the Board of Education members concurrently with his term of office.

The political impasse between the district and the state came to a head during the summer of 2000 when the district faced a projected budget deficit of $205 million. Under pressure from the state takeover law to balance the budget, the Philadelphia Board of Education made cuts and adopted a budget of nearly $1.6 billion, which contained no new money for the programs that the superintendent felt were required to fully implement the Children Achieving reform agenda. As a result, the implementation of new promotion and graduation requirements was postponed and the number of days allocated for teacher professional development was reduced. Not willing to remain to oversee the piece-by-piece dismantling of his reform agenda, Superintendent Hornbeck announced his resignation on June 5, 2000.

RELATIONSHIP WITH PROFESSIONAL UNIONS. The school district's relationships with its professional unions, the Philadelphia Federation of Teachers (PFT) and the Commonwealth Association of School Administrators (CASA), were strained over the course of Children Achieving. Both the PFT and CASA sought salary schedules that were more competitive with the surrounding suburbs. And they offered strong objections to key components of Children Achieving, particularly to its accountability provisions. Alleging that the pay-for-performance system for school principals was not objective, CASA brought suit against the district. The PFT repeatedly questioned the alignment of the SAT-9 assessment with the new district standards and the use of the PRI to assess schools. It also criticized the clusters as increased bureaucracy and argued that money would be better spent on early childhood education, smaller classes, and a district curriculum that would provide more direction to teachers. In addition, the school district, under pressure from the state and the business community, sought major changes in the work rules in the teachers' contract in the negotiations that began in January 2000. Specifically, district officials wanted

- a longer school day and school year without explicitly paying teachers for the additional time. The teachers' work day was one hour less than the state average;

- a change in how teachers were assigned to schools. Rather than rely on seniority, the district wanted to give principals greater voice in hiring and to be able to assign the most qualified teachers to schools with the most need; and

- a pay-for-performance system. Under the current contract, teachers' salaries are based on years of service and their educational attainments. The district would like salary increases to be based on classroom performance.

The PFT was adamantly opposed to asking teachers to take on additional burdens without commensurate increases in compensation, and they were reluctant to give up work rules fought for and won in earlier contracts. At the time of this writing, the city's mayor has used his new authority to impose the new work rules desired by the district, and the possibility of a strike over these issues looms large.

PRINCIPAL AND TEACHER TURNOVER. Philadelphia, like other urban districts, faces serious shortages of high-quality personnel, especially principals and assistant principals, to guide and support the reforms. Leadership is particularly problematic at the high school level. In the 18 comprehensive high schools (out of 22) for which we have data on the length of principal tenure, only five principals have been in their current schools for two years or more. Most high schools have had multiple principals over the course of Children Achieving. The district is at a disadvantage in recruiting and retaining qualified school leaders because its salaries are the lowest in the region, and because state legislation has made retirement an attractive option for many. Additionally, increased accountability under Children Achieving combined with loss of authority to the clusters has lowered morale among principals in the system. Our qualitative research indicates that many principals feel that they have not been shown respect by district policy-makers and have had little influence over the course of reform.

Philadelphia is also failing at the job of recruiting and retaining teachers. Teacher turnover is high. From 1995 to 1999 in the average school in Philadelphia, nearly 40 percent of teachers were new to the school in which they were teaching. In some elementary and middle schools, turnover rates were as high as 60 percent. The district's analyses show that their teacher-transfer policies (as spelled out in the collective-bargaining agreement with the teachers' union) result in the least-experienced faculties serving in schools with the lowest achievement, highest poverty, and greatest proportions of African-American and Latino students. Studies conducted by the Philadelphia Education Fund show that many prospective and current teachers are being lured to positions outside of the city, where salaries are higher, class sizes are smaller, and teaching conditions are generally more appealing (Useem 1999).

Implementation Issues

Perhaps the most fundamental lesson to be gleaned from research on policy implementation and change in education is that it is difficult, even in the best of circumstances, to alter education practice. Reform takes time and requires tremendous support and patience. Altering classroom practice requires the development of new skills that have to be learned and practiced. For successful implementation to occur, teachers must believe that the reforms are both desirable and doable. Implementation ultimately depends on the smallest unit of the organization (McLaughlin 1991). In this section, we examine some of the implementation problems that limited the effects of the Children Achieving reforms and are obstacles to continued improvement.

REFORM OVERLOAD. The research literature is clear in that maintaining focus over time is essential to substantive educational improvement. This was difficult in Philadelphia due to the number of reforms being implemented and the amount of time required at the school level to implement them. Teachers in Philadelphia faced development of new curriculum in every subject, new assessments, new work arrangements and relationships, new demands for professional development, new procedures for obtaining services for students, new evaluation procedures, and other related changes. All of this was asked of them at once, following the superintendent's dictum of "all at once." Reform overload was a strong contributor to school staffs' inability to focus their efforts around clearly defined and manageable instructional priorities. Furthermore, reform overload resulted in rampant frustration and alienation among principals. They felt angry, disempowered, and disrespected as they received one mandate after another that had not been shaped by their input and that was not accompanied with the necessary supports for implementation.

Additionally, the burden of the reforms being implemented overwhelmed cluster staff. Many clusters were unable to fully develop or implement their own reform strategies, because so much time was spent disseminating information about new district policies and programs that the schools were required to put into practice. The staffs in all 22 clusters worked hard to win teacher support and to assist them, but they were hampered by the sheer number of district initiatives and directives that they had to carry out. The staff of the Teaching and Learning Network was too often serving as conduits for new district programs rather than as sources of help to teachers seeking to improve instruction.

SEQUENCING AND ROLL-OUT OF THE REFORMS. One of the primary implementation flaws of Children Achieving was the sequence in which the district rolled-out the reforms and supports. The accountability system was put in place prior to the supports. Schools were held accountable for performance targets before teachers had received the new standards, before the Teaching and Learning Network and all 22 clusters were in place, before the development of curriculum frameworks offered a modicum of guidance, before the summer institutes offered teachers rich opportunities to examine their practice. All of this contributed to the perception of teachers and principals that they were being asked to carry a disproportionate amount of the burden for improvement—and that they were carrying it alone. It also put the focus squarely on the district test rather than on the standards, and on test preparation rather than curriculum development.

UNDERESTIMATION OF TIME AND SUPPORT. Implementing standards-based instruction requires much of those who work in schools. It requires new curriculum and deep changes in teaching that occur only over extended periods of time and with intensive support. The district did not provide teachers with adequate curriculum materials needed to do the job, nor enough guidance and time for them to develop their own units of study. Teachers were not trained adequately for standards-based instruction, and many held beliefs that ran contrary to it. Opportunities to participate in content-based professional development, work collaboratively with other teachers, observe expert colleagues, and receive coaching in their own classrooms were eventually provided, but they came on the scene late— after the direction of the reform and teachers' attitudes toward it were shaped by the accountability system.

CONFUSION ABOUT GOVERNANCE. Another implementation issue that plagued Children Achieving was confusion surrounding the development of the new governance structures. Understanding which decisions should be made by the streamlined central office or by local school councils or small learning communities was difficult. For example, the new roles of the central office often conflicted. While central office staff was committed to decentralization and wanted to let schools make more decisions, it was also cognizant of the problems that teachers, principals, and other staff faced as they struggled to respond to standards and a high-stakes accountability system. Confusion and indecision about how much guidance to provide and, in some cases, superficial understanding of the elements of the reform, led central office leaders to temporize and delay actions. This contributed to the poor sequencing of supports for teachers and to frustration in the schools.

The creation of local school councils (LSCs) also proved difficult and their legitimacy and authority were ambiguous, at best. From the beginning, schools had difficulty simply establishing them. In order for a council to be considered "operational," one adult from at least 35 percent of all student households had to participate in the election of the parent representatives. A number of schools were never able to get 35 percent of parents to participate. LSCs that became operational lacked the legitimacy and authority that is afforded by legislation or contractual agreements. They did not have the power to hire staff, and their discretion over budgets varied considerably by school.

Another site of school decision-making was the small learning community (SLC), but its effectiveness was also limited by confusion over leadership and governance. By the fourth year of the reform, most SLC members were being given common preparation time and other opportunities to meet, but they lacked budgetary authority and the autonomy to act on their own decisions. Schools grappled with the implications of these new organizational arrangements for staff roles and responsibilities: What is the role of the principal in this new school organization? Where should small learning community coordinators focus their energy and attention? In the name of decentralization, the central office provided little guidance about these issues, and support from clusters was uneven. Not surprisingly, implementation of small learning communities and their functioning varied widely across the schools.

CREDIBILITY OF THE ACCOUNTABILITY SYSTEM. Another of Children Achieving's implementation flaws was its reliance on an accountability system that was perceived as inaccurate and unfair. Challenges to the Performance Responsibility Index (PRI) were constant throughout the course of Children Achieving and contributed to a lack of credibility in the index. Among other things, critics objected to the way the PRI was calculated, its assumptions about progress, and its lack of incentives for deep improvements in instruction.

As described earlier, the PRI score for each school was a composite figure made up of five indicators: mean student scores in reading, mathematics, and science; staff and student attendance; and the promotion or persistence rate. School staff objected to several of the indicators, but particularly to the measure of staff attendance. District officials measured staff attendance strictly, counting even staff out on long-term disability and maternity leave as "absent." This struck many teachers as unfair and contributed to the perception that teachers were the only people being held accountable for students' low performance. Although district officials made changes to the PRI in the second cycle, they did not change the way staff attendance was calculated.

The calculation of school targets and progress on the PRI was also questioned, because it failed to take into account error in measurement. Measurement error is based on the concept that the scores of an individual repeatedly taking a test will fluctuate, within a certain band, around a hypothetical "true" score. This phenomenon occurs not only in standardized tests of individuals, but in any kind of measurement. In the PRI there was no attempt to take this fluctuation into account for schools. The PRI was measured precisely: if growth was equal to or greater than the target, it was counted as progress. If growth was less than the target, even minutely so, it was considered problematic. In many cases, the error bands, if calculated, would have been larger than the growth targets themselves. That means that a school could have made adequate progress but the PRI would show stagnation or failure, or, alternatively, that a school might actually regress and still be rewarded.

The questionable assumptions about progress underlying the PRI were another problem. Targets and baselines were developed based on an assumption of consistent, linear progress. School targets were calculated by taking the baseline score, subtracting it from 95 to get a measure of the growth needed for the school to reach 95 in 12 years. That figure was then divided by six to get the amount of growth needed in each two-year cycle. It was assumed that progress would occur in equal increments. We know that improvement happens this way only rarely and that there are many other potential growth patterns. Performance might get better quickly and then level off. It might be flat for several years, before shooting up exponentially. None of these other potential growth patterns could be accommodated by the PRI.

From afar, school progress on the PRI looks promising. Almost all schools have met their performance targets in the first two accountability cycles. However, even schools making significant progress as measured by the PRI have struggled instructionally, and some have implemented the reforms only superficially. The PRI did not provide strong incentives for organizational learning. Only schools identified as making low progress received systematic feedback on the quality of their instructional efforts. This meant that schools encouraging extensive test preparation of the worst kind might be rewarded as much as those undertaking deep changes in instruction. And this method of reviewing only those schools that did not meet their targets reinforced the idea that feedback was a form of sanction and that reflection was only necessary when there was measurable failure. Rather than promote a district-wide culture of continuous progress, it encouraged many schools to seek quick fixes and adopt coping strategies. Additionally, reconstitution proved to be an empty threat in a context where staff turnover was high. There was no pool to replace principals who might be removed from their schools.

CONCLUSION: SOME LESSONS LEARNED

By the fall of 2000 Philadelphia public education appeared grid-locked, with the unresolved teachers' contract emblematic of a lack of agreement about the values underlying Children Achieving and its means for bringing about improvement. Advocates of the reforms felt that considerable progress had been made, but that inequities in state aid and resistance from the teachers' union were threats to continued progress. Critics, in turn, pointed to the flattening of test scores, budget problems, increased expenditures on administration, and the emphasis on test preparation as evidence that the reforms were deeply flawed.

Without doubt, Children Achieving offered the city a powerful set of ideas for school reform and changed the nature of the debate over public education. Central ideas—such as that results matter; that all children can learn at high levels—and that all means *all*; that everyone must be held accountable; and that professional development is a necessity—have generated a new set of expectations for local policy-makers.

However, the leadership of the School District of Philadelphia paid too little attention to implementation lessons from the past. They often criticized teachers rather than attempting to win their support for reforms. They adhered to the dictum of the Children Achieving plan that everything had to be done simultaneously, which placed enormous burdens on teachers and principals. They assumed that teachers would embrace the reforms in exchange for more freedom to develop curricula. They put pressure on teachers before they provided supports, and they underestimated the difficulty of developing standards-based curricula and instruction.

Capacity was lacking at all levels of the system, yet efforts to build it were late, sporadic, and weak. Left without the necessary supports and feeling overwhelmed and overburdened, many teachers, principals, and administrators left the district, seeking higher salaries and better working conditions outside the city—making implementation of the reforms even more difficult.

Individual schools also varied in their capacity for change, their professional cultures, and their reform histories. The experience in Philadelphia suggests that differentiated reform strategies are needed for elementary, middle, and high schools. Each level of schooling brought different organizational issues, professional norms, and cultures that needed to be addressed. Their past experiences with reform varied, and the challenges they faced in motivating students and staff were different. However, Children Achieving only offered a "one size fits all" reform strategy that was difficult to adapt to varying school contexts, and it was left up to the cluster and school staffs to figure out how to address variations in school capacity and needs.

The case of Children Achieving reminds us of the importance of context and of the hard lessons learned about implementation of reforms in the previous, more piecemeal reforms of the 1970s and '80s. It also illustrates a central problem with the practice of systemic reform—as opposed to its theory. In attending to all of the conditions affecting teaching and learning, the architects of systemic reform can easily lose sight of instruction itself. Instruction remains at the heart of the enterprise, and improving it is the key to raising performance. If the reform theory does not explicitly lay out strategies for doing this, it is likely to generate a range of responses—some productive, some not—and early gains will not be sustained. In the last few years the leaders of Philadelphia's reform seemed to recognize that they had to move beyond new structures to address core problems of teaching and learning. They organized summer institutes around curriculum content, began to shift their professional development from workshops to coaching, and supported work on curricula in early literacy.

To sustain the reform momentum in Philadelphia and to make further achievement gains, the leaders of the Philadelphia schools are going to have to do more than solve their financial problems. They are going to have to re-examine their theory of reform, and ask themselves what the mechanisms are for building school capacity and improving classroom instruction. They will have to provide more guidance, more tools, more time to develop curricula. They might continue and extend the work of capacity-building and instructional improvement that was initiated under Children Achieving, but the work will have to be more focused, more collaborative, more persistent to build professional cultures in the city's schools that embrace high standards and work towards continuous improvement.

NOTES

1. In 1993 philanthropist Walter Annenberg pledged $500 million to help improve the quality of education for America's neediest children, and he challenged private donors to match these funds. Nearly 60 percent of the resulting challenge grants have gone to eight of the nation's largest school districts, including Philadelphia's. The goals of the challenge are to support an unprecedented number of public schools to work directly with their local communities; to manage their resources in ways that meet the needs of their particular student population; to set high expectations for all students; and to assess progress through careful and continuous review. The challenge encourages communities to develop their own strategies to reach these goals. Instead of giving funds directly to school districts, the challenge works through nonprofit collaboratives in each of its sites, which in turn are supported by staff of the Annenberg Institute. In 1995 the School District of Philadelphia submitted a reform proposal called Children Achieving to the Annenberg Foundation and received a $50 million challenge grant that has been successfully matched with $100 million from Philadelphia corporations, foundations, and federal grants.

2. In 1996 the Children Achieving challenge commissioned the Consortium for Policy Research in Education (CPRE) and Research for Action (RFA) to conduct a four-year evaluation of Philadelphia's Children Achieving initiative. Over the past four years, CPRE has conducted two system-wide surveys of teachers about the impact of the reforms on their daily work and about the character of their instruction. CPRE and RFA staff members have also collected data from 48 Philadelphia schools: observing classrooms, meetings, and professional-development sessions, and interviewing teachers, principals, and other school officials. We have interviewed district officials and civic leaders and observed numerous meetings in which the reforms were debated, designed, and revised. We have examined the SAT-9 test results and other indicators of system performance.

3. Initially, performance and opportunity-to-learn standards were also envisioned, but they were never fully developed.

4. Soon after the 1996 baseline scores on the SAT-9 were announced, the school district also announced its plans to reconstitute two high schools. The Philadelphia Federation of Teachers was outraged and charged that the reconstitution plans had been made without the appropriate consultation and before mutually agreed-upon criteria had been set. An independent arbitrator agreed with the union and the reconstitution plans were abandoned, but not without cost. The episode seriously disrupted the two high schools marked for reconstitution (the principal of one of the schools had her car vandalized and was the subject of threats for her support of Hornbeck's plans) and embittered an already tense relationship with the teachers' union.

5. Philadelphia began using the ninth edition of the Stanford Achievement Test (SAT-9) in 1995–1996, the first full school year of Children Achieving. This analysis includes data from testing conducted in the spring of each year from 1996 to 1999.

6. Under Children Achieving, schools who do not test all their eligible students are penalized in the district's accountability system.

7. While these improvements in achievement were encouraging, it must be noted that the overall performance of students in the district remains low relative to other Pennsylvania districts. By 1999, the average 11th-grade reading score was still more than 150 points below the state average, and mean 5th-grade reading scores were nearly 200 points below the state average. (Data from the Pennsylvania State System of Assessment, <www.paprofiles.org>.)

8. Using the hierarchical linear modeling (HLM), we examined the relationships between teacher and school characteristics, measures of professional community, measures of reform implementation, and growth in test scores over four years (1995–1996 to 1998–1999). The HLM analysis showed that both the poverty level of students and the degree of professional community in a school were directly related to its growth in achievement in fourth grade. Interestingly, poverty did not depress growth in achievement. Schools with the highest concentration of poor students actually improved faster than schools with lower concentrations of poverty. But poverty was also a significant predictor of the baseline scores (1996 SAT-9 scores), so these poorest schools also had lower baselines and therefore more room for improvement. The only measure of professional community that was significantly related to growth in achievement was teacher collaboration. Schools with greater teacher collaboration experienced higher rates of growth in achievement from 1996 to 1999. The measures of reform implementation were not significant predictors of achievement growth in our HLM models, but subsequent analyses using logistic regression did reveal significant relationships between small learning community implementation and school conditions, as well as between small learning community implementation and professional community measures. For a more detailed explanation of this analysis, please contact the authors.

9. Efforts to create a quantitative measure of the level of test preparation in schools were not fruitful.

10. This sample of 21 schools included 11 elementary schools, 5 middle schools, and 5 high schools.

◙   ◙   ◙

CHAPTER THREE

Balancing Autonomy and Control in the New York City Public Schools

using the Double-ACE model

BRUCE S. COOPER

DAVID C. BLOOMFIELD

> When Americans grow dissatisfied with public schools, they tend to blame the way they are governed. There is too much democracy, or too little, critics insist, too much centralization or too little, too many actors in the policy formulation or too few. Although Americans have recurrently demonstrated a profound distrust of government (Farnham 1963), they have also asserted a utopian faith that once Americans found the right pattern of school governance, education would thrive. (Tyack 1993, 1)

A T FIRST GLANCE, IT APPEARS that urban historian David B. Tyack's statement above applies to New York State. For, on December 17, 1996, the New York State Legislature in an extraordinary session passed a new statute (the Act), significantly altering the organization and governance of the nation's largest urban school system, the New York City Public Schools. The Act considerably weakened the authority of the (decentralized) community school boards and district superintendents, instead giving the chief executive officer, the schools chancellor, much greater latitude and responsibility to hire, evaluate, train, transfer, and fire community superintendents and to remove or supersede elected community school boards or individual board members. Was this just another swing in the pendulum, a change from a decentralized to a re-centralized system, or was something more profound and important happening—the introduction of strategic management, making the system more flexible and performance-driven?

The seesaw between centralization and decentralization has a long history. We know, for example, that the 1996 Act was not the first time the State Legislature had changed the governance arrangements in the New York City schools. As summarized by the Marchi Commission in *Governing for Results: Decentralization with Accountability* (Marchi 1991), until the late nineteenth century most big-city school systems were decentralized according to wards and other political subdivisions. Even after the consolidation of the five boroughs of New York City in 1898, each borough had its own school board and its own superintendent of schools. Only in 1902, with the appointment of William Henry Maxwell as the city's first school superintendent, was a single system created with a standardized curriculum throughout the city (Marchi 1991, 58). Since then, lawmakers have continued to tinker with this centralization–decentralization paradigm to create what Tyack calls "the one best system" (1974). For example, in 1969, the New York State Legislature devolved power to its 32 regional community school districts under the New York City Decentralization Law (Chapter 330 of the Laws of 1969) to meet demands for community control. And later, an effort was made to decentralize still further—to school-site governance—under former State Commissioner Thomas Sobol's 1990 directive, *A New Compact for Learning* (Hannaway and Carnoy 1993; Ravitch 1983).

The 1996 Act might appear to be just another round in the centralization–decentralization effort, vesting new control in the office of the schools chancellor, formerly Dr. Rudolph Crew and Harold O. Levy. The metaphor often used is that of a pendulum, swinging between lesser and greater centrism and decentrism, of more central bureaucracy versus more local autonomy (Sharpe 1979; Wohlstetter 1995).

Richard Elmore (1993) explains that shifts from centralization to decentralization and back again are virtually meaningless, because these reforms focus more on changing the status quo than on finding the best organizational structures for school improvement. Elmore writes:

> In any specific case, decentralizing reforms seem, at least on the surface, to provide very plausible answers to the ills of public education. In general, however, repeated cycles of centralizing and decentralizing reforms in education have little discernible effect on the efficiency, accountability, or effectiveness of public schools. . . . A debate ensues about the merits of centralization and decentralization. At any given point in the debate, the "co-effect" or "enlightened" position is usually clear. It is the opposite of whatever was previously correct. Each doctrine is well-developed, to the point where it can be recited more or less as a mantra by reformers and practitioners. (1993, 34)

Even though the pendulum metaphor has a certain appeal and fits our notions of "history repeating itself" in dynamic cycles, we shall argue in this chapter that, for the effects and meaning of the 1996 Act, this image is both incorrect and misleading; that the new powers of the chancellor introduce a shift from procedural controls to the key elements of strategic management, constituting a sea change in urban school governance (Osborne and Gaebler 1992). Instead of changes along the centralization–decentralization continuum, the 1996 New York State statute granted the chancellor and others throughout the system the discretionary authority and resources to attain qualitative outcomes, not merely to engage in mandated protocols geared to achieving regulatory compliance.

STRATEGIC MANAGEMENT THROUGH STATUTORY REFORM

The Act's corporate model of strategic management differs from "re-centralization" in three ways: (1) as a non-zero-sum game, (2) as a dynamic, interactive model, and (3) as a reactive and proactive process. First, traditional views of centralization and decentralization tend to treat political power as a zero-sum game; that is, when authority is increased at one level or for one party—say the superintendent—then subordinates (e.g., school principals and teachers) lose a concomitant amount of their control. This bifurcated thinking ignores the possibility that greater central activity and authority—when directed at standards and enforcement and recognition of quality—may, in fact, *empower* and enliven local decision-makers and improve classroom performance.

Instead of treating the New York City schools structure as an "either-or" proposition (with either one party or the other having increased power), we see the change as an opportunity for a "both-and" situation, where *both* the chancellor *and* school-site leadership now have control over resources, but just at different levels. Thus, the Act ingeniously maintains the same basic structure (community boards, superintendents, and school-site management) but alters the role and relations among these levels.

Interestingly, Fuhrman and Elmore (1993) likewise have considered and rejected the zero-sum game in their major study of "the balance between state government and local school districts" (p. 82)—relationships analogous to this study of school board and school-site interactions. Fuhrman and Elmore explain:

> The concept of state–local relationships as a zero-sum game simply does not fit the facts. Such a model cannot account for the strong impact of a number of state policies in the absence of significant state efforts to enforce or monitor those polices: it does not explain why locals comply in the absence of such enforcement or clear directives; and it cannot accommodate evidence of increased local activity coinciding with increased state activity. (1993, 89)

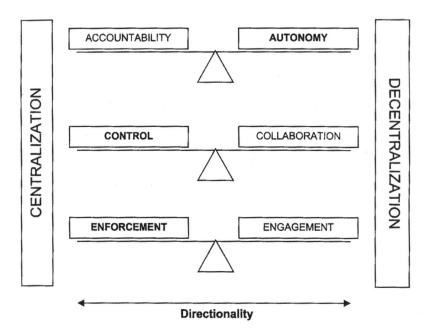

FIGURE 3.1 Balancing centralization and decentralization: the Double-ACE model.

A Balancing Process: The Double-ACE Model

Second, through the allocation of these new powers, the state law creates a dynamic, interactive model of strategic management among central administration, community school district, superintendent, and school principals, so that education decisions are in the first instance the responsibility of school-level leadership, with the central staff monitoring and evaluating these decisions to ensure that schools meet education benchmarks. Strategic management, then, is leadership directed at stated goals, shared activities, and improved performance through collaborative decision-making at all levels of the organization.

Strategic management requires recognition of the need to balance the centralized responsibilities of accountability, control, and enforcement with the decentralized concerns of autonomy, collaboration, and engagement in the school and classroom. As shown in figure 3.1, this model is called "Double-ACE" and allows leaders to explore the central–local relationship in three ways:

- *Double-A: Accountability–Autonomy* can be seen as extremes, as a dichotomy, or as complementary, balancing qualities, whereby the central authority holds local actors responsible (accountable) but permits them the autonomy to meet standards in ways best for them. This model is strikingly different from the typical governance statute—one that allocates authority among the actors but fundamentally ignores their interaction, leaving that process to politics and the courts. John Anderson, president of the New American Schools Corporation, puts it this way: "A growing body of evidence demonstrates that neither top-down system changes nor bottom-up school changes alone can lead to improvements in student achievement. What is needed is system change specifically targeted to support the improvement of classroom practice . . . both kinds of action are necessary but not sufficient" (Anderson 1997, 48).

- *Double-C: Control or Collaboration* is likewise a possible dichotomy, with greater central control squelching local cooperation and collaboration. However, a balance—of sufficient clarity of top-down expectations and oversight with the full opportunity for local participants to share ideas and reach mutually acceptable decisions—is critical if urban school systems such as New York's are to work. Strategic management is thus both reactive and proactive—that is, leaders often combine a role of overseeing local school affairs with a strong long-term mission, specific objectives for carrying out that mission, and the means of motivating and measuring the results (Anderson 1997).

  This combination of roles contrasts with the rudimentary weapons available under the centralization–decentralization model, where schools are held in check in only two ways: either (a) by imposing standards and procedures and taking action against the most egregious laggards and outliers; or (b) through active devolution of authority (i.e., decentralization), assuming somehow that those closest to the students (parents, teachers, and building administrators), "freed from state and district prescriptions," to quote Hannaway and Carnoy (1993, 137) "would focus their efforts on ways that would lead to greater student achievement."

- *Double-E: Enforcement or Engagement/Empowerment* poses similar concerns, for an overemphasis on centralized control and enforcement can reduce a sense of engagement and empowerment within the organization. Double-E, then, speaks to the results of the centralization–decentralization battle, where highly centralized systems seek to enforce rules and regulations, while decentralized ones are after greater engagement, while somewhere in between might be a balance point.

Thus, this dichotomous view—local is good, central is bad, or vice versa—ignores the unique and important contribution of both top managers and local educators and the synergistic, dynamic, and self-reinforcing relationship that can occur between the top and the bottom of the organization. Central leadership, in a strategic-management context, holds the "big picture": the benchmarks across settings, access to macro-resources, and the authority to intervene when things go wrong. Strategically, top management should make a conscious effort to forge ties with local school leaders, to engage in a highly interactive process, and to motivate schools to improve. Meanwhile, the delivery units (schools and classrooms)—having the close-up picture and the best knowledge of students and families in their schools—are free to determine means and proximate ends, leaving final, summative assessment to those at the top of the system.

And when the decentralized units (schools) go afoul of the rules, laws, or basic tenets of quality education, they need city-wide leadership to set them back on track. Thus, as Anderson found, school district leaders "set the direction for the schools and run the accountability system, while at the same time freeing schools to do the hands-on work to accomplish their performance goals" (1997, 34).

Opportunities for Strategic Action to Meet Performance Benchmarks

The 1996 state law reflected Chancellor Crew's background as an advocate for applying private-sector management techniques to public education and the new focus on national, state, and local educational standards. Crew's successor, Harold O. Levy, an attorney, is in fact even more "corporate," having served as an executive at Citibank prior to his appointment as New York City schools chancellor. Rather than relying on procedural norms that have been so long associated with "decentralization-style" thinking, the new law focused on the application of performance benchmarks to individual principals and community superintendents—a striking and revolutionary statutory concept, as shown in figure 3.2 depicting the new governance model (see, for example, Education Law § 2590-h [8]). The law required the chancellor to "promulgate minimum clear educational standards, curriculum requirements and frameworks, and mandatory education objectives applying to all schools and programs throughout the city districts, and examine and evaluate periodically all such schools and programs with respect to compliance with [replacing "maintenance of"] such education standards and other requirements."

Thus, the first step in strategic management is setting the goals clearly for all divisions, schools, programs, and locations, which must then be evaluated. While this sounds like "good-old" centralization speaking, the means for reaching goals are very much strategic and information-dependent if units are to improve. The Act makes possible mutual, highly interactive activities, multiple levels of accountability, sanctions for poor school performance, and the identification of responsible, accountable parties. This synergy of reallocated functions, as described below, is a clear departure from traditional "top-down" public administration where the game is zero-sum and the conditions favor win–lose outcomes.

SCHOOL PRINCIPAL ACCOUNTABILITY. This performance-driven formula-

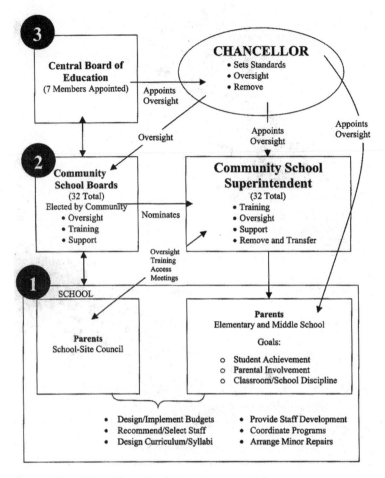

FIGURE 3.2 New York City school governance model.

tion creates rich, interactive relationships among the system's actors—hardly zero-sum thinking and quite apart from the chancellor's authority. For example, the Act at § 2590-f (5) requires the 32 community superintendents to evaluate principals annually to determine their "educational effectiveness and school performance, including the effectiveness of promoting student achievement and parental involvement, and maintaining school discipline." Thus, in a single legislative stroke, the law ties together students, parents, principals, and superintendents in a critical evaluative relationship unique in American education law.

The importance of § 2590-f (5) and similar provisions of the law (see *infra*) is that beyond mere words, the statute has teeth. Principals are not only annually evaluated by superintendents, according to the foregoing criteria, but these building administrators are also directly appointed by

superintendents—with input from parents, teachers, and support personnel—and with final review and possible rejection (for cause) by the chancellor as spelled out in Education Law §§ 1590-f (1)(d) and 2590-i (2)(c).
Supplemented by the new supervisor's contract with the city, which eliminated principals' tenure, these changes offer true accountability at the
building level.

In a clear break with the earlier propensity of some community school
boards to mete out patronage through principal appointments ($5,000 was
rumored to be the "going rate" to buy a position), community school board
members are now banned from any role in the appointment of staff other
than a limited one in hiring community school board superintendents. In
fact, community school board members are subject to removal "for will-
ful, intentional, or knowing involvement in the hiring, appointment, or
assignment of employees other than as specifically authorized" by statute
(Education Law §§ 2590-e [4]; 2590-i [2][a]). While such actions are "cen-
tral-like," they mainly empower subordinate community superintendents,
not the chancellor. These provisions also "clean up" the graft and corruption in local districts and make it more likely that teaching and learning
will be a priority.

SANCTIONS FOR PERSISTENT EDUCATIONAL FAILURE. The New York State
Legislature deemed the strategic reorganization of failing schools to be so
important that the Act permits the chancellor to declare "martial law" and
take over schools that exhibit "persistent educational failure" and combine them into a free-standing "chancellor's district" under his direct
authority. Principals may also be

> removed or transferred by the superintendent or by the chancellor for per-
> sistent educational failure of the schools or other causes. . . . Persistent
> educational failure of the schools shall be defined in regulations of the
> chancellor to include a pattern of poor or declining achievement; a pat-
> tern of poor or declining attendance; disruption or violence; and continu-
> ing failure to meet the chancellor's performance standards or other stan-
> dards. (Education Law § 2590-i [2][a])

Principals may also be ordered "by the chancellor or the superintendent to
participate in training or other forms of staff development or to address
identified areas of educational need and promote student achievement
and school performance" (Education Law § 2590-i [2][b]).

The chancellor and community superintendents thus have clear
authority to hold principals accountable in a strategic manner to promote
school performance. This "cradle-to-grave" authority to hire, review, stip-
ulate training, evaluate, and remove, though perhaps intuitive, has never
before existed so explicitly in the New York City schools. Appointments,
mandated evaluations according to explicit criteria, and potential required
re-training, transfers, or terminations without tenure protection are heavy
weapons in the arsenal of any school administrator. Through the new gov-

ernance statute, these armaments are for the first time available in New York City, not just with "top" or "central" management (e.g., the chancellor), but spread throughout the system among the 32 local-district superintendents and four borough-based high school districts—middle or unit managers in the system.

Schools identified as "persistent failures," therefore, are subject to drastic action. With the cooperation of the teachers' and administrators' unions (the United Federation of Teachers and the Council of Supervisors and Administrators), the chancellor can transfer teachers and administrators to other settings and replace them with new staff. Such actions were previously difficult, because administrators were not held accountable for school performance and radical reorganization was constrained by notions of seniority and school-specific tenure. Unfortunately, at this time, efforts to improve schools by transferring qualified teachers into these buildings are severely restricted by the teachers' contract.

SUPERINTENDENT ACCOUNTABILITY. Given current contractual limitations, under the statute chancellors now have the perfect opportunity to shape the actions and behaviors of over a dozen new community-school-district superintendents, given the early retirement of nearly one-third of the district superintendents. Each superintendent is required to submit to the chancellor a comprehensive strategic plan for identifying and solving their district's problems and improving performance. The strategic plan is linked to each superintendent's contract through performance standards, which are periodically evaluated and used in determining contract renewal.

The Act is thus strategically proactive: it pushes superintendents to use these new powers fully and consistently. An argument could be made that such actions were long available to "creative" superintendents. Implied power, however, only works when leaders have the initiative and courage to use it. Bureaucratic inertia created by the earlier (1969) law and its resulting local school board politics dampened rather than stimulated such initiative. Why should a community superintendent, under the watchful eye of the community board, take the risk of evaluating and replacing weak school principals, when these actions were not required?

The Act mandates that superintendents take action against failing principals or else face their own termination or other sanctions at the hands of the chancellor. The new statute requires that the chancellor establish an inclusive public process for the recruitment, screening, selection, and review of candidates for district superintendent, and further to "[s]elect community superintendents from a list of candidates recommended by community boards and consistent with regulations and a model contract developed by the chancellor"; and the policy further reads: "Remove a community superintendent who fails to comply with" . . . all applicable laws, explicitly including "performance standards addressed by administration and educational effectiveness, and any requirements for continuing training and education."

SCHOOL-LEVEL AUTHORITY. Rather than a top-down or bottom-up pyramidal structure, the Act is careful to allocate sovereignty in various arenas, among different educational actors and groups. Thus, while the chancellor and superintendents have monitoring roles, their focus is on performance, not procedure, which effectively lies at the discretion of school-based stakeholders: students, parents, staff, and principals. In this context the new law is noteworthy in addressing the powers of superintendents, beginning with the qualification of these powers, thus explicitly devolving district authority to principals and schools

Among the important powers reserved to schools (i.e., usually the principal, in consultation with parents and staff) consistent with central and district policies are the authority to:

1. *Design and implement budgets*, in keeping with the chancellor's regulations;

2. *Make recommendations for staff selection*;

3. *Develop school-based curricula*;

4. *Enhance teacher and staff development* relevant to increasing pupil achievement, support extended day programs, school-reform programs, and public-support services;

5. *Coordinate programs* related to public-support services;

6. *Make or arrange for minor building repairs*; and

7. *Identify and purchase equipment and supplies* that can be purchased for less than if purchased through purchasing arrangements entered into through the city board, the chancellor, or the superintendent.

While not going as far as to give principals appointment authority or the ability to contract out services (rather than goods), this new statutory constellation goes a long way toward putting principals in control when it comes to school performance rather than isolating them in their former "middle-management" positions, which largely required them to respond to district or central orders—rather than to initiate action.

PARENT POWER. Parents—who were largely absent from the power formulations of procedurally intensive governance laws—were required to send their children to school and, except in special education or long-term suspensions, any further involvement was largely a matter of administrative discretion and parental organization.

The Act contains a number of explicit, innovative provisions making parent powers yet another key force in holding educators accountable and in motivating them to act. In addition, parents have roles in the selection of superintendents and principals. And parental involvement is one of three major criteria for evaluating a principal's performance—student achievement and school discipline being the other two.

The chancellor is also required annually to prepare an updated parent-training program. School-based management, "which balances participation by parents with participation by school personnel in advising the decisions regarding powers delegated to schools," is also stipulated, with the appropriate training "to any parent and school personnel who participate in the school-based management and share decision-making." Uniquely, the new law also requires the chancellor to promulgate a "parental bill of rights" that, at a minimum, must provide for the following:

a. Reasonable access by parents, persons in parental relations, and guardians to schools, classrooms, and academic records of their children;

b. The rights of parents . . . to take legal action and appeal the decisions of school administration;

c. The rights of parents . . . to have information on their own child's educational materials;

d. Access to and information about all public meetings, hearings of the chancellor, the city board, the community superintendents, the community boards, and the schools; and

e. Access to information regarding programs that allow students to apply for admission where appropriate outside the student's own attendance zones.

LIMITING THE POWERS OF CENTRAL AND COMMUNITY SCHOOL BOARDS. Limitations on community board powers under the law have received much attention as a result of the corruption that catalyzed the reform. Lost in this discussion, however, but of great importance to the strategic nature of the new law, is the similar loss of power by the Central Board of Education—a seven-member group appointed by the mayor (two appointees) and the five borough presidents (one each).

In parallel language, the community school boards "shall have no executive or administrative powers or functions," and the Central Board "shall exercise no executive power and perform no executive or administrative functions" except as otherwise provided by the law. Whether these bodies are willing to acknowledge and comply with their newly constrained powers or not is a matter for speculation. The statute clearly contemplates an end to the politicization of appointments and contracts at the central level, in an identical manner to its strictures on this kind of activity by the local community boards.

CASE STUDIES

The application of the centralization–decentralization model to actual situations in the New York City schools shows the complexity of urban school governance, and how a mix of central and local control is important in understanding actual developments. Three education issues are treated in the New York City context: (1) a struggle to raise student standards; (2) a move to create another level of administration and governance: the appointment of five borough-wide "super" superintendents; and (3) the movement to privatize services in the city's worst/poorest performing schools. Each of these case studies illustrates the ways in which governance occurs between centralized and decentralized means, again using the Double-ACE model.

Standards

New York City, like most urban districts, has struggled to raise standards, improve test scores, and meet expectations for improved student performance. Ostensibly, Chancellor Crew's battle to implement the state legislation strove to accomplish these by gaining more authority over principals and community district superintendents. This drive for Authority, Control, and Enforcement—as the Double-ACE model presents—was extended to the principals' contracts that, when renegotiated over a four-year period ending in 1999, eliminated tenure for principals and required them to work a 12-month year (in exchange for a 16 percent salary raise). Crew, thus by his own definition, had a full arsenal to meet the challenge of raising standards.

In the spring of 1999 Crew used his powers to remove six superintendents (of the 32 community school districts) who in his opinion were failing to sufficiently improve the performance of students. In addition, 51 of the system's 1,100 principals were also replaced. According to the then-deputy chancellor for operations, Harry Spence, these actions were coordinated to create "pressure to make the new culture of accountability stick." However, Crew's dramatic actions were immediately criticized on several fronts. First, the body count was disputed, as many of the fired superintendents were arguably retiring anyway, so that Crew's numbers were, according to critics, purposely inflated. Second, the low test scores upon which these removals were based were suspect and were indeed revised upward at a later date. Finally, Crew was accused of racial discrimination by purposely spreading his personnel actions across all major ethnic and racial groups.

For example, his removal of a White female superintendent, Phyllis Gonon in Community School District 18, seemed designed less to improve scores than to show the public that White and Black administrators were equally subject to his control. Another White superintendent, Robert Ricobono, is suing the Board of Education for reverse discrimination, even as he teaches educational administration at the prestigious School of Education at New York University. In pursing his decisions to remove superintendents of all colors and ethnicity, Crew also removed superintendents in Districts 5, 12, 18, 19, and 29.

Applying the Double-ACE model to efforts to improve standards and student performance might lead to the conclusion that changes in leadership at the district (and the school levels by replacing principals) had little or no impact on pupil achievement. It seems to us that the chancellor's attention to standards became enmeshed in the political push/pull between the central office and district superintendents, who, after all, were used to exercising their previous autonomy. One might argue, therefore, that in a system as large and complex as New York City's, the ability of top executives to positively influence student achievement by replacing middle-level administrators is quixotic. We prefer a counter-argument: that in large urban districts, top-down centralized actions must be met by bottom-up efforts at autonomy, collaboration, and engagement. These qualities of school culture are not easily changed by the short-term replacement of staff.

"Super" Superintendents and High School Governance

Another move toward decentralization has led Chancellor Levy to make two widely heralded structural innovations: first, the appointment of five "super" superintendents to monitor district operations in the five boroughs (Manhattan, Queens, Brooklyn, Bronx, and Staten Island); and second, the shifting of the management of the city's nearly 200 high schools from the central office to the 32 school districts that already run pre-K, elementary, and junior high/intermediate schools.

The 1996 Act empowered the chancellor to name "borough deputies," but previous Chancellor Crew never embraced the idea and never appointed any of an array of upper-mid-level bureaucrats to those positions, even as they continued in their other responsibilities. Levy, on the other hand, has removed *the* High School Division staff at central and has replaced it with five borough-wide superintendents to oversee and monitor the 32 community superintendents.

Levy's deputy chancellor for instruction, Judith Rizzo, explained that neighborhood high schools—which even under decentralization were run centrally—had become choices of last resort and suffered from neglect as resources were poured into city-wide magnet schools. Thus, she believes, local control (high schools managed by boroughs instead of the central office) will result in better, more appealing, and responsive local programs.

While being highly consistent with the Double-ACE framework, several practical problems emerge from this reorganization. For example, how exactly will the new super-superintendents interact with their "subordinate" colleagues at the 32 district offices? In the transition, some of the new borough-wide superintendents continue to be acting "district executives." And what does this restructuring say about the confidence the chancellor has in the 32 districts' ability to actually run schools, even as he devolves power downward from central to borough?

Regarding high schools, other problems exist. First, the elite schools like Stuyvesant High School and the Bronx High School of Science are state chartered and draw students by admissions tests from throughout the city. Therefore, since these schools and others (Brooklyn Technical High School and the LaGuardia High School for the Performing and Visual Arts) are not borough-based (and thus have a much larger catchment area), the new arrangement creates *de jure* a two-tiered system of high schools.

Second, Schools Under Registration Review (SURR schools) and the Chancellor's District high schools—which suffer from endemic low performance and have been "taken over" by both the state (SURR) and the city (Chancellor's District schools)—may require direct central oversight and control. Thus, in effect, the new arrangement creates an unwieldy three-tier structure that includes (1) borough-run regular "zone" high schools under the five new super superintendents; (2) elite city-wide high schools that are managed centrally; and (3) schools in trouble that are at various stages of *state* or *system* takeover under SURR or Chancellor's District arrangements.

Third, the *community* district boards and *their* superintendents have no experience with high school programs and curricula. Further, high school personnel widely disdain the performance and politics of these district offices, creating a cultural divide that seems to obviate the goals of the chancellor's plan. Who will provide instructional and curricular support to high school teachers in academic areas not taught at the lower *grades*, including calculus, physics, and Latin? How will high school principals react to control by district superintendents with no experience working in the upper grades with older adolescents?

The success of this restructuring and apparent decentralization may depend more on attention to the cultural differences than to structural "rationality." Ironically, consistent with the dynamics of our Double-ACE model, the new chancellor appears to be re-inventing decentralization by *pushing* control of the high schools down to the districts, while inserting yet another layer of bureaucracy around himself with the five borough super-superintendents. How this restructuring will affect the tenuous balance of accountability and autonomy, control and collaboration, and enforcement and engagement remains to be seen. More importantly, will these changes stimulate any improvement in student learning and test-score results?

Privatization and Choice

Another example of Levy's use of his new statutory power is his plan to privatize the management of persistently low-performing schools. In New York, these state-designated SURR schools have become educational albatrosses hanging around the necks of the last three or four chancellors. Crew had *shifted* the SURR schools into his Chancellor's District for special resources and attention, thus removing these schools from the control of the publicly elected community school boards. However, these SURR schools have not prospered under direct Chancellor's District control, despite new funding streams and efforts to improve them *by lifting them* from under New York State review.

Crew refused Mayor Giuliani's importuning the Board of Education to privatize these schools through the use of student vouchers. Surprisingly, the idea had been floated in 1996 by the left-leaning New York State Regents Advisory Committee on Low-Performing Schools. That committee had recommended that children "trapped" in low-performing schools be given preference in admissions to other public schools of choice—or even to private schools, if no public placements were available. Giuliani went further, calling for a pilot program based on New York City's popular Student-Funded Fellowship Program, which, under private auspices and using private donations, places poor children into the city's parochial schools on scholarship (a kind of private voucher program).

The privatization movement picked up steam as the mayor's proposal was embraced by a powerful Black congressman and education entrepreneur, Rev. Mr. Floyd Flake. Flake ran a successful private school for his largely minority parishioners in Queens, a borough of New York City. Flake noted that the city was "not alone in its failure." He continued:

> But we should not take much comfort in being in the same boat as cities like Philadelphia, Atlanta, Indianapolis, Los Angeles, and Detroit. Our city, more than other places in the world, has the intellectual and financial capital to deal with these issues of school failure. But we are not—even though other cities have already taken up their crosses to deal with their school crises. (Flake 1998, A4)

While Crew's rebuff of the mayor's suggestion about using vouchers for the most needy students in the worst schools may likely have led to the chancellor's resignation, Levy, with his private-sector experience, embraced the idea but with a twist. Rather than giving vouchers to parents, an idea that is anathema to the liberal establishment, Levy suggested "outsourcing" the management of the SURR schools to corporations such as the Edison Project and Victory Schools. Not coincidentally, Rev. Mr. Flake was by then an executive with the Edison Project, which is run by Benno C. Schmidt, Jr., who was appointed by Giuliani as vice-chairman of the City University of New York (CUNY). Victory Schools, another private school-management firm in New York City, is run by Margaret Harrington, a former high school executive under Chancellor Crew.

Thus, in the complex political and organizational landscape of New York City schools, issues of privatization illustrate how, in the face of system failure, the chancellor can wrest control of individual schools—and categories of schools (SURR schools)—from the public sector altogether, forcing change from "without" the system. While in the past the central authority tended to take over (re-centralize) failing schools, only to return them to the districts several years later but in no better shape, Levy has maintained his central authority and oversight while permanently outsourcing (contracting out) schools' management to the private (even "for-profit") sector. The signal to the field was that when decentralized failed, the central office would no longer "take over the problem" but would dramatically remove the source of authority from the local domain.

Perhaps the lesson is this: that greater *autonomy, collaboration,* and *engagement* may not always accompany traditional forms of decentralization, and that more dramatic, and real, "uncentralization" (privatization through outsourcing, if not vouchers) is the next step for failing systems management.

DOUBLE-ACE: PUTTING IT ALL TOGETHER

When read as a series of regulations, we may fail to see the overall combined effect of the Act's provisions. But when the parts are read together, several principles of the Double-ACE model emerge:

1. *Power is specified and shared:* The net effect of this new law is to enable each power center to work with other units while specifying where accountability begins and ends. The chancellor now has authority to ensure that community boards, superintendents, principals, and schools are working together effectively.

2. *Policies are both proactive and reactive:* The new law makes each level both reactive (to educational standards and avoiding, for example, "persistent educational failure") and proactive—anticipating problems and providing training to stop difficulties before they happen.

3. *Leaders have separate authority and work with others:* The new law gives certain key actors major new responsibilities, while requiring group process and engagement as well. Thus, the net effect of the Act could be to empower the chancellor, boards, and superintendents to do their separate jobs, while also engaging groups at the central, district, and school levels to work together.

4. *Policies treat both means and ends:* The law looks at both the "ends" (performance standards, tests, and results) and the "means" of getting there, while leaving the process to those closest to the teaching/learning actions (school principals, teachers, and parents). Perhaps it is too early to tell how well this strategic-management process will work in a system of this size. But it is obvious that the new role of chancellor calls for the ability to balance centralized accountability, control, and enforcement to improve standards, while encouraging local autonomy, collaboration, and engagement.

□   □   □

PART TWO

Increasing Mayoral Influence
over Urban Schools

◙   ◙   ◙

CHAPTER FOUR

Mayoral Takeover

the different directions taken in different cities

MICHAEL W. KIRST

KATRINA E. BULKLEY

C HANGES IN AMERICAN big-city school governance often focus on reforming a prior reform. At the turn of the twentieth century, "progressive" reformers wanted to overcome excessive decentralization caused by ward-based school boards of 50 to 100 members and corruption from mayoral influence in teacher hiring—the symbol of city government in 1900 was Tammany Hall in New York City (Tyack 1974). The committee system, often large and unwieldy, provided opportunities for extensive and complex political influence.

The solution to this alleged excess of representation was to install a nonpartisan school superintendent—hence the turn toward executive leadership and neutral competence (Tyack 1974). By 1910 the conventional educational wisdom among school leaders, as well as among leading business and professional men, was that smaller boards in conjunction with professional superintendents who would select teachers and work with certified administrators to create a uniform city-wide curriculum was the solution. The watchwords of reform during this era became "*centralization*," "*expertise*," "*professionalism*," "*nonpolitical control*," and "*efficiency*," all of which would inspire "the one best system" (Tyack 1974). The governance structure rooted in ward-based committees needed to be revised so that schools would operate "above politics." To achieve this, school boards had to be small, elected at large, and freed from all connections with political parties and regular government officials such as mayors and councilmen. School districts in this new design would raise their own property taxes so as to not become fiscally dependent on city hall. Mayors were seen as part of a discredited, inefficient, corrupt regime that did not fit with the industrial model of governance in which the school superintendent was a CEO.

It was not until the 1960s that this Progressive Era governance pattern was challenged as undemocratic and not sufficiently representative of minorities because of its focus on city-wide representation. There was a partial reversion to the earlier pattern of electing school boards from geographic subdistricts of the city and tighter board oversight of the superintendent. Unions became omnipresent, major players in board elections, and voluminous collective-bargaining agreements grew annually. In the 1970s some cities adopted models of administrative decentralization, consisting of area superintendents for subdistricts within a city. New interest groups created a political pluralism that represented such interests as handicapped, bilingual, disadvantaged, and gifted pupils. Boards responded to these multiple governance pressures, superintendent turnover accelerated, and the era of the administrative chief ended. Alongside these changes, the conditions of children deteriorated into massive poverty.

From 1960 to 1995 some large cities like Chicago and Philadelphia preserved a role for the mayor in appointing school board members. As city school performance stagnated nationally, various governance prescriptions, such as subarea decentralization and weakly implemented school-based management, failed to improve performance. In some cities, school board members increasingly saw their role as redistributing school jobs and contracts to benefit residents in the geographic slice of the city that they represented.

From the late 1960s, mayors (including Lindsey of New York City and Cavanaugh of Detroit) became increasingly concerned that city economies could not be improved substantially without good schools and middle-class children. However, these mayors hesitated to seek control of the schools, because they feared that there would not be enough school improvement to justify their re-election. Similar to Italian and Irish mayors earlier in the century, new African-American mayors such as Washington in Chicago and Young in Detroit focused during the 1980s in part on redistributing school jobs and services to minority communities (Beinart 1997).

The 1990s produced an 180-degree reversal of the negative 1900–1920 mayoral Tammany image. Many mayors projected an image of efficient public managers who were less interested in redistributing jobs, and more interested in improved services. Some mayors argued that city hall needed to provide more integrated and coherent public services, including those directed at children. Anti-union Republican state legislatures in Illinois, Michigan, and Ohio were ready to cut back the influence of teachers' unions and elected urban school boards that faced repeated financial crises. Education reformers stressed that a host of new policies with each new superintendent created lots of policy "wheel spinning" but little change in educational achievement (Hess 1999).

Consequently, the long-standing independence of the schools from city hall has recently been re-examined in some of the nation's major cities where policy-makers, often with the support of the electorate, are putting the mayor in charge or enhancing mayoral power. Chicago, Boston, Detroit, Philadelphia, Washington, D.C., Oakland, Harrisburg, Pennsylvania, and Cleveland have all moved in this direction, while other cities like Rockford, Illinois, and New Orleans are discussing it. And, even without substantial formal changes in governance structures, mayors in cities such as New York, Los Angeles, and Milwaukee exert much more influence over school policy than did their predecessors. In this power shift, school boards are the big losers. Mayors increasingly make major decisions that were the providence of the school board, including the selection of superintendents in Chicago, Boston, Philadelphia, and Cleveland.

In the first section of this chapter we examine the underlying political and institutional theories policy-makers are embracing as they approve these new mayoral regimes. What has fostered this recent governance change, reversing the century-old progressive effort to remove mayors from school governance? The second section describes some of the different models being used in cities around the nation. In the third section we focus on the reasons why policy-makers in Boston and Chicago, as well as other cities, have been interested in giving more power to mayors. The final section examines some of the early changes that resulted from the governance changes in Boston and Chicago, and provides an introduction to the case studies of these two cities that follow this chapter.

THE MAYORS AND INSTITUTIONAL CHOICE

In the 1980s and '90s frustration mounted in many cities regarding the state of public education, and especially the governance of the city school systems. Policy-makers responded by investigating different institutional choices to address the perceived problems. The concept of "institutional choice" focuses on the crucial policy decision of which institution(s) should be the key policy decision-maker(s), and what authority should be vested in different institutional actors (Clune 1987; Plank and Boyd 1994). As Plank and Boyd note: "The politics of institutional choice is preeminently concerned with 'deciding who will decide' about issues of public policy" (Plank and Boyd 1994, 265).

New institutional choices have a long history at all levels of U.S. government. For example, courts were reluctant during 1960–1985 to delegate civil rights protection to the institution of local school districts in Mississippi. The 1983–1993 state education reform movement included an institutional choice to enhance the curricular and testing role of state government. Another type of institutional choice is whether to place various functions in the hands of markets (e.g., vouchers) or politics (e.g., school board elections) (Chubb and Moe 1990). The institutional choices that are made may reflect concerns about policy goals, the ability of the existing system to address goals, and the relative political power of various actors. In most cases, however, institutional choices are due to a combination of policy and political forces (Komesar 1994).

Institutional choice is complex, uncertain, and subject to continual political change. The balance of control in education will never be settled by policy-makers making a purely logical analysis, but is rather part of a series of evolving political bargains and changing perceptions about the capacity of alternative institutions. In selecting the mayor as the primary institutional actor in education, policy-makers implicitly assert that mayors are capable of making the changes needed to improve school performance. Moreover, they are making a choice to decrease the influence of school boards—boards that are often seen as being incapable of making necessary changes and/or as having different substantive goals than the policy-makers who decide institutional arrangements.

Why Mayoral Takeover?

There are a number of different reasons for the shift to mayoral takeover of the public schools, including bureaucratic dysfunction, decreasing faith in urban school boards, and new demands placed on mayors and urban governments as a result of diminished federal funds for urban areas and changing urban coalitions. In addition, mayors were both under more pressure to address educational problems and more interested in increasing their power in the public schools.

BUREAUCRATIC DYSFUNCTION. During the years 1890–1920, progressive reformers operated on the assumption that a professional bureaucracy would guarantee efficiency, accountability, and neutrality. However, considerable research has suggested that professional hierarchies, despite claims to the contrary, are not politically neutral, because different ways of organizing school bureaucracies necessarily biases allocations of scarce school revenues in favor of particular outcomes (Knott and Miller [1987] suggest this about bureaucracies in general). Critics argue that professional bureaucracy often leads to the very inefficiency and unaccountable political power that reformers had sought to eradicate in the first place. Professional education bureaucracies can create unanticipated consequences and tensions between hierarchy and specialization, and between written rules and reliance on expertise (Wirt and Kirst 1997). The inability of dysfunctional city-education systems even to provide adequate school facilities was illustrated in a 1997 analysis of Washington, D.C. (Perl and Wilgoren 1997).

Ironically, this sad current state of affairs can be seen as the legacy of reforms enacted at the turn of the century by progressives who favored the executive centralization model. This model hindered the flexible responses that education requires, generating instead the red tape associated with rigidity and dysfunction. At the school level, bureaucratic routines often become a way to protect bureaucratic authority and to deal with inadequate resources, but this often occurs at the expense of innovation and productivity. Goal displacement spreads as bureaucratic procedures replace educational goals. Bureaucracy may create "trained incapacity," or an inability to think beyond narrow specialized roles (Knott and Miller 1987, 119).

Electoral mechanisms of popular control, including those involving school board members, are predicated on the assumption that officials voted into office are in full command of policy and program, and that other components of governmental machinery are little more than executors of their collective will. But the control by the educational bureaucracy and fragmented political power in cities like Chicago and Boston undermined the Progressive model—no one seemed to have real command over systems perceived as spiraling out of control. Reformers in the 1990s have contended that it took the mayors to restore the central executive accountability element of the Progressive model (Rich 1996). The perception of a lack of control by existing boards was exacerbated in Boston by the School Committee's behavior. Specifically, the School Committee was often seen as a disorganized and fractious entity that engaged frequently in fights both internally and externally (especially with various mayors). Boston superintendents criticized the Committee for having an excess of staff and for becoming too involved in the details of management and personnel.

During the 1980s integrating children's services became more of a priority. Many analysts stressed that the 1900–1920 separation of schools from city government hindered services coordination and the ability of educators and city officials to use school sites as one-stop centers for services. The hope has been that mayors might be able to overcome this fragmentation of services better than school systems (Kirst and McLaughlin 1990).

Federal/state grants exacerbated this independence of school systems from central leadership. Categorical grants like special and vocational education created vertical bureaucracies from local educators to the federal and state grant-making units. A 1995 study of Detroit, Gary, and Newark found that attempts by mayors to influence schools were thwarted by a cartel of educational administrators, teachers, school boards, and community activists (Rich 1996). Moreover, the dispersal of local power to nonelected bureaucrats has made it extremely difficult for low-income people to influence policy. In short, progressives during 1900 to 1920 cleaned up big-city corruption but may have destroyed the basis for sustained central, popularly based action and mayoral accountability in education policy (Goldberg 1995). A recent study of Los Angeles demonstrates that problems with bureaucracy are not confined to the older Eastern and Midwestern cities (Portz 1996).

DIMINISHING FAITH IN EXISTING STRUCTURES. Another explanation for large-scale city school governance changes is the perception that there is a "major operational failure" in the existing system and diminishing support for the existing governance system (Allison 1971). Cibulka argues that dismal performance and negative publicity of big-city education has undermined the legitimating values upon which the old governance structure was built (Cibulka 1997). Prior to the 1995 legislation that gave the mayor more power over schools, the Chicago school district, for example, had considerable negative publicity due to frequent teachers' strikes and budget deficits that often led to schools not opening at the expected time. As Easton put it, the failing political system in Chicago lost its "diffuse support" (Easton 1965). One effect of this diminishing support may be increased in-fighting and dissension among school board members, such as that found prior to mayoral takeover in Chicago and Boston (Portz 1996). Media reports of dismal test scores and school violence also undermined the legitimacy of the old regimes.

THE ACCOUNTABILITY PUSH. During this period when there has been increasing interest in mayoral control, there has also been a push for greater accountability in public education. This focus on accountability is linked to concerns about bureaucratic dysfunction and the overall diminishing faith in public education in large cities.

Reformers in both Boston and Chicago were particularly concerned with issues of accountability. The primary goal in both cases was to establish clearer lines of political authority and responsibility, making the city's mayor ultimately accountable for the progress of the public schools. The logic was in keeping with Cibulka's description of "political integration," which is "premised on the notion that the policy works most effectively where there are clear and direct lines of accountability from public elected officials to the public" (Cibulka 1997, 322).

In Boston, the purpose of moving from an elected School Committee to an appointed one, Yee argues in chapter 5 of this volume, was "to clearly identify who was responsible for improving the schools and to 'take the politics out of schools.'" Despite the arguments of Progressive Era reformers decades earlier, the direct election of board members was perceived as increasing the political nature of the School Committee. Similarly, Illinois legislators sought a system in which the mayor would be accountable for the schools. In addition, reform supporters, including the mayors, in both cities were concerned about the ongoing flight of middle-class White (and to a lesser extent, minority) families from their city and their city's public schools. They hoped that the mayors would use their newfound power over the schools to reverse this long-term trend.

NEW DEMANDS. In addition to both real and perceived problems in urban education, new pressures have been placed on urban governments that can impact school governance structures. As Beinart points out, two of these added pressures have come from lessened federal aid and changing racial coalitions (Beinart 1997). In recent years, federal aid to cities has declined drastically. This has put increased pressure on urban governments to compensate for diminishing federal support for children's services, spurring frequent school budget shortfalls in cities such as Chicago and Boston where schools are dependent on the city treasury for funds (see U.S. Conference of Mayors 1994).

Also, the loss of public tolerance for large-city employee costs has occurred as the traditional civil rights coalitions have disintegrated (Beinart 1997). Alliances of Democratic mayors with business evolved in such cities as Detroit (Archer) and Cleveland (White). Where Blacks had once been the starting point for liberal coalitions, Black votes in many big cities declined significantly as a percentage of the total vote (Meyerson 1998). It became easier politically to depose Black city school boards and central education district leaders. Consequently, the focus of some big-city mayors has changed from providing municipal employment to improving student test scores. Hence the broad coalition of generally Democratic voters—including poor people, unions, school employees, neighborhoods, and civic reformers—has been weakened (Meyerson 1998). Into this vacuum have stepped Republican mayors in New York and Los Angeles who have pressured the school boards to appoint different central education administrators.

While Chicago and Boston are held up as examples of mayoral takeover, it is important to recognize that both cities have long had strong mayors, and have not relied on more "apolitical" city managers. As well, the public schools were never as separate from these city governments as was the case elsewhere, or as Progressive Era reformers would have liked. Both districts have historically been fiscally dependent on city government, and this fiscal dependence has often provided a justification for mayoral involvement in Boston and Chicago school issues. Chicago is among the minority of cities that has never had an elected school board, and thus the district has never been fully separated from city politics. Boston's mayor has historically influenced the total spending of the Boston public schools, but not the spending priorities of the elected School Committee. In addition, the role of the courts in Boston during the desegregation era limited the influence of the School Committee. Nevertheless, Chicago and Boston leaders *did* follow the ideals of progressive reformers in creating large professional bureaucracies using civil-service-type exams and classifications. Benjamin Willis, the General Superintendent of Schools in Chicago during the 1960s, was a model of the professional education CEO (Cuban 1976).

A contributing factor to a climate for reform in both cities was a very active civic elite, particularly as represented by a business community with a history of involvement with public education reform. According to Shipps, in chapter 6 of this volume, "Chicago's new regime is the consequence of long-simmering frustrations with the performance of the Chicago Public Schools . . . coupled with an extraordinarily engaged and active civic elite." The Vault in Boston and the Commercial Club in Chicago were, and continue to be, powerful city organizations comprised primarily of leaders of large businesses. In Chicago, the Commercial Club was intricately connected to the education system, and the role of this dominating organization is closely tied to the business community's role in the fiscal matters of the city's public schools. The history of a strong business role in education is much longer in Chicago than in Boston, where the Vault became more active in the 1980s.

   CONTEXTUAL FACTORS. General trends in recent years, including a growing frustration with bureaucratic structures and a diminishing faith in governance structures, including elected school boards, have encouraged policy-makers in a number of cities and states to consider enhanced mayoral control over education. However, there are also local reasons for interest in this type of reform. For example, some of the specific issues that the 1995 structural changes in Chicago were designed to address arose out of the recent 1988 education reform that granted considerable powers to local school councils (LSCs) comprised of teachers, parents, and community members. The decentralized nature of the 1988 reform, combined with prior governance changes, created a system in which there were many levels of political accountability, and no clear ultimate responsibility. This fragmented system created a situation in which the School Finance Authority, LSCs, the school board, and the mayor were all in some way accountable for the successes and failures of the Chicago public schools.

   Other issues combined with those directly related to governance in creating an environment in each city where policy-makers were willing to make substantial structural alterations. Both cities, but especially Chicago, were plagued by continual fiscal problems in the school district. In Chicago, regular cost overruns and the difficulty of raising money through bonds contributed to a series of fiscal crises that required the business community to help bail out the school system. These budget problems were very public and contentious. While the Boston public schools' financial woes were not as dramatic as in Chicago, by the late 1980s the district's steadily rising budgets were causing concern among city leaders (especially the mayor), who were also having to contend with cuts in state aid due to the state's financial difficulties. Related in part to budget issues were ongoing labor problems in both school districts, especially between the school system and the teachers' unions. Labor disputes had been a continual problem in Chicago since the late 1960s and strikes were not an unusual response. Bitter contract negotiations were also common in Boston.

   WHY MAYORS WANTED CONTROL. The growing problems in urban education and the increased pressures placed on urban governance created a crisis situation in many cities, leading the public and policy-makers to demand a major overhaul. In the past, mayors avoided the political tangle of education, but this has become more difficult in the current climate that focuses on the role of education in a city's overall health. Cibulka (1997) argues that mayors can no longer avoid school-related issues politically, because of the increasing view among business leaders and others that schools are a critical piece of urban economic development. In addition to an interest by mayors in using education as a part of a broader urban-improvement plan, there are financial incentives for mayors to become more involved with education. As Cibulka notes: "Increasingly tight city budgets also place pressure on mayors to keep taxes down. Schools consume a large portion of that tax dollar, and in some cities the mayor has little direct control over decisions made by urban school officials" (Cibulka 1997, 322). Thus, there are both ideological and budgetary reasons for mayors to seek greater control over their city's system of public education.

Current mayors such as Daley, Menino, and White have received support at both the city and state level—support that was critical in order for them to assert more control over education. One reason they received this support was due to the belief that highly visible mayors are more likely to be held accountable by voters for the state of public education than relatively unknown school board members. Political integration, with mayors at the head of urban governance, "is premised on the notion that the policy works most effectively where there are clear and direct lines of accountability from public elected officials to the public. This is achieved by having fewer officials to elect and only one set of elections" (Cibulka 1997, 322). In addition to policy reasons, such as greater accountability, city and state politicians have political motivations for removing control over education from a publicly elected local school board that they cannot direct to a mayor over whom they may have some influence.

THE "NEW IMPROVED" MAYOR GAINS CONTROL

The impetus for turning to mayors to solve problems in urban education systems stems in part from the belief that there is a "new breed" of mayor that can improve education and avoid past mistakes. The new improved mayor is

> largely about managing city government efficiently in the public interest
> rather than using it as a mechanism for arbitrating competing interest
> groups. . . . They have an ideology: that cities can dramatically alleviate
> seemingly endemic urban afflictions without a massive redistribution of
> wealth, that the way to achieve this is by using competition to make city
> services radically more efficient. (Beinart 1997, 16)

These "new" mayors have formed an informal network and symbolize a radical break with their predecessors. Some of these mayors include

Daley (Chicago), Rendell (Philadelphia), White (Cleveland), Goldsmith (Indianapolis), Riordan (Los Angeles), Giuliani (New York), and Norquist (Milwaukee). They allegedly realize that in a tight budgetary climate more city jobs to pay off constituencies will not work, so part of the answer is to privatize and contract out services. They are a marked contrast to the old-style "civil rights" mayors of the 1970–1990 era:

> While calling for dramatic change nationally, the civil rights mayors pre-
> served the status quo at home—appeasing the municipal employee unions
> with generous contracts, using city jobs to cement their coalitions and
> leaving education, that most intractable and politically dangerous of prob-
> lems, to elected school boards. (Beinart 1997, 20)

Beinart suggests that changes in the urban environment discussed ear-lier—including the decline in federal aid, disintegration of the civil rights coalition, and new coalitions that include Hispanics and immigrants with less electoral reliance on Blacks—can help to explain big changes in may-oral behavior and ambitions. New policies have caused these reform may-ors to become estranged from their own political parties, which cling to older paradigms. For example, Daley's 1995 takeover of Chicago schools would not have happened if the opposite-party Republicans who sup-ported him did not control both Illinois state houses in 1995. These may-ors appeared to be willing to confront strong interests on both sides of the political fence, including teachers' unions, civil rights leaders, and the Christian Coalition. The new mayors speak the language of modern public management: reinvention, innovation, privatization, competition, strategic planning, and productivity (Eisinger 1997). They hope these concepts will enable them to make the most of the dwindling resources they control, and that privatization will provide better services. Mayors like Daley in Chicago and Menino in Boston use their sophisticated media skills and staff to reiterate these new public-management approaches and contrast them to fractious school boards.

In sum, mayoral takeover or an increased role for mayors in schools is justified by proponents as providing a single point of electoral accounta-bility, more integration of children's services with schools, and a better pupil attainment. Such developments will spur city economic develop-ment, stimulate more middle-class people to live in cities, and forge a closer alliance between city government and businesses. Political losers in this shift will be the central school district professionals and the school boards. Opponents assert that a school board appointed by the mayor will result in less democracy, because the voters will have fewer electoral choices and cannot vote for a board member from their section of the city.

FORMS OF ENHANCED MAYORAL PARTICIPATION

While mayoral takeover has garnered most media attention, there are several forms of mayoral influence. Chicago is the most extreme form of mayor impact. Mayor Daley installed his trusted employees as the chairman of the school board and superintendent, as well as moving about a hundred of his office staff to take over key functions such as personnel and contracting. Mayor Menino picked a new superintendent and made him part of the mayor's cabinet, but did not transfer any of his own office staff to take over key operational units of the school system. Mayor Archer in Detroit appointed a new school board, but the board appointed the superintendent who has prerogatives invested in his office that cannot be overturned by the Detroit board. Moreover, the one Detroit member appointed by Michigan Governor Engler vetoed the board's first choice for superintendent. Oakland's mayor, Jerry Brown, led a successful city charter amendment to appoint three added members from the city at large to the current seven-member board.

But other mayors have relied primarily upon backing a slate with endorsements, financial support, and campaign workers. Mayors Serna of Sacramento and Riordan of Los Angeles were successful in electing their slates that led quickly to the replacement of the superintendent. Mayor Riordan, who raised $2 million for his slate, plays an active role in discussions about where to build schools and in teachers' union elections of its leadership. In November 1999 Philadelphia voters passed a referendum to allow the mayor to appoint all board members at one time. In June 2000 Mayor Street of Philadelphia negotiated a new finance plan with Pennsylvania Governor Ridge that led to the resignation of Superintendent David Hornbeck. Mayors have integrated city services more closely to the schools. For example, Mayor Gonzalez of San Jose, California helped to provide subsidized housing for teachers. Mayors have linked city services for children, transportation, safety, museums, and community-development organizations more closely to schools (Finn and Petrilli 1999). The Republican mayor of Jersey City advocates vouchers for the city schools, but has not been successful in making this change.

Some observers of the switch to mayoral control have suggested that this institutional change is not a panacea for education problems and is unlikely to improve education. Skeptical education administrators point to mayoral control of schools in Baltimore, where the mayor never lost much influence over schools as a result of Progressive Era reforms. Richard Hunter, a former Baltimore superintendent who has served in a number of cities, observed:

> The best way to gain the [mayor's] support is to do something for the mayor: contribute to the campaign fund; work on the re-election effort; deliver votes or support from a constituency; or convince the mayor his

or her support of your project will attract political advantage, positive media publicity, or additional campaign contributions. In short, you must help keep the mayor in office. When public education becomes part of the political process, education policy decisions become commodities bought, sold, bartered, and bestowed like patronage positions and building permits. (Hunter 1997, 219)

Hunter believes that the spread of interest in mayoral control stems from "scape-goating educators" that began with the National Commission on Excellence in Education in 1983 and the efforts to placate insistent business leaders in 1985. Hunter and others stress that control by the Baltimore mayor, where mayoral control of schools has always been the case, has not resulted in better school performance. In 1997 the Maryland legislature reduced the power of the mayor, creating a CEO appointed by a "New Board of School Commissioners" appointed jointly by the mayor and governor from a list submitted by the State Board of Education. This new CEO can change the Baltimore school-personnel system. In Baltimore, "political control of the schools [by the mayor] has not proven to be a panacea" (Cibulka 1997, 322).

Critics of mayoral control contend that the use of contracts by mayors for services such as building repairs will lead to machine politics whereby school contracts are traded for campaign contributions to the mayor. The idea of a "new breed of mayor" does not carry much weight with these critics. Despite these concerns, favorable publicity about Boston and Chicago under mayoral control has led state politicians and other mayors to think more about mayoral takeover (Newton 1997). In Los Angeles, Mayor Riordan formed his own slate of candidates to overthrow the incumbent school board. This new board appointed former Colorado Governor Roy Romer as superintendent. In Milwaukee, Mayor Norquist led a movement to allow the city to establish charter schools.

However, some mayors stress that the mayor's capacity to change schools is politically risky if there is no prerogative for the mayor to appoint the board. As Mayor Stephen Goldsmith observed: "I don't mind tilting at windmills, but I like to win every now and then. It's funny: the best thing for my career is to be Pollyannaish. The more I agitate for change at Indianapolis Public Schools, the more I get blamed for the problems" (Grunwald 1998).

WHAT HAS MAYORAL CONTROL IN BOSTON AND CHICAGO DONE?

In both Boston and Chicago, new powers granted to mayors quickly resulted in fundamental changes in the governance of these large urban education systems. In this section we explore two central issues: first, what are some of the basic differences in the directions taken in these two cities? And second, why have these different outcomes resulted from similar structural changes?

Governance Change in Boston and Chicago

As a result of the factors discussed earlier and other political and historical issues, formal governance changes enhancing the role of the mayor were introduced in Boston and Chicago in the late 1980s and early '90s. In Boston, a series of decisions between 1989 and 1996—both legislative and electoral—gave the mayor the power to appoint the School Committee. Up until this time, the School Committee had been directly elected in some form. This change gave the mayor a much stronger role in the operations of the school system and created a direct line of authority to him. Mayor Flynn in Boston spearheaded the charge to alter the governance structure of the Boston public schools. He was supported by the state legislature, which was becoming increasingly concerned with the Boston schools, and by the business community. Much of the African-American community was skeptical of eliminating an elected School Committee, and the Irish of South Boston (who had long held power on the elected committee) also opposed the change.

In Chicago, the governance changes of 1995 granting an enhanced role to the mayor were layered over the earlier reforms instituted in 1988. The 1988 reform, which was supported by state Democrats and civic activists, shifted power from the district to the local school councils. In this legislative change the mayor's ability to appoint the city's school board was decreased. However, the impetus for this decentralization was not a desire to increase the influence of educators. Rather, Shipps (1995) argues, it was designed to enhance the influence of parents and community members; she comments that "educators were blamed for the problems and their discretion curtailed." While the 1988 reforms pushed control towards the school site, the legislation passed in 1995 shifted power up the ladder to the mayor. Although Chicago's Mayor Daley favored this shift, he did not pursue it publicly as Mayor Flynn had. Instead, the 1995 reform was a Republican legislator-led governance change that emphasized centralizing political accountability. It was placed over the structure of the 1988 reform, rather than replacing it.

These changes gave the Chicago mayor "more authority than any mayor since before the Progressive Era . . . effectively turning the [public education] system into a department of city government" (Shipps, in chapter 6 of this volume). Specifically, the legislation in 1995 eliminated the school board nominating committee, which had effectively minimized the mayor's ability to select school board members, and replaced the traditional board with a new corporate-style one. In this new structure only one member of five was to be focused on education (the chief education officer) and there was a CEO, rather than a superintendent. The legislation also limiting the rights of the unions to strike was temporarily curtailed, and a large number of issues that had been bargained in the past were defined as nonbargainable issues. State legislation enabled Chicago to contract-out many more building repairs, services, and purchases rather than using the numerous unions within the old system.

In both cities, the primary initiators of the governance changes that granted more power to the mayors were the business community, the mayor (especially in Boston), and the state legislators. Local groups, such as community activists and minority-group representatives, were not directly involved, and educator organizations including the teachers' unions were also peripheral to the debates or opposed the changes.

While the goals of those who pushed through the governance changes in Boston and Chicago had certain similarities, especially the desire to improve accountability, there were also some important differences. In Chicago, there was a strong emphasis on improving the efficiency of the public schools—particularly the fiscal efficiency of the district. As Shipps notes, the 1995 governance changes were "a continuation of a long-standing effort to improve efficiency and restructure accountability." This emphasis reflected the interests of the business community. While improved efficiency was also a factor in Boston, it was not nearly as central to the discussion.

Another difference between the reforms in these two cities involved the role and purpose of the district's "leader." Reflecting the focus on efficiency, the Chicago public schools were to be led by a business-style CEO rather than a traditional superintendent. In Boston, on the other hand, Flynn explicitly wanted a strong educator-leader at the head of the school system. While Mayor Flynn wanted to be held accountable for the state of the Boston public schools, he claimed he was not interested in being directly involved with the district's operations. Rather, he sought to place a strong superintendent in charge of the district—a superintendent who would not have to contend with the many demands of an elected School Committee. The intentions of those who initiated the governance changes in Chicago and Boston were reflected in the implementation of these changes, and especially in the interests and styles of the new leaders chosen with the input of their city's mayor.

Finally, the view of city and state leaders about the capacity of educators to reform education was rather different. In Chicago, there was continual skepticism about the ability (and motivation) of educators in improving schools—both the 1988 reforms that shifted power toward parents and community members and the 1995 reforms that granted additional power to the mayor moved control away from educators. While Boston's leaders shared some of these concerns, they were still interested in vesting considerable authority in public-education professionals.

Similar Change, Different Directions

The governance changes that shifted power towards the mayors in Chicago and Boston only set the stage for the substantial shifts in these two school systems. The mayors themselves, and the individuals whom they helped to select as the leaders of these districts, took advantage of structural changes to implement substantive reforms. In Chicago, Paul Vallas, a former budget director for the city, moved to the new position of CEO of the Chicago public schools. The selection of Vallas reflected the business community's interests in having someone from outside of traditional public education at the helm of the city's schools. Vallas believed that clear accountability combined with a district run more like a business would lead to an improved organization. In this top-down change model, management creates a vision and defines clear sanctions for individuals and schools who do not make progress toward that vision.

Superintendent Tom Payzant in Boston was a much more traditional choice for a district leader, and his selection reflected the mayor's interest in having a professional educator who would stay away (at least to some extent) from the political issues that had consumed much of the time of previous superintendents. Payzant's approach was much more within the framework of traditional education reform, and his primary focus reflected a professional-education model involving higher standards and capacity-building.

The changes that resulted from the combination of a new governance structure in each city and mayors and school-system leaders who sought to alter these districts also reflect some of the differences in the intentions of those who sought governance change. In each city there were shifts in both the practical and governance aspects of the district and in the overall message about teaching and learning sent by the mayor and superintendent/CEO.

In Chicago, some very visible and practical changes occurred in the first years following the 1995 reform. For example, for the first time in years, the school district's budget appeared to be in reasonable shape. (However, part of this change may be due to Mayor Daley's willingness to support the school system through property tax increases and money from other parts of the city budget.) In addition, for the first time in years there was relative labor peace in the Chicago public schools, and the pattern of teachers' strikes was broken.

At the district central office there were also some major changes following Vallas's arrival. City employees were placed immediately in the key budget, personnel, and facilities positions. The leadership of the district, in addition to Vallas, came partially from the business sector rather than from education. This new administrative team has repaired schools, begun professional development for principals, expanded preschool and after-school programs, ended social promotion, and put a quarter of the elementary schools on probation.

While LSCs (created through the 1988 reform) continued to exist at all the Chicago public schools, their influence was reduced, and the new central office leaders increased their own role in the functioning of the city's schools. But the LSCs still appoint the school principal and "principals continue to act with more freedom and control of resources than ever before. In elementary schools this change has been accompanied by a broad-based gradual increase in achievement" (Sebring and Bryk 2000, 105). This combination of no budget crises, no strikes, and a generally positive view among the public of the reforms that Vallas instituted appears to have improved the general public perception of the school system during this period.

The direct impact of the governance changes in Boston on the actual governance structure of the public schools was not as marked as in Chicago. The most notable change was the elimination of the bitter battles within the School Committee and between the Committee and the mayor—a predictable outcome of having the School Committee appointed rather then elected. The Committee included allies first of Mayor Flynn, then of Mayor Menino, and many members had close connections with the business community. As in Chicago, labor relations, particularly with the teachers' union, improved during the years following the governance change. Also similar to Chicago, some of the most blatant budget problems disappeared in Boston. While Boston's mayor has always influenced the amount of money spent by the public school system, these changes allowed him to also impact how those dollars are spent. Unlike in Chicago, however, there were no dramatic changes in the structure or staffing of the district's central office, and no transfer of city employees to key positions within the school system's central office.

The style and substance of the education reforms that were put into place during this period, in the context of these governance changes, were quite different in the two cities. In Chicago, the initial focus was on accountability—defined largely as success on test scores—and taking action with schools and students that do not meet predefined goals. According to Shipps, there was been an emphasis on "strong and immediate sanctions" for principals whose schools do not meet Vallas's performance goals. This is especially true for schools whose students fell into the bottom 25 percent of test scores within the district—these schools faced such high-stakes consequences as probation and reconstitution. The state's 1995 mayor takeover law removed some bargained items from the teachers' contract and allowed the superintendent to terminate teachers on short notice in reconstituted schools.

For students, there were also new and high-stake repercussions for low test scores. The most public example of this involved Vallas's call for an end to social promotion (which was put into place following the conclusion of this study). Vallas has met with some success in terms of test scores, as there was an increase in scores on the Iowa Test of Basic Skills (ITBS) soon after he began his new program. It is unclear, however, exactly what is responsible for this improvement.

While these accountability measures generally focused on minimal standards and raising the educational outcomes of students faring the worst in the city's schools, there were also changes for those students at the upper end of the performance spectrum. For example, Vallas supported the creation and expansion of alternatives such as magnet schools, accelerated programs such as International Baccalaureate options, and charter schools. Alongside efforts to remove "troublesome or slow-learning students" from regular public schools to other settings such as transition centers and alternative high schools, there was a push for more "upper-end" options linked with the goal of bringing middle-class families back into the Chicago public schools.

One hope for increased mayoral control of schools was that mayors would be more able to link together currently fragmented programs designed to support students and families (Kirst and McLaughlin 1990). In Chicago, Daley and Vallas were able to help schools through support from a variety of other city agencies. In addition, Vallas pushed the expansion of after-school programs that have been well-received publicly. In the past two years Chicago's reform scope has expanded and now encompasses much more than its initial foci. Vallas has aggressively utilized the takeover legislative permission to contract-out services and purchases rather than having to go through one of over 20 unions within the school system.

Vallas has pursued instructional improvement through highly structured lesson plans and less capacity-building than Boston. He stresses that in a system where one out of every four students changes schools, consistency is crucial. A team of one hundred Chicago teachers developed the plans for 30,000 teachers. These lesson plans are very specific for each daily topic, but successful implementation will depend in part on how well principals provide support. The style of the education reforms being undertaken in Boston, while arising out of a similar governance change, is quite different than in Chicago. Although Mayor Flynn and Superintendent Harrison-Jones were the first leaders to experience the mayorally appointed School Committee, the major changes can be seen as largely resulting from the actions of Mayor Menino and Superintendent Payzant. In contrast to Vallas, who came in as an education outsider, Payzant was very much the professional superintendent who sought to work primarily within the existing structures. While Vallas relied heavily on the existing capacity of the school system, Payzant's plans focused on increasing capacity. According to Yee (in chapter 5 of this volume), "Payzant emphasized his long-term commitment to steady, resolute progress through staff training, new materials, and high standards." A big question is whether this long-term change strategy will produce enough results to buffer it from political opposition.

Some of the methods Payzant used included raising standards, leadership development, whole-school change, and creating a "Reorganization Plan" focused on student performance (Hill, Campbell, and Harvey 2000). His focus on teaching and learning issues involved relying to some extent on professional norms as a means to increased performance rather than sanctions. Unlike Chicago, there was little change in Boston in the tenure of administrators or teachers, and no talk of reconstitution or making major changes in the teachers' contract. Initially, Payzant introduced school report cards that included results on the Stanford-9 test. Currently, Boston is focusing on the new state assessment, called MCAS (Massachusetts Comprehensive Assessment System). Payzant has used funds from the Annenberg Foundation to implement an elaborate instructional-change strategy including school-site coaches, joint teacher planning time, literary specialists, formative assessment, school quality reviews, and district resource-action teams. High-performing schools get autonomy similar to charter schools. Payzant has merged state-wide standards expectations with a $10 million Annenberg grant that helps schools choose and implement instructional strategies that will help meet those standards.

THE FUTURE OF MAYORAL CONTROL

The new reliance on mayors as the primary elected official overseeing a city's education system may result in changes in the effectiveness and efficiency of the involved urban school districts. However, it is always difficult to predict the outcome of governance changes. The effects of such changes involve an ongoing pattern of interpretations of those effects by different actors, actions taken based on those interpretations, and new political stresses resulting from those ensuing actions. Inevitably, this feedback process leads to yet more and new demands being placed on the administrators and creators of the governance change (Wirt and Kirst 1972). The theory underlying the shift to mayoral control may be reinforced through this feedback process, or the institutional change may lead in unexpected directions. Mayor Daley's school control was re-authorized in 1999 by the Illinois legislature without significant opposition. Boston voters, by a 70 percent majority, approved extension of mayoral control in 1996.

Some literature on institutional change suggests that efforts to change institutions often lead but to permutations of the institutions that previously existed (DiMaggio and Powell 1983; March and Olsen 1989). This literature suggests that mayorally controlled schools may well end up operating in a similar manner to the institutional structures that they replaced, thereby demonstrating some of the "problematic" aspects of the pre-existing system (such as bureaucratic dysfunctions). Hence, the need to keep reforming older "reforms."

Mayor takeover can lead to a more coherent education system at the central office level, reduce some of the conflict caused by fragmentation, and stabilize the budget (Wong 1999). Greater coherence can improve the public image of the school system and provide more favorable media coverage. Policy changes will reflect the preferences of the newly empowered actors through mayoral takeover, rather than any essence of the structural reforms themselves. Mayors in Chicago and Boston have addressed classroom instruction and not merely focused on fiscal issues. A potential downside of mayoral takeover is the minimized voice of dissenters. Without the possibility of gaining influence through an elected board or city council, those who disagree with the mayor's preferences have less access to forums in which to voice their displeasure and possibly change policy.

A key issue is whether mayoral control can improve classroom instruction and the everyday lives of teachers and children. Historically, governance change has not had much effect on classrooms, but Chicago and Boston demonstrate the crucial differential impact of local context for school-improvement strategies (Tyack and Cuban 1995). Mayor Daley focused initially upon daily lesson plans and schools and students that score very low on the ITBS. Mayor Menino in Boston opted for a strategy that gives high priority to staff development. An interesting political development in several cities is the effective role mayors have played in negotiating with governors and the White House. Mayors have more access and influence at these top levels of government than do school superintendents.

Whatever its impact, there are political and geographic limits to the spread of mayoral control. Many cities are not contiguous with school districts—San Jose, California has 20 school districts within its city boundary, and Southern cities are part of county school districts. But city test scores in many cities have not risen sufficiently to offset state and local dissatisfaction nor created large-scale changes in bureaucratic standard-operating procedures. Current studies of new governance techniques in large cities contribute to our understanding of mayoral influence (Cuban and Usdan 2002). More efforts at mayoral takeovers are possible. And, if the mayors do not succeed in cities like Chicago, Boston, New York, and Cleveland, voucher advocates will have a stronger case—at least for the worst-performing big-city schools.

ACKNOWLEDGMENTS

This chapter is based on research supported by the Consortium for Policy Research in Education (CPRE), which is supported by a grant (No. OERI-R308A60003) from the National Institute on Educational Governance, Finance, Policymaking, and Management (U.S. Department of Education). The views expressed in this chapter are those of the authors and are not necessarily shared by the U.S. Department of Education, CPRE, or its institutional members. An earlier version of this chapter was presented at the AERA Annual Meeting in Seattle in April 2001.

◨   ◨   ◨

CHAPTER FIVE

From Court Street to City Hall

governance change in the Boston public schools

GARY YEE

S TANDING ON THE STEPS of the Jeremiah Burke High School in 1996, Boston's Mayor Thomas Menino said, "If I fail to bring about these specific reforms by the year 2001, then judge me harshly" (Anand 1996). He urged voters to trust him, by voting to keep a mayor-appointed school committee. His speech may well be repeated by urban mayors across the country as they seek greater control of their city's school systems. Policy analysts have suggested that mayoral control of schools may align city resources and leadership with district efforts to reform urban education (Portz 1997). At the 1998 U.S. Conference of Mayors, both Menino and Richard Daley, mayor of Chicago, were featured as "revolutionary heroes" who were transforming education (Rakowsky 1998). Polls have placed educational reform at the top of the domestic agenda and mayors have declared that educational reform is their highest priority.

Mayors have become increasingly involved in the governance and even operation of their city school systems, either directly or indirectly, at the same time that state and federal government agencies have increased their involvement in school funding, curriculum and instruction reform, and goal and standards setting (Hunter 1997). Until 1997, Baltimore schools operated like a city department; in Oakland and Boston, mayors now appoint all or some school board members; and in Los Angeles and Sacramento, mayors have actively campaigned for slates of board members.

Schools matter for cities, and city support matters for schools. Good school systems attract families, provide steady jobs for local residents and contracts for local businesses, and increase property values. They are a source of civic pride. Schools need the financial and political support of voters, and mayors can help to attract and maintain community-wide support. But poorly functioning schools are a drain on a city. A poorly educated local workforce frustrates employers, and social pathologies associated with poorly educated students increase the cost of doing business in cities and limit business investment. In contrast to earlier times, when mayors avoided involvement in school issues, today's candidates are developing their own educational-reform agenda.

City leaders have begun to question whether school districts led by a professional superintendent under the direction of an elected school board are even necessary. Some mayors argue that school districts would be more efficient and effective under themselves. Does mayoral involvement "take politics out of education," or does it inject politics into education? Do incidences of mayoral takeover signal a historic shift away from a professional superintendent with an elected school board toward direct governance by city or state governments? Or are mayoral takeovers simply political strategies that are irrelevant as educational innovation?

In Boston, mayoral control was preceded by several other governance shifts of equal importance in their time; this study documents those shifts, from the elected school committee to the federal courts in 1974, to the strong superintendent in 1985, and, finally, to the mayor. Two important interests in the city—the business community and the Black community—also sought and played critical public, prominent, and system-focused roles. Throughout the decades the conflicts were intense, with the outcome always in doubt. Contrary to the straightforward explanation that poor-performing schools and a chaotic school board resulted in the necessity for mayoral intervention, I argue that the Boston public schools have been the arena where various stakeholders have tried to take an active role in governing Boston's schools.

Data for this study came from an analysis of official reports by the Boston public schools, other studies that provided a detailed history of the Boston public schools, and news articles culled from the computerized archives of the *Boston Globe*. In addition, I conducted a set of interviews with 12 individuals who have had a long-term interest in the Boston public schools to provide perspective and points of view that provide contrast to the mayor's and the superintendent's. After the case history was completed, local scholars were asked to provide comments and corrections.[1]

THE BOSTON PUBLIC SCHOOLS: 1960–1997

Until 1975, the Elected School Committee

Flight to the suburbs by middle-class residents began well before 1960, the result of regional policies supporting newly developed suburbs where jobs were being relocated (Tyack 1974). According to Schrag (1967), compared to the suburban school systems that surrounded it, Boston's teachers earned less, its schools were poorly maintained, and most of its academic programs were notably mediocre. Families who could had already abandoned the public schools and sent their children to parochial or prep schools in Boston, or simply moved to the suburbs; 30 percent of the high school students in Boston attended parochial or private schools. This left much of the school system to working-class Irish Americans, except for the nationally acclaimed examination high schools, and the schools located in Black and Jewish neighborhoods such as Roxbury and Mattapan.

The school district was governed by the elected school committee and its superintendents. Firmly established teacher recruitment and placement policies and informal familial and patronage networks ensured employment for Irish-American residents, differential expenditures for schools in different neighborhoods, selection of compliant superintendents (until 1962, all were Irish-American Bostonians), and rigid student-placement rules that segregated schools by race. In 1960 the city-wide Black population was 9 percent, yet the Black student population had reached about 25 percent, and most of it attended schools that were over 80 percent Black (Lukas 1986).

The mayor had little obvious influence over schools during this time, but the mayor, the city council, and the school committee were elected in the same city-wide elections, and the council had final budgetary authority over schools. The five committee members, elected at large but representing neighborhoods, drew more votes by ignoring or even insulting the small but growing Black electorate (Schrag 1967).

In 1965 the Massachusetts legislature passed the Racial Imbalance Act, which acknowledged the harmful effects of segregated schools on both Black and White students and tied state financial support for public school systems to their adoption of plans to eliminate "racial imbalance" in their schools. A school was considered racially imbalanced if more than 50 percent of the students were Black. By the mid-1960s, 45 of Boston's 200 schools were declared by the state to be racially imbalanced. Suburban and rural legislators supported this measure, since only the three largest urban areas—Boston, Springfield, and Cambridge—would be affected.

While the district's planning department developed numerous desegregation plans, most involved redistributing Black students through busing to schools with large White majorities and the school committee consistently rejected all of them. It argued that the imbalance was the result of neighborhood housing patterns, that it was more important to respect parental choice, and finally that it was resisting judicial tyranny (Dentler and Scott 1981). Instead, the committee adopted an open-enrollment plan giving parents the "choice" to transport their children to nonneighborhood schools. This resulted in greater racial imbalance in minority–majority schools, since some White parents took this opportunity to move out of schools that were becoming "too Black" (Golden and Lowery 1982). Black parents organized private transportation so that their children could attend "open" schools in White neighborhoods. They later created the METCO program to send their children to willing suburban schools. Even though little improved for Black students in the Boston schools, the Racial Imbalance Act set the stage for new, external forces to enter into the governance arena.

The Federal Court: Judge W. Arthur Garrity (1974–1985)

By 1971, 62 Boston schools were racially imbalanced. When the school committee refused to transport Black students from overcrowded, imbalanced schools to underutilized, largely White schools, Black parents sued in federal court. In 1973 the State Board of Education itself drafted a plan to reduce racial imbalance, but it was rejected by the Boston school committee. Newly elected Mayor Kevin White, who sent his own five children to private schools, argued that a shift should be made from using busing to create racial balance in the schools to using magnet schools and voluntary transportation to suburban schools to improve educational opportunities for Black students, a position also advocated by President Richard Nixon (Lukas 1986; Spring 1994).

In 1974 Federal Judge W. Arthur Garrity ruled that the Boston school committee had violated the constitutional rights of students by intentionally maintaining a segregated school system.[2] He cited its assignment of students to neighborhood schools, its unfair hiring and transfer policies with respect to minority staff, and its inability to successfully implement any policies to address the racial imbalances. The plaintiffs' compelling data demonstrated that schools with large Black student populations had fewer resources, lacked modern facilities, were assigned less-experienced teachers, and that overall Black student performance lagged well behind White students (Dentler and Scott 1981).

In September 1974 court-ordered busing began in Boston. With violence increasing, Mayor White denounced "forced busing" but appealed to Whites for "law and order" (Lukas 1986). He suggested that the school committee be abolished and the school department be made a city department of city government, with the superintendent a department head. Finding little interest and concerned about the effect on his re-election campaign, he abandoned this effort and receded from any significant educational-leadership role. In 1976 he was nearly defeated for mayor; his victory was made possible only by overwhelming support from the Black electorate, earning him the derisive title of "Mr. Black" (Golden and Lowery 1982).

With little official support from either the school committee or city government, Judge Garrity appointed his own "panel of masters" and directed them to develop a plan that would address his "deep educational concerns" (Dentler and Scott 1981)—a signal that correction of racial imbalance was not the only goal, but that educational quality was an expected outcome. The revised plan, adopted in 1975, restructured student school assignments through a geocoding system that bused both Black and White students. It also introduced a one-for-one minority-teacher hiring policy, assigned them to schools across the district, and upgraded rundown schools in Black neighborhoods.

By most accounts, administrative decision-making shifted to the courts during the 1970s (Lukas 1986) and the school committee's power declined, as each element of its authority was stripped away, except that of appointing the superintendent. Even the stark patronage system that had controlled not only civil-service positions but also administrative appointments began to ebb as Garrity installed a professional-rating system to select new administrators and established an equity department.[3] As a *Boston Globe* investigative report (1982) described,

> [t]hree major factors characterized the operation of the School Committee during most of the 1970s: patronage, personal ambition, and a desire to be heavily involved in daily administrative matters. [But] patronage appointments began to cease in 1978 for two reasons. First, a professional-rating system was instituted by Judge Garrity. Second, the School Committee went outside the system to name Robert Wood and Robert Spillane as superintendents. (*Boston Globe* 1982)

The Strong Superintendents: Robert Spillane and Laval Wilson (1982–1988)

After the approval of Boston's desegregation plan, state funds helped to fuel significant capital improvements and new school construction. In 1977 a coalition of parents and teachers whose platform included parental involvement, quality education, and desegregated schools elected two members to the school committee, including its first Black. That committee hired the first outside superintendent, Robert Wood. He, in turn, hired equal numbers of Black and White new teachers. By 1980, in Boston about 17 percent of the teaching force was Black, Black students made up about 50 percent of the school population, and Blacks made up 20 percent of the city's population.[4] During this period, state legislation restricted school boards to an "educational policy" role, with the superintendent responsible for district-management decisions. Nevertheless, in 1980, the committee, unwilling to acknowledge his role as school chief, fired Wood after a three-to-two vote (*Boston Globe* 1982).

ROBERT "BUD" SPILLANE. In the summer of 1981 Robert Spillane, who had served as New York Deputy Commissioner of Education, was appointed superintendent. Spillane declared that Boston's school system was a "national disgrace," with little capacity for budget management or prioritizing academic reforms and no system of accountability (*Boston Globe* 1982). Spillane made several moves to establish his authority. First, citing the need to cut the budget, he completed a layoff plan for teachers.

Then he insisted that a new district curriculum, the first in recent history, be written by his own team. Third, he insisted on authority to make personnel decisions. This initially put him in conflict with Black committee members, whom he felt were protecting Black administrators and interfering with his executive prerogative.

While Spillane's supporters saw him as a decisive, candid, and strong manager who got things done, his opponents viewed him as impatient, impulsive, and unwilling to address Boston's underlying sociopolitical realities. Spillane chafed under Garrity's "rigid" student-assignment policy, which he believed would never encourage a return of White students to the Boston schools (Cooper 1982). Still, Garrity, being sufficiently assured that his plan was being implemented, in 1985 stepped back from his direct oversight, assigning that role to the State Board of Education.

Under Spillane, the business community, whose leaders lived in the suburbs and had little to do with the Boston public schools, began to play a more public, active role (Dooley 1994). Through their coordinating committee, known as the "Vault," they developed their own city-wide strategy to improve schools. In September 1982 they signed the "Boston Compact," along with Mayor White, Spillane, and others. The business community agreed to fund after-school and summer employment and to hire all qualified Boston graduates who sought employment, in exchange for the district's commitment to public accountability for improved organizational and student performance. At the same time, the Bank of Boston established the Boston Plan for Excellence, donating $1.5 million to endow a fund to support creative classroom initiatives as a gift to the city. Its purpose was to provide an endowment "to be used as a catalyst for innovation" (Dooley 1994, 19).

The 1983 election brought in a new mayor, former City Councilman Ray Flynn, and a significantly changed school committee. City council and school committee membership grew from five to thirteen seats, with nine elected in district-based elections and four elected at large. Joe Cronin, Massachusetts's Secretary of Education, urged Flynn to resist interfering with the school committee and instead serve as an advocate for the schools to the governor and the state legislature:

> This can be a year when inexperienced city officials squander their leadership potential by squabbling over positions, patronage, or perquisites of office, or a year when the new mayor, City Council, and School Committee could rise to the occasion and raise Boston schools to their former reputation of competence, even excellence. (Cohen 1983)

In 1985 Spillane left Boston to accept a superintendency in Virginia. In his final interview, he warned that "the school committee is going to be a very serious problem. They get too concerned with management and personnel issues" (Sege 1985).

LAVAL WILSON. In 1985 the school committee replaced Spillane with Laval Wilson, an experienced and highly regarded superintendent. Mayor Flynn and School Committee President Nucci both declared him the consensus choice. They chose Wilson for his toughness, his "instant professionalism and credibility, someone to pay attention to the details of managing a system" (Hernandez 1986). In other words, they chose a man who would serve in the best tradition of the professional superintendent.

Wilson, like Spillane before him, viewed Boston's school problems as essentially educational and managerial, not racial—poor performance was the result of ineffective teaching and instructional support, not racism. Wilson had widespread support from the business community. Both the mayor and the business community steadily increased their visibility and influence in education. In addition to its funding for the Compact, the business community expanded its direct support for various programs.

In early 1987 Wilson presented his Boston Education Plan, which focused on literacy and student accountability through the adoption of a single basal reading text and a back-to-the-basics approach to instruction. In 1988 he presented a new student-assignment plan and a school-facilities-renovation plan. While each was a significant and necessary change, together they created resistance about what would be expected of teachers, where students would go to school, where teachers would be assigned, and who would raise the additional taxes. The expanded board's public bickering over local issues only increased and seemed to exacerbate its inability to support any educational agenda, or even to support its superintendent.

Community support for Wilson weakened in light of lukewarm public approval of his Boston Education Plan. But business executives, his strongest supporters, urged the school committee to renew Wilson's contract for at least two years, noting that another change in leadership would disrupt major reforms. They renewed the Compact in 1987, adding the teachers' union as a full partner. Political, business, and educational leaders joined in a show of unity to announce a new teachers' contract that included a provision to improve the schools through a school-based management strategy, directing power away from the archaic central-office bureaucracy and toward principals and parents.

But the regional recession of 1988 ushered in a series of belt-tightening moves and subsequent budget deficits.[5] The city council and mayor reduced city expenditures to eliminate budget deficits, but they had little control over the school budget, which included salary increases for teachers. The school committee was unwilling to reduce its budget, which would require it to lay off newly hired teachers. Its budget was rejected by the city council, and Mayor Flynn was faced with the unenviable task of resolving this budgetary crisis.

During 1988 Flynn's interest in education matters was becoming more visible. Some observers speculated that he was simply creating a re-election campaign issue, but others saw his interest coming from concern about finding a way to re-attract young middle-class families to Boston (Wen and Marantz 1988). Parents frustrated with their school system voiced their concerns to the mayor, and the mayor listened.

THE INITIAL REFERENDUM. Flynn created an advisory panel to consider a plan to shrink the school committee and allow him to appoint its members. He argued that appointing a board would keep politics out of the schools (Wen 1989). After some hesitation, in November 1989 Flynn placed a referendum on the ballot to gauge voter interest in an appointed school board.

Black elected officials feared that the referendum would undermine political power in minority neighborhoods and were concerned that "instead of the masses being empowered [by being able to vote for a school committee member], you will have an elitist group of individuals made up of the mayor's cronies" (Ribadeneira 1989a). They believed that after years of being a minority on the school committee, they were on the verge of electing a working majority in the next election. They worried that the mayor, elected from a voter group of which only 10 percent of the voters had children in public schools, would ultimately reduce support for schools that served a mostly Black student population.

The school committee unanimously opposed Flynn and created a bumper-sticker that read: "Keep democracy. Elect your School Committee" (Ribadeneira 1989c). The mayor, they argued, should focus on building a slate of qualified committee candidates to stand for election. Flynn responded that in fact "people who have never had children in the schools tell me that I have to do something about the appalling conditions of the schools."

Flynn's referendum picked up support from members of the business community, who argued that voters could always vote mayors out of office. They agreed that changes in school governance was not a panacea, but Flynn suggested that at least "a new school board will stop wasting time and tax dollars." The chairman of the Vault was quoted by the *Boston Globe*: "We cannot afford to have efforts at reform go by the wayside because the School Committee process has been a drag on reform, and frankly, it has been" (Ribadeneira 1989a, b).

Referendum supporters and opponents framed the problem with the Boston schools in two contrasting ways: that petty interference and lack of leadership by uninformed and parochial committee members were paralyzing the schools, or that poor and minority parents would lose political advocates that could protect their interests. While Flynn argued that schooling was being endangered by the unprofessional behavior of the elected school committee, his opponents argued that community participation and debate about fundamental educational decisions were only preserved when the committee was responsive to its constituency.

The advisory referendum was approved by a slim 869-vote margin of victory out of 57,497 votes cast, which represented less than 10 percent of Boston's eligible voters. After Flynn's advisers warned him that taking control of the school district could become "the mayor's Vietnam," he put his plans on hold (Howe 1989).

The 1990 school year began with the same pressing problems: how to pay for the teachers' contract and how to implement the revised, zone-based student-assignment plan? Garrity had delegated responsibility to the school committee for designing the student-assignment plan and fulfilling the mandate of high-quality desegregated schools. Mayor Flynn's own consultants devised a "controlled-choice strategy," which divided the district into four regions; families living in each region could select schools for their children, so long as their selection did not adversely affect school racial balance. His plan was ultimately accepted by the school committee and Wilson.

In 1990, after an acrimonious debate that split along racial lines, the committee voted to buy out Wilson's contract—a vote that a committee member called "a lynching" (Ribadeneira 1990a). Two supporters did not run for re-election, eroding his support, and a key opponent was elected board president. Wilson's firing renewed calls to restructure the school committee. The Vault had supported Wilson and now considered collectively endorsing the appointed committee, which individual members had supported. They blamed not the mayor for Wilson's troubles but the infighting they observed in the committee. Meanwhile, city council members criticized the committee for terminating Wilson's contract, while at the same time requesting additional funds for the new teachers' contract.

In Wilson's view the problem was not how the committee was selected, but the shortness of the term (two years), the inexperience among individual members, and its large size (13 members). He stated that he spent most of his time making sure that he had secured seven votes for each decision. He reiterated the widely held view that the committee should select a superintendent, give him a broad outline of policies, and then let him operate. He ended his last interview in Boston by observing:

> Until this city addresses the critical issue of the governance of the schools, then you are going to see the same revolving-door scenario with superintendent after superintendent. After a few years, you find you've made enough enemies on the committee that they have the right number of votes to replace you. If you owe your job to the mayor, then it's going to influence your decision-making. But it's clear that something has to be done about the governance. (Ribadeneira 1990b)

The Education Mayors: Raymond Flynn and Thomas Menino (1988–present)

MAYOR RAYMOND FLYNN. Throughout 1990 the mayor's chief and overriding concern was the chronic fiscal crisis—the result not only of a very large budget increase proposed by the school committee, but by the state's fiscal crisis that triggered deep cuts in local aid to cities and towns. Committee members believed that the mayor had manufactured the budget deficit by withholding funds necessary to meet the teachers' contract increase in an attempt to make the committee look bad, but Flynn noted that of all city services, only the schools were slated for any increases whatsoever, despite a declining enrollment.

That autumn, four members of the city's legislative delegation proposed the establishment of a nine-member board, with five members elected from districts and four appointed by the mayor. However, others repeated the Boston Teachers' Union's refusal to support any proposal that would "diminish the citizens' right to vote and select their own representation because that would be hypocritical [to] the democratic process" (Ribadeneira 1990c). Indicating its frustrations with the school committee over both the search and the lack of a balanced budget for the coming year, the city council considered abolishing the committee altogether, instead creating a city department to take over its functions.

Once again, the Black electoral delegation and legislators from poor White neighborhoods voiced concern that an appointed board would dilute the strong voting bloc that served neighborhood interests. They feared that the few jobs that minorities had gained over the decade would be lost if the mayor himself was responsible for distributing patronage jobs in the schools. They doubted the mayor's real commitment to deal with poor neighborhoods, White or Black: "Fix my neighborhood first. Give me better service in Dorchester and Roxbury. Deal with the violence. Clean the streets and abandoned lots. Give us more police service. If you do some of these things, then maybe we'll consider giving you the school system" (Rezendes and Marantz 1990).

While an overwhelming majority of Boston residents believed that the current school committee should be dismissed, they were reluctant to turn the district over to the mayor; some preferred devolving power to the schools, as was occurring in Chicago. Finally, in June 1991, with legislators, Black activists, and past opponents agreeing to compromise on some type of change, the Massachusetts House and Senate overwhelmingly approved a home-rule petition for an appointed board: Chapter 108 mandated that Boston's 13-member board would finish its term at the end of the year and be replaced by seven members appointed by the mayor (Biddle 1991). A referendum would be held five years later to determine voter willingness to continue this governance change.

At almost the same time, the search committee finally nominated Lois Harrison-Jones, an associate superintendent from Texas. Flynn intended to replace the 13 members that selected her, therefore he sought to cancel any appointment so that his new committee could select the superintendent. When that was rejected, he asked the incoming superintendent to reduce the length of her contract from five years to three. In an editorial, the *Globe* pleaded for "a climate of continuity in a school system mired in chaos. Despite all the talk of removing politics from the educational process, a contentious debate about the superintendent's contract smacks of the political bickering that has marred the Boston public schools for too long" (*Boston Globe* 1991).

In the autumn of 1991 the council's budget allocation required Harrison-Jones to make severe cuts, including staff layoffs, but at their last meeting the elected committee refused, saying that such unpopular cuts would have to be made by Flynn and his new board. While Harrison-Jones was not enthusiastic about what she considered to be an educationally unsound budget, she said that she "could care less about politics—this is a fiscal matter" (Ribadeneira 1991).

Flynn's appointments to the school committee made it clear that he intended to control the educational decision-making and policy-making apparatus. He appointed close political allies and an aide, Bob Consalvo, as the committee's secretary. Harrison-Jones's supporters feared that Consalvo's appointment created a shadow superintendent who would eventually undermine her credibility and authority with employees within the system. Bob Marshall, of the Black Educators Alliance, pointed out that contrary to Flynn's pledge to remove politics from the school system, Consalvo's appointment would ensure that politics would be part of any future educational agenda (Aucoin 1991).

Within the school system, Harrison-Jones was well-regarded by teachers and administrators for her openness and encouragement of school-site innovation. Her meetings in the heavily minority neighborhoods generated public support. But an impatient business community urged her to quickly implement necessary structural reforms. Over the summer of 1992 she unveiled a new management plan to reduce the number of top administrators from 16 to 8 and to establish school-site councils for shared-site governance that would shift authority for curricula, personnel, budgeting, and professional-development decisions to the schools.

But as school started in September, Consalvo publicly criticized Harrison-Jones for not making enough staff changes and for the poor performance of high school students on the annual standardized test. He proposed a voucher plan to help parents of at-risk students pay for private schools. Harrison-Jones suggested that his desire for control of patronage was the basis of this criticism. She argued that the controlled choice-assignment-plan modifications she proposed would give parents more choice and at the same time prevent the return of racially segregated schools (Robinson 1992). Committee Chairman Paul Parks publicly rebuked Consalvo, reminding him that he worked for the school committee, not the mayor, and demanding that he stop "public lobbying" for his voucher plan and end his public criticism of Harrison-Jones. Others pointed to the school committee's failure to support Harrison-Jones or to reprimand Consalvo for speaking for them as evidence that the mayor himself was taking over the schools (Aucoin 1992).

In November 1992 Consalvo resigned, portraying Harrison-Jones as a defender of the status quo who blocked reform efforts, in part because she was hired by and therefore loyal to the elected school committee rather than the present appointed board (Chow 1992). Until she was ousted, he said, the mayor could not be held accountable for poor school performance (Rezendes 1992). Flynn kept up the public pressure for the school committee to adopt more sweeping reforms, including a new curriculum and "pilot schools"—a public variant of charter schools. As Flynn continued to criticize the school district for working too slowly, the school committee seemed to side with Harrison-Jones and suggested that Flynn was relying on incorrect information from Consalvo. Long-time observers noted that Flynn's power to appoint the school committee had not taken politics out of the school system. But he argued that the consensus to change school-board governance mandated that he take leadership of the school system. "When I demand more from our schools, I am accused of meddling. And if I don't speak out, I am criticized for not showing leadership. You have to step on a lot of toes; that's how change comes about" (Rakowsky 1993).

MAYOR THOMAS MENINO. In March 1993 Flynn announced that he was leaving for an ambassadorship at the Vatican. In his last major speech as mayor, he urged his audience to continue to pressure the schools to move forward on reform. City Councilor Thomas Menino, as council president, became acting mayor. Known as an "urban mechanic" for his attention to constituency "pot-hole" interests (Walker 1995), Menino tied his leadership to the quality of public education and to his ability to retain employers and businesses and create new jobs. In a landslide victory in November, Menino became Boston's first elected Italian-American mayor.

Shortly after the election, Harrison-Jones announced that Boston student performance was improving across 12 of 17 areas and was well above the level found in other urban areas. By this time, about 80 percent of the students attending schools were minority, including significant numbers of Asian and Hispanic students, while only 38 percent of the staff were.

The new committee approved the new school budget, but by now, Boston was spending $331 less per pupil than it did in 1991. In June 1994 education, business, and city leaders jointly announced that a new three-year teachers' contract had been signed. The agreement included pilot schools, site-based management, full-day kindergarten classes, higher system-wide standards, restoration of specialty classes, and a new job category for teachers that allowed for more pay for teacher-leaders. Business representatives of the Boston Compact flanked Menino and Harrison-Jones to express support, and they credited Menino for his leadership in the collective-bargaining process (Benning 1994). Also present were parent representatives and community-service organizations, which were new members of the Compact. During the summer, Menino named Harrison-Jones to his mayoral cabinet.

But the prospects for stability and political peace were mitigated by impatience with the institutional changes that observers believed were necessary for system-wide improvement. Two issues continued to plague Harrison-Jones—her unwillingness to fire principals and the slow pace of the reforms (*Boston Globe* 1994). Finally, despite earlier public displays of cooperation, Menino urged Harrison-Jones to step down.

Supporters once again rallied to her defense, believing that she was being railroaded out by politicians because of her commitment to poor and minority students. They suggested that the criticism was motivated not by a desire for her to move more quickly, but by pressure from the "good old boys network" that blocked the very changes she initiated, especially those focused on improving the education of minority children (Hart and Walker 1994).

While the school committee continue to urge her to resign, Harrison-Jones responded that reforms take time and that the lack of respect for the superintendent undermined school morale (Hart 1995a). Nevertheless, shortly thereafter, the committee announced that it would not extend her contract. She agreed to leave; it was apparent that while she worked well with the minority community, the mayor's support, not theirs, was the critical ingredient for staying in the superintendency.

Menino created a search committee and said that appointment of the next superintendent was his administration's highest priority (Hart 1995b). With the opportunity to hire his own superintendent and having a school committee loyal to him and a teachers' contract firmly in place, Menino said that he wanted the city's business leaders and voters to hold him accountable for reforming the public schools. In July the search committee identified four candidates, all from outside the district.

Harrison-Jones, in her departing interview, reviewed her efforts to develop a caring district; to do that, she said that she had to protect children from the machinations of intrusive politicians, who, as she saw it, would run roughshod over the city's public school system (Hart 1995c). With the search in its final stages, a new group of 40 city leaders formed the "Critical Friends"; they included members of local colleges and universities, civil rights and educational-policy organizations, and members of the Vault. They pushed for a role in the selection process, urging the mayor to call for the resignations of all the district's senior administrative staff in preparation for the new superintendent, but they were rebuffed (Hart 1995d).

In August 1995 the school committee unanimously selected Thomas Payzant as the city's superintendent. Boston-born Payzant had been a Department of Education's Assistant Secretary since 1993, and prior to that was superintendent for the San Diego Unified School District. Anthony Alvarado had received considerable support from the minority community and the *Globe*, because of his work in New York City and his charisma, but Menino clearly wanted Payzant. The Critical Friends remarked that Payzant had "failed to energize our intellect and our spirits" (Hart 1995d).

Without delay, Payzant appointed six principals to his management team to oversee mixed "clusters" of elementary, middle, and high schools organized in geographical areas. He restructured the central office and eliminated several positions. He assigned one administrator to address the accreditation problems with Boston's high schools (8 of 15 were on probation, warning, or had lost accreditation). In July 1996 he presented his comprehensive plan, *Focus on Children: A Comprehensive Reform Plan for the Boston Public Schools* (Boston Public Schools 1996a). The primary goal of the plan was to "improve teaching and learning for all children." Key strategies included: "New City-wide Learning Standards" in each subject area; a "Center for Leadership Development"; a single, school-wide planning document for whole-school change in each school; and a "Reorganization Plan" that focused schools on student performance. In the plan, Payzant described how, for the first time, the Boston public schools had all of the elements moving in the same direction:

- A mayor with school improvement as his top priority.
- An appointed school committee that provided stable leadership on educational policy.
- A superintendent with experience in managing reform and a mandate for making change.
- The support of the Boston Teachers' Union and a contract with many reform provisions.
- The Boston Compact that partnered the schools with the city's economic, political, educational, cultural, and community resources.

THE QUESTION 2 REFERENDUM ON THE ELECTED SCHOOL COMMITTEE. The 1991 home-rule petition establishing the appointed school committee called for a public referendum five years later to determine whether or not it should become a permanent governance structure. Despite the initial lack of public support, Menino urged voters to retain the appointed school board, staking his political career on it: "We need stability in the system. *We've taken politics out of the school board now*, and, with our new superintendent Tom Payzant pushing for educational reform, I'll be involved, speaking for the appointed board, along with a lot of other people" (Mooney 1995 [emphasis added]).

In his 1996 State of the City address Menino unveiled his own five-year plan to reform the schools: higher academic standards, rebuilt schools, extended day programs, and more computers in the classrooms. Underscoring his commitment to the schools, Menino said:

> I want to be judged as your mayor by what happens now in the Boston public schools. Don't undercut our efforts by introducing narrow politics back into the schools [a reference to the vote on the appointed school

committee]. If I fail to bring about these specific reforms by the year 2001, then judge me harshly.. (Anand 1996)

Payzant noted that Menino "has the right goals and they're achievable depending on the availability of resources—in terms of the city and school department and public–private ventures" (Avenoso 1996), but others noted that he did not specify any academic targets such as test scores or attendance-rate improvement.

Arguments against the referendum were similar to those that had occurred five years earlier. Opponents of the appointed committee claimed that it was little more than a rubber stamp for the mayor, that its members had failed to cultivate active relationships with parents and teachers and instead focused on the priorities of the business community and the mayor. Meetings were short and poorly attended, and decisions were usually unanimous and made with little discussion or input. Some city councilors said they would not vote for new taxes without a commitment to terminate the controlled-choice student-assignment plan and return to a neighborhood-schools plan (Avenoso 1996).

Most elected officials representing the Black community still publicly favored an elected board, but there was now more division in the community leadership, especially among church leaders. Similarly, in the predominately White working-class neighborhoods of South Boston, there was significant dissatisfaction with the changes over the past two decades, but their interest was more in finding a way to return to neighborhood-based student-assignment plans rather than who was going to make the decision. But the most convincing argument for an elected board was that parents should have some say about the school-district's agenda, and that because the appointed board seemed largely ceremonial, both poor White and minority parents had lost the attention of the school administrators who now only served the mayor and his business interests.

Supporters of the appointed committee argued that its unanimity simply meant that Payzant's staff was doing an excellent job of policy planning and presentation, that committee members had done their homework, and that there was a broad consensus over the new strategic direction of the district. There was more ethnic diversity with the appointed committee than ever existed in the elected one. Test scores overall continued to decline, but Payzant emphasized his long-term commitment to steady, resolute progress through staff training, new materials, and high standards. There was a widespread belief that Payzant was making modest but steady progress in improving schools and thus there was little interest in changing directions.

Several initiatives signaled to voters that their educational interests would be addressed in meaningful ways by the mayor. Schools could apply for grants provided by the Boston Compact to undertake whole-school change (Boston Public Schools 1996b). Twenty-seven schools were selected, including a majority that served poor and minority students. Menino established a task force in the summer of 1996 that would review the 1988 student-assignment plan and consider more slots at "neighborhood schools" for elementary children, thus chipping away at desegregation strategies of the past (*Boston Globe* 1996a). Two of six planned "pilot schools" were opened.

Supporters of the appointed board raised nearly $700,000 from the Boston business community for their eight-month drive, while opponents raised less than $4,000. The privately funded Boston Municipal Research Bureau (1996) wrote a series of briefing papers urging support for the appointed committee. Elected committees were accused of "placing politics over sound policy" by

- Grand-standing and finger-pointing in long and chaotic meetings.
- Consistently budgeting more than the city was willing to allocate and incurring operating deficits in 11 out of 14 years, even though school spending increased.
- Micromanaging and being concerned with day-to-day operations rather than with broad educational policy.
- Spending over $1 million on staff, stipends, and benefits for themselves.
- Being unable to make decisions efficiently and to serve the whole school district.
- Generally creating a climate of uncertainty.

In the month before the November vote, Menino was able to turn many of his strongest opponents into supporters. Black ministers urged their congregations to support the appointed committee, arguing that the chaos of the old elected board was far worse for Black children than the stability of the new one. Four days before the election, the *Globe* reported that the Boston schools had just received a $10 million challenge grant from the Annenberg Foundation, based on Boston's new "relentless focus on children and schools":

> Things are different now, thanks to a mayor who has linked his legacy to public education, an appointed school board that values children more than politics, a flexible teachers' union contract and renewed partnerships between individual schools and business. It was this "alignment of business, educational and political leadership" that convinced the foundation that major school reform is possible in Boston. (*Boston Globe* 1996b)

Voters responded with an overwhelming vote of confidence for the appointed board—70 percent rejected the referendum. Only in largely Black neighborhoods in Roxbury and traditionally poorer White neighborhoods in Dorchester and South Boston was there any significant opposition. *Education Week* noted that the vote confirmed Menino's membership in "a small fraternity of big-city mayors who have moved aggressively to assume responsibility for their troubled public schools" (Hendrie 1996).

AFTER THE REFERENDUM. The year 1997 began with Mayor Menino and Superintendent Payzant firmly in control of the schools. Rejection of Question 2 by voters meant that the appointed committee was firmly institutionalized. Payzant announced the appointment of 15 new principals/headmasters over the summer of 1997. The school committee extended Payzant's contract for an additional three years, to 2003. Menino, riding a crest of unprecedented popularity, won re-election in 1998. The Boston Plan for Excellence (1999) added more "21st Century Schools." The school committee changed the admission process for the examination high schools, eliminating set-aside slots reserved for minorities. Results from the Stanford-9 (SAT-9) standardized test generally pointed to continued poor performance across the school district, with small improvements in the middle-school scores. Payzant, discouraged by the disparities in testing outcomes between Black and Hispanic students and White and Asian students, reiterated his goal to eliminate that gap by 2003.[6]

Only the Critical Friends have publicly critiqued the Payzant–Menino tenure; Hubie Jones, the chair, noted several successes, but believed that the pace of reform was too slow, the foundation was not yet in place, and that leadership was "disengaged" from the parents and community leaders. He described continuing central-office problems, the disparities in test scores, and the lack of a strong evaluation process that removed ineffective teachers and administrators. Finally, he criticized the administration for not acknowledging the value of "constructive criticism" (Jones 1998).

In a recent address, the mayor reviewed the success of Boston's school leadership. He announced that Boston's schools were fully wired to the Internet and that the computer-to-student ratio reduced to 1:7, near what he had promised during his election campaign. He also pointed to the city's funding of full-day kindergartens, after-school programs, and his literacy initiative, and he praised the collective effort of businesses, foundations, and local colleges in partnership with the city and the school district. Notably absent was any acknowledgment of the role played by parents or community activists.

DISCUSSION

Even though this chronology has traced the shift in apparent control of the Boston public schools from the elected school committee to the courts, the professional superintendents, and the current mayor and his appointed committee, all three mayors in this study have argued for an increased role for the mayoral office. Several questions arose from the review of this history that provide a framework by which to consider the likelihood of mayoral control effecting significant educational change.

1) Does Mayoral Control Take Politics Out of the Schools?

School boards have given politics a bad name; acrimonious personal attacks and posturing were regularly observed on the board, and, in earlier years, there were regular criminal convictions for corruption. Administrative decisions are no longer being contested at school committee meetings. Even if there are problems at the local school site, those problems are handled administratively at the site or within the school district bureaucracy. The appointed school committee has worked on policy committees and largely accepted that role; it does not use the media for campaigning for future office. The average length of a committee meeting fell from three hours, to half that (*Boston Globe* 1996b). Without the public spectacle of contentious school committee meetings, according to some informants, what has really happened is that the district has become "quiet."

At one level, the political trades and tirades that occurred at the elected committee's meetings are gone, yet setting school policy is inherently a political process. The lack of debate suggests that all voices have not necessarily been heard. At its extreme, only certain voices are validated, contested issues are not likely to be given extensive coverage, and there is little point for community interests to lobby the board, leaving the agenda to elites (Jones 1997; Tyack and Cuban 1995).

But Menino has publicly staked his political future on the quality of the schools, and the public supported him in the votes for the referendum and his re-election. Furthermore, instead of weekly political debates, the mayor has four years between re-election campaigns with which to evaluate program effectiveness around such indicators as test scores and student attendance. This allows a longer lead time for new strategies and for voters to weigh the quality of the mayor's education agenda against satisfaction with his other work—for example, fire, recreation, or police services. In an ironic twist on a familiar topic, when student performance did not show rapid improvement, Hubie Jones, of the Critical Friends, criticized the slow pace of the reforms in Payzant's plan (Jones 1998) in much the same way that Flynn and Menino criticized Harrison-Jones (Robinson 1992).

2) What Changes in Schooling Have Resulted from Mayoral Control?

Most of the changes directly related to teaching and learning can be attributed to the strategies and leadership of Superintendent Payzant, and he is a member of the mayor's cabinet. The superintendent's ability to maintain a steady implementation pace for the *Focus on Learning* and the "whole-school change" strategy reflects Menino's support. Menino has been instrumental in attracting significant corporate support and providing increased city services. These reflect the mayor's "urban mechanic" reputation (Walker 1995).

At the same time, some board members have acknowledged that they do not spend as much time in schools as did their elected counterparts, do not feel as responsible for individual schools, and so are not as personally knowledgeable about successes and problems at individual schools. And, despite changes in central-office titles, there is little evidence that Payzant has made radical changes in his administration, and little significant change in the teaching force. According to recent reports, over the past three years less than ten teachers were dismissed for incompetence.

There can be no doubt that desegregation decisions have significantly impacted schooling over the past 30 years—busing, affirmative action, and the selection of Black administrators and superintendents—and the debates regarding mayoral control raised many concerns that Boston may be returning to separate and unequal education for its Black students—in short, resegregated schools (Orfield et al. 1996). The ouster of a popular Black superintendent, the rollback of the district's controlled-choice student-assignment plan, and the end of raced-based admissions to the examination schools all occurred under mayor control. Observers fear that the decisions will negatively impact minority students the most, and they want the mayor to be more vocally explicit in his commitment to the education of Black youth. Otherwise, some analysts believe, re-segregation of the schools will be the inevitable consequence and, reminding listeners that earlier mayors resisted court decisions to integrate schools, urged the mayor and school committee to mount a challenge in court "because it is right [to facilitate integration]" (Goldberg 1999).

3) Does Mayoral Control Create the Climate that Attracts Business Support and Is Able to Re-attract the Middle Class?

Business support for schools in Boston, through the Private Industry Council, the Boston Fund for Excellence in Boston, and the Boston Compact have not only contributed money but have adamantly supported a whole-school change strategy. Their financial and technical support during the referendum was considered to be critical to its success. Political alignments exist today, but it should be recognized that they are under conditions of financial prosperity in Boston, and therefore should an economic downturn occur, there is fear that school funding will be left unprotected.

Efforts to preserve the middle class in Boston have been a steady theme articulated by all three mayors, and yet eight years of mayoral control of education have not stemmed that slide. Even though the changes at the top, in terms of governance, are strong, it is not yet clear whether the public schools have attracted the middle class back to Boston. In reality, the middle class has not used the public schools for quite a while, and its flight from Boston was not solely the result of the schools. The percentage of White students using the Boston public schools declined from 20 percent in 1992 to 15 percent in 1998. However, changes in admission policy to the elite examination high schools have increased the numbers of acceptances for students from local private schools; this was not a policy promoted by the mayor, but he, the board, and even the NAACP believed that their opposition to the lawsuit would be met with defeat in the courts, unraveling desegregation policies across the country.

4) How Did Mayoral Control Occur?

Did it occur because mayors were disgusted with the chaos of the school boards or the poor performance of the schools?

Far from being a quick process, the change that occurred in Boston was the result of a series of demands, responses, and changes that occurred over a 25-year period. What started as an effort to wrest privilege away from political leadership in order to gain access to better schools for Black children in the 1960s became a reform to transform what was being taught (1982) and how it was being taught (1992) to a whole-school change process focused on teaching and learning (1996). In order for it to have succeeded, it required first the reduction in overall power of the elected school committee by the courts, then the establishment of a history of strong superintendents with commitment to improved student achievement, and then the willingness of the mayor and the business community to support these efforts.

A key factor in this shift was the emergence of strong superintendents who were not cut from the same local cloth of Boston Irish Catholic neighborhood politics, and who were considered strong, professional educators. If anything, this change seems to represent the final conquest of "managers of virtue" (Tyack and Hansot 1982), the ascendancy of a "nonpolitical" leadership of the schools embodied in the professional superintendent. Mayor Menino's choice of Payzant, a career educator with a reputation of solid, if somewhat colorless, leadership ability, over a more charismatic and populist finalist signaled the mayor's desire for steady, incremental school improvement. Payzant's background gave him positive connections with the Boston elites but not necessarily with the Boston neighborhoods that lost their advocates when the elected committee was changed.

5) Does Mayoral Control Improve Student Achievement?

Measuring the independent effects of various elements of a comprehensive reform agenda like Boston's is extremely difficult. But many believe that a coherent systemic strategy that builds capacity, leverages, and generates resources that focus on teaching and learning and that mobilize community-wide support has the best chances for long-term success. Such is the general impression of Boston's current reform—Menino takes great pride in many of the supports and initiatives that the city has supported. Using test scores as an achievement indicator is risky, but recent results seem to confirm that Boston was moving in the right direction, but not quickly enough to meet Payzant's self-imposed five-year goal of system-wide improvement and significant reductions in the achievement gap. There continue to be significant differences in performance between Black and Hispanic students and White and Asian students, and efforts to close those gaps such as mandatory summer school and the elimination of social promotions are met with skepticism.

The Critical Friends initially endorsed the alignment of resources, authority, and mission (Critical Friends 1997), but more recently reported that the current reform strategy had not actively engaged poor and minority residents in improving schools for their children. They have not seen renewed effort or innovative teaching strategies by the professional staff in schools with large numbers of Black children. If anything, some believe that the supervision of instruction has declined, not increased. There is fear that pressure to comply with the wishes of White middle-class families will mean a return to the schooling disparities that existed before the Garrity era. They question Payzant's ability to remove ineffective administrators and teachers and to bring residents into the schools (Jones 1998).

The challenge for the mayor and his superintendent is to ensure that the coherence in place will serve the interests of all children and families, including those traditionally underrepresented. Success requires that the strategy is just for all, that it will work over time, that access and distribution of goods and resources does not violate constitutional rights. As recently as 1970, the city government, school governance, the school bureaucracy, and the electorate were generally in alignment with regard to their expectations for the Boston public schools. Teachers, administrators, and politicians along with most White parents agreed with the direction in which the schools were headed. But Black families were left without a voice in the process and did not benefit from any of the employment or social-mobility advantages that were possible for others. Yet, even with the Racial Imbalance Act in place, the elected school committee, in alignment with the school district staff and the city government, resisted state and local pressure to increase educational opportunities for its Black minority, moreover encountering little opposition from any elected city officials.

The most difficult aspect of this is that educational reform at its most fundamental level—if its goal is to improve educational outcomes for all children—may not be politically popular. It may include policies that increase opportunities to learn for poor and minority students—for example, early childhood opportunities, after-school programs, in-school health clinics, and small class sizes with more educational specialists. Policies that provide differential support may not be politically popular and will take a skilled and committed mayor to provide political and administrative support. Under Mayor Menino and the benefit of the current economic boom, that seems to be very possible. Whether that commitment will remain under other mayors will test whether or not mayoral control will succeed in improving schools for all.

CONCLUSION: WHO BENEFITED AND WHO WILL BENEFIT?

Mayoral control of school districts is seen as an answer for troubled school districts. People believe that what mayors do will be different from what elected school committees did—that they will not be susceptible to local neighborhood politics, that they will root out inefficiencies inherent in school bureaucracies, and that they will articulate a single agenda and course of action that will align the disparate forces that have fragmented schools. The purpose of this case study was to suggest that the final decision and confirmation of Mayor Menino's role in schools was in fact itself the result of decades-long political debates that have not yet subsided. These debates reflect questions about who controls the schools—the jobs and contracts within the system, the real access of specific groups of students to a quality education, the nature of the response to judicial as well as legislative mandates, and the speed with which change can be effected.

Supporters of every persuasion have argued that administrators don't move quickly enough. That impatience reflects the fundamental dilemmas facing most urban school districts, that may or not in fact be solvable. How does a city provide equal educational opportunities for all children? What is its responsibility to children whose parents can select multiple alternative educational strategies? How do you improve teaching and evaluate teachers within tight legislative and collective-bargaining constraints and short timeframes? And with each question must be asked, who will pay?

Whether Menino's active commitment will remain, whether Payzant's initiatives will lead to the end of the achievement gap, and whether education will draw the same priority for other mayors remains to be seen. As the 1980s came to an end with a regional recession, the cost of the superintendent's efforts to improve education for Black students was pitted against other demands for services for city residents. The current changes have had little effect on efforts to return Boston's White middle-class children to attend the public school system, and, more to the point, to increase the appeal of a Boston residence for corporate leaders and professional staff and their families. By that standard, the governance change has had little effect: the percentage of White students in the schools continues to fall (from 20 percent in 1992 to 15 percent in 1998), except in the examination high schools. While there is little apparent intent to diminish the quality and opportunity for education for Boston's Black residents, it is possible that Black residents will feel that the attention and responsiveness of the school system to their needs has been compromised and that Boston will re-segregate its school system (Jackson 1999). If that occurs, then it is possible that another lawsuit could be filed, as the NAACP did in the 1970s.

Finally, most voters agreed that political alignment, stability, and accountability, and the initiatives introduced by the mayor and Superintendent Payzant were sufficiently important benefits that they were willing to forego the opportunity to vote for district representatives. While test scores have been rising for the system as a whole, little was mentioned of the achievement gaps between Black and Hispanic students and Whites and Asian Americans during that process, except by Superintendent Payzant, who set as his personal goal the elimination of those gaps by 2003—the end of his contract. The achievement of those students, who make up three-quarters of the city's student population, became his explicit success indicator.

Judge W. Arthur Garrity's death in 1999 sparked a heated and emotional exchange that underscores the powerful influence of race and racism on urban schools and sounds a cautionary note for the future. For some, Garrity destroyed the life opportunities of a generation of Boston's children by his decisions to force busing on the city, and yet for others he was a truly courageous leader who held accountable a school district and Boston's residents for their neglect of, and disregard for, the education of Boston's Black children (Feeney 1999; Jackson 1999). Ironically, in 1997, he ruled that Boston's Latin High School had unlawful admissions criteria that favored Black students, thus opening the door to the unraveling of 25 years of school-desegregation policies, including some based on his decision in 1974.

Effective governance is not simply aligning political, civic, professional resources, leadership, and accountability around a clear educational mission. It arises out of a fundamental willingness to respond to widely disparate and often competing demands for access to limited resources. The elected committee sought to respond by ensuring that their constituency, the Irish-American poor and working class, had schools that preserved culture and provided both steady employment and job-skills preparation for its youth. The courts sought to ensure that Roxbury's Black students had access to the same educational opportunities as South Boston's Irish. Superintendents sought to make the system work. Mayors saw fractious school decision-making as tearing the fabric of community life and scaring away opportunities for economic growth.

A popular mayor can reduce political chaos and provide hope for schools in the short term, but mayoral control cannot guarantee any better outcomes than did the elected committee, the courts, or the superintendents, because mayors themselves are also subject to political pressures. Businesses, which began by funding individual teachers, now seek a voice in school system change. The state continues to establish high-stakes, test-based outcome standards. The Black community continues to wonder whether its children will be left behind once again and thus political organizing and judicial relief remain options. Effective schools require strong and lasting relationships among the various parties that have exercised their power in the past and can still do so today, under the right conditions. In the end, a school system that works for all must have the same elements no matter what entity governs them: neighborhood involvement and oversight of schools, a vision of social justice that recognizes the rights of every student and the responsibility of residents to them, an efficient organization that focuses on teaching and learning, city-wide political and civic support that includes stability in leadership and mission, links to other social services such as after-school tutoring, health care, leadership development, and recreation, and opportunities for job training and internships.

Boston's case of mayoral control certainly can test whether political alignment, a professional focus on teaching and learning, and a growing local economy can produce high student achievement. Mayor Menino's extension of Payzant's contract demonstrates a desire to provide this test with enough time to succeed. Whether the youth who benefit will be the Irish from South Boston, Blacks and Latinos from Roxbury, or children from re-developed, newly occupied middle-class neighborhoods in Back Bay or Hyde Park remains to be seen. It will depend on the willingness and ability of future mayors to support and sustain that agenda in every neighborhood, their commitment to eradicate the consequences of racial policies past and present, and the capacity of individual schools and its teachers to become just, learning communities.

NOTES

1. I thank Marcia Pointdexter, a teacher in the Boston public schools, for her initial assistance, perspective, and contacts; John Portz and Ralph Edwards, Northeastern University, for comments on this manuscript and important political analyses of the Boston schools; and numerous teachers, administrators, and civic leaders who sat for interviews that informed this study.

2. *Morgan v. Hennigan*, Civil Action No. 72-911-G, United States District Court, District of Massachusetts, June 21, 1974.

3. Each administrator was expected to contribute to campaign funds for school committee members and campaign for the incumbent. This allowed committee members to intrude into day-to-day operations at the school site according to the Boston Finance Commission (1975).

4. The number of students in the Boston schools plunged from about 80,000 in the early 1970s to 60,000 by 1980, fueled by White flight to the suburbs that offered new jobs and new housing. The numbers have increased consistently though the 1990s, to about 63,000 in 1998.

5. Prop 2 1/2 mandated that taxes collected by the state for programs such as schools be capped at 2 1/2 percent of the assessed valuation for property. This in effect limited the amount of money available for cities and towns to fund their schools.

6. In 1990 San Diego's Superintendent Payzant committed the district to addressing similar disparities as the result of institutional racism and specific deficiencies within the city schools (Traitel 1990).

◙ ◙ ◙

CHAPTER SIX

Regime Change

mayoral takeover of the Chicago public schools

DOROTHY SHIPPS

To MANY THOUGHTFUL OBSERVERS of school politics, governance change has been a routine and repeated method of reforming urban public education. Alternating initiatives and eras have sought to increase the efficiency of public schools, and/or to increase their public accountability, often with the goal of improved equity, by either decentralizing or re-centralizing school system governance structures (Tyack 1993).

Leaders come and go, laws are passed and new contracts are bargained, but rarely has there been a *new regime*—a fundamental change in the institutions and individuals that formulate and execute education policy. Regime change involves not only a change in leadership, but also a change in the institutions and the "informal arrangements that surround and complement the formal workings of government authority." Clarence Stone analyzes such fundamental political change as requiring an examination of "who makes up the governing coalition . . . how [their] coming together is accomplished . . . and with what consequences" (Stone 1989, 3–6), because "those who would . . . alter current policy can do so only by making use of or generating an appropriate body of nongovernmental resources" (Stone 1993, 18).

Chicago's recent history of school reform is one case of contemporary regime change in urban school governance, and a much-touted model for the rest of the nation (Beinart 1997; Office of the Press Secretary 1998). In 1995 Mayor Richard M. Daley took over the leadership of the city's schools and now directs a hierarchy of city bureaucrats with the help of civic elites. Key decision-makers are no longer educators, and the Chicago

Teachers' Union (CTU) has been weakened as a force capable of blocking change. Daley's new regime elevates the status of business-like solutions to the city's schooling problems and increases the influence of business leaders. Latinos, the city's fastest-growing minority, have also benefited from the new regime in smaller ways. In contrast, the city's African-American population, despite having for decades produced a majority of the system's students, has much-reduced access to decision-making. Moreover, there is reason to be concerned about the effects of the new regime for poor students of color.

This chapter focuses on coalition-building and the mayor's role in Chicago's complex regime-change process. I outline the laws that enabled change and describe the informal relationships and decisions that have had the effect of shaping policy in practice. In the process, I show that Chicago's new regime is the consequence of long-simmering frustrations with the performance of the Chicago public schools (CPS), coupled with an extraordinarily engaged and active civic elite. The Chicago case is an extreme one. As such, it emphasizes the importance of legacy and contingency in mayoral takeovers, and reveals, in high relief, the impact that a regime change can have on issues of power and access in school governance.

CHAPTER ORGANIZATION

Below I highlight the differences between three Chicago school-reform laws. The first was a business-led oversight committee in response to fiscal collapse in 1980, followed by a decentralization law enacted in 1988, and a 1995 law that established the mayor as the school system's central governance figure. All mandated a complete change in system-wide leadership, and all changed the system's formal governing institutions. All are important to understanding Mayor Daley's role in Chicago school governance and the roots of the current regime. Elements of each linger on.

Shifts in reformers' intentions stand out when these formal governing statutes are contrasted, but changes made to the informal arrangements of governing clarify the underlying trends and patterns by concentrating on *who* was involved and *how*. These informal arrangements include the legacy of governing expectations that residents and leaders take for granted, the motivations and coalition partners of those who support change, and the informal uses policy-makers have made of their formal authorities.

To reveal these informal processes, I describe key aspects of the legacy of mayoral influence on Chicago's schools inherited from the early twentieth century, then examine the development of each law, and place each within the city's mayoral politics. The coalitions that initiated each law are described, including the ways that each law responded to perceived inadequacies of the one before it.

In conclusion, I return to the political consequences of urban school regime change in Chicago. What might it suggest about Mayor Daley's role and what are the implications for other cities seeking mayoral control of the schools?

Sources and Methods

This chapter draws on published and unpublished research conducted over the past nine years. The historical and political discussion of the years prior to 1995 rely heavily on my own work and on the many primary (e.g., archival research, elite interviews) and secondary sources consulted in its development (Shipps 1995, 1997, 1998; Menefee-Libey and Shipps 1997; Shipps, Kahne, and Smylie 1999). Discussion of the current regime (1995–2000) relies on the voluminous literature on reform effects and 72 semi-structured interviews of civic leaders in 1997 and as many collected in 1998. The city's key business, community, foundation, government, higher education, labor, and media organizations involved in the public schools are represented in these interviews. I sought confirmatory evidence through systematic reviews of documentary sources (e.g., PA 85-1418, HB 206, district records), and media accounts (e.g., *Catalyst, Chicago Tribune, Chicago Sun Times, Chicago Defender, Education Week, National Press Club*) collected for the years 1994 through 2000.

Interviews were taped, transcribed, then analyzed using a variety of methods. Content analysis permitted identifying key themes for tabulation and cross-comparison. Modified network analysis permitted an examination of the influence relationships between informants, and of the information sources that guided their opinions. Answers to one series of questions were grouped to create typologies of belief about change in the CPS, thus clarifying the motives of the mayor and his management team as compared to those of other civic leaders.

THREE LAWS

Chicago is an especially interesting case of regime change because new governance arrangements came gradually, over 15 years. Layered changes in three successive laws helped to forestall a return to the status quo. The coalitions behind each law were different and new structures empowered different constituencies, cumulatively broadening support for change. From the start, the city's powerful business associations have been central actors, involved initially because of a fiscal crisis.

The School Finance Law of 1980

In November of 1979 Chicago's banking leaders refused to refinance about $85 million in school debt. Their decision sparked a fiscal crisis that had been smoldering for a decade, quickly overshadowing an equally long-standing struggle to desegregate the city's schools.

Legislators were persuaded to give an emergency loan to the school system if the entire Board of Education resigned (the superintendent and his budget manager had already resigned), a joint House and Senate investigating committee was impaneled, and a business-led School Finance Authority (SFA) was created to oversee district finances and approve all major budgetary decisions. The governor and the mayor were jointly responsible for selecting the five members of the SFA. Their first appointments set the pattern for the life of the organization: all were active or retired business executives sitting on the city's largest boards of directors (SFA 1993).

The SFA was empowered to oversee the annual budget of the board, monitor the board's receipts and disbursements, and require it to produce three-year financial plans with every budget after 1982. The SFA also oversaw a mandated downsizing of the central office and appointed an independent financial officer for the district. Although initially expected to fade away after six years of balanced budgets, business oversight through the SFA remained until 1995, constraining central-office decision-making throughout (Shipps 1997).

The School Reform Act of 1988

Eight years later, a new school law created an elected, 11-member school board for each school (dubbed the "local school council" or LSC), giving each one the power to hire and fire the school principal and set school goals and improvement plans. In addition, substantial state Chapter 1 antipoverty funds ($500,000 to $800,000) were redirected from the district office to each LSC.

The 1988 law added other layers of citizen governance to the system as well. It created an elected council for each of 11 reorganized subdistricts, a central School Board Nominating Commission (SBNC) designed to limit the mayor's discretion in selecting central board members, and strengthened the SFA by giving it oversight of district restructuring in addition to fiscal oversight.

Educators were blamed for the school system's problems and their discretion was curtailed. Principals lost their tenure and teachers were limited to only two seats on the new LSCs, ensuring that the six parents could dominate in all votes. The law created professional personnel advisory committees (PPACs) at each school made up of teachers who were expected to assist the principal; but unlike the other new governance structures, PPACs were given no statutory authority. Simultaneously, the superintendent's authority was constrained by fiscal and managerial oversight from the SFA, and by the added layers of governance between him and the schools (Shipps 1997).

The School Reform of 1995

The 1995 law gave Richard M. Daley more authority than any mayor since before the Progressive Era, effectively turning the system into a department of city government. He has unfettered power to select a small (five member, seven as of 1999) corporate-style school board, eliminating the SBNC put in place in 1988. It also gives him the authority to select the system's chief executive officer (CEO), who is no longer required to have educational training. The CEO, in turn, tops a corporate-style hierarchy made up of a chief financial officer, chief operating officer, chief purchasing officer, and a chief educational officer. The elimination of subdistrict councils and the suspension of the SFA underscore the centralization of authority in the hands of the mayor and his management team.

The new law nullified many financial and labor constraints in the Chicago school code that had made balancing the system's budget difficult in previous years. Twenty-five separate funding streams were consolidated into two state block grants, and seven separate tax levies were merged in the operating budget. Thirteen previously bargained workplace issues were removed from the code and the CTU was forbidden to strike for 18 months after the law's enactment. To encourage the mayor and the CEO to further restructure the system in line with popular notions of business efficiency, the law lifted all obstacles to outsourcing, privatization, and contracting for all types of school services.

The 1995 law also gave the CEO sweeping new authority over individual schools. It identified sanctions that the CEO could apply to whole schools, principals, teachers, and LSCs when he felt them in need of his "intervention," and underscored his discretion by providing no specific criteria (Shipps, Kahne, and Smylie 1999).

THE INFORMAL PRACTICE OF REFORM

Contrasts in the successive laws sketched above appear to lurch between extremes of centralization and decentralization. Different actors (e.g., business, parents, the mayor) were empowered in each. Yet informal rules of political behavior in Chicago and the implementation strategies policy-makers and constituents engaged in after each law reveal three underlying patterns. First is the legacy of uncommon governing arrangements to which these laws respond. Second are the changes in mayoral power that began before the 1979 fiscal crisis and continue to influence school politics today. Finally, powerful organizational actors in the civic arena—business associations, unions, and racial and community groups— weighed in to tilt the balance of reform implementation after each law was passed. In this mix of context and agency some groups have gained while others lost ground in school decision-making. The most problematic aspects of regime change have been the effects on the city's large and historically underserved African-American community.

Building on a Legacy

Chicago's schools have always been atypically governed. Chicago has a separate school law, originally written into the 1870 State Constitution as applying only to cities with over 100,000 in population. This means that when governance changes are enacted into law by state legislators, a majority of legislators do not bear the electoral consequences of their decisions, since the effects will only be felt in Chicago. Hence, downstate Republicans have been able to limit funding for the CPS for decades. At the same time, groups with legislative access and influence have privileged status in the politics of Chicago schools.

As important, CPS governance has been tied to the mayor's office for more than a century. Since 1872, the mayor has appointed the Chicago school board. Periodic changes in the Chicago school code fettered the mayor's discretion and freed it in turns, but the appointed school board has never been abrogated. Beginning in the 1940s, successive mayors voluntarily appointed advisory groups to nominate candidates for the school board, although none felt obliged to accept their advice (Herrick 1971) until the 1988 law mandated it. Chicagoans have come to expect the mayor's hand in school board selections and no attempt to limit the mayor's board-appointment authority has lasted.

The system's financial ties to city hall also began with formal statutes that became increasingly informal over the century. The 1872 school law gave the city treasurer control over all school funds, to be withdrawn only upon authorization by both the mayor and the city clerk, while city council approval was required for raising and collecting taxes (Herrick 1971). By the 1970s the mayor's formal authority was constrained to establishing the overall school budget level, while the city council rubber-stamped final agreement (Cronin 1973). Despite the district's increasing legal autonomy, however, mayors for much of the century have used the schools for patronage and as a source of contingency funding. These informal and unorthodox arrangements were occasionally publicized (Counts 1928; Joint House and Senate Chicago Board of Education Investigation Committee 1981), but concerned citizens have had little formal recourse. Downstate legislators have been unsympathetic to increasing Chicago's state aid, and there is no popular referendum authority in Illinois.

Financial Collapse Emboldens Business

During the recession years of 1978 and 1979 it became increasingly apparent to Chicago's business elite that Mayor Richard J. Daley's successor would not be able to finesse the city's finances in the way the "pharaoh" had (Cohen and Taylor 2000). Mayor Jane Byrne did not command his party loyalty and patronage, nor did she have his mastery of budgets. Both the city and the school system were on the verge of bankruptcy. The CPS had accumulated a total debt of over half-a-billion dollars, having spent that plus a $2.6 million surplus in the previous eight years (Joint House and Senate Chicago Board of Education Investigation Committee 1981, 12).

The joint legislative investigation committee that convened in 1980 to look into the financial collapse identified several reasons for the system's fiscal problems. These included unpaid property taxes, deflated leases on board real estate, and below-standard tax rates, but drew special attention to the costly union settlements Mayor Daley had negotiated in amounts that the board was unable to raise. About half of the rise in costs in the previous ten years had been for labor.

Unions were an important partner of Daley's governing coalition, actively supporting his Democratic machine. After he granted teachers collective-bargaining rights in 1966, Mayor Richard J. Daley (1955–76) had set the tone for labor accommodation by siding with the CTU in every contract dispute during his administration. He also had appointed a majority of machine-loyal school board members and convinced legislators in Springfield to make changes in state aid and loosen the legal constraints on school borrowing. He prevailed upon the city's corporate leaders— themselves recipients of deflated school leases, extended school-tax deadlines, and other favors from city hall—to ignore the unusual accounting and financial procedures used to keep the district's bond ratings high (Joint House and Senate Chicago Board of Education Investigation Committee 1981, 57–69). It was simply assumed that the next mayor would continue the pattern.

It turned out, however, that neither his immediate interim successor, Michael Bilandic (1976–79), nor the next elected mayor, Jane Byrne (1979– 83), had Daley's control over the Chicago Democratic party machine. This loss of patronage and loyal workers in the office of the mayor altered relationships with the mayor's governing partners: corporate business and unions. As power shifted from the office, those who occupied it increasingly sought out the powerful (Byrne 1992; Granger and Granger 1980).

After watching businessmen successfully negotiate a bailout for the schools that put them in charge of district finances, and faced with replacing the entire school board under the 1980 law, Mayor Byrne asked an elite business association to provide her with the slate from which she selected the new board, among the most racially balanced ever seen in the city. This business-vetted board then chose the city's first African-American superintendent, the Californian Ruth Love, passing over the Black community's choice of Manfred Byrd in the process.

In the summer of 1980, 82 loaned executives of the same elite business group conducted a comprehensive analysis of the school system that served as a management audit for Superintendent Love, and clarified what business leaders expected of a reformed and fiscally viable school system. Primary among its 253 recommendations was administrative decentralization—a goal that several successive management reports were to reiterate over the decade (Chicago United 1981). As business leaders worked with the dispirited Manfred Byrd—whom Ruth Love had put in charge of implementing the recommendations—they became frustrated with what they characterized as central-office resistance, reinforcing their view that the central office had a stranglehold on the system (Shipps 1997).

AFRICAN-AMERICAN REACTION. Jesse Jackson's PUSH, the Chicago Urban League, The Woodlawn Organization (TWO), and other Black organizations believed that African Americans should be making district decisions. A majority of students were Black, yet the board had actively resisted desegregation for more than a decade under White leadership. Business's focus on the fiscal stability of the system in 1979 meant that the school desegregation they had been fighting for became a secondary issue, trumped by what was cast as the very survival of the school system. Despite business's selection of African Americans for the top school posts, when Mayor Byrne turned to business rather than established Black community organizations for assistance many mistrusted her motives. SFA-mandated cuts had already hit the central office hard (Hess 1991)—in 1980 about 40 percent of the board's employees were African American. Fewer jobs not only meant a decrease in services for the district's mostly African-American students, it meant fewer middle-class jobs for their parents.

A few Black activists interpreted business interest in the schools as a plot to disenfranchise African Americans just as the schools were becoming theirs to control. Activist Lu Palmer explained: "I don't understand why White guys would want to fix the public schools when their own children go to Catholic schools or the suburbs. I can only think that they want to be able to say 'We tried' [in order] to pave the way for a voucher system" (quoted in Shipps 1995, 259). An African-American businessman clarified: "This Black community response to the school reform has in part to deal with the fact that it is about saving jobs that Blacks have only recently gotten in the last decade and a half" (quoted in Shipps 1995, 259). Tension and mistrust between the city's business elite and many Black activist organizations over job-advancement opportunities were to remain (Jarrett 1991).

Latino community activists had a different reaction. Concerned that the system's strained finances would adversely affect the relatively few schools in which Latino students were concentrated, they began to organize around issues like bilingual education and neighborhood schooling that had not been salient under the Black–White polarization of desegregation politics in the 1970s (Kyle and Kantowitz 1992).

White education activists also began to extol neighborhood schools and decentralized governance. As they studied the system's high dropout rate and the poor reading skills of those who *did* graduate, they became convinced that Chicago's schools needed greater community links and that bureaucrats were hiding serious performance deficits (Moore 1990; Hess 1991; O'Connell 1991).

Daley's death had emboldened the Chicago Teachers' Union (CTU) to make separate and independent demands on city government. The CTU withdrew its endorsements of machine candidates and threatened the school district with another round of strikes (Grimshaw 1979; Rakove 1982). After striking for two weeks in January 1980 to protest payless paydays and $60 million in cutbacks ordered by the SFA, the union was again on a two-week strike for pay increases in 1983, and yet again in 1984. By that time the city had a new mayor, and businessmen and activists were both looking for opportunities to push their reform agendas further.

Competing Reform Agendas

For different reasons, the unlikely coalition of White and Latino community activists and elite business leaders who wrote and lobbied for the 1988 law agreed that devolving many educational decisions to schools would improve the quality of the decisions made. The coalition was short-lived and each group poorly understood the others, but it was possible at all because they constructed compromise legislation after it became clear that none of their separate proposals could attract enough votes to pass. The law passed the state legislature with no Republican votes.

Business executives based their reform plans on their experience with the latest management wisdom about the importance of "front-line" leadership and the devolution of accountability and responsibility to the shop floor. Firsthand experience gained since 1979 gave business executives credibility when they complained that the school system's central administration was bloated and bureaucratized, and that school officials lacked management expertise and bargaining power with the CTU. Better, these executives reasoned, to empower school principals and cut back on the number of decisions that were made centrally. That would lower the stakes in contract negotiations and diminish the disruptive potential of strikes. It would also improve the return on their financial investment and encourage parents and school personnel to take more responsibility for student learning and behavior (Shipps 1995).

At the same time, results from their own research reports describing dismal school performance encouraged White and Latino community activists to begin organizing for a different form of decentralization: community control. In their definition of the problem, activist organizations adopted some of the executive's arguments about the dysfunction of large organizations, but also sought to avoid the reputation for corruption and fragmentation that decentralization had spawned in the 1960s by relying on parents and individual schools as the agents of change (Moore 1990; O'Connell 1991). Some found confirmation in the educational literature that identified strong principals and supportive parents as key elements of "effective" schools (Hess 1991). Others saw an opening for alternative instructional techniques and experimentation with the teacher–student relationship (Shipps, Sconzert, and Swyers 1999).

Widely disparate groups heard in this rhetoric an opening for their own desires. White ethnic parents fighting integration saw an opportunity to use decentralization to further the distinctiveness of their schools, reasoning that the ultimate aim ought to be vouchers for all children (Walberg et al. 1988). In addition to bilingual education, Latino activists saw opportunities to press for more Latino principals (Kyle and Kantowitz

1992). Other activists adopted the populist ethos of the city's new African-American mayor, seeking to improve schools by making them key institutions in the social and economic development of neighborhoods (Clavel and Wiewel 1991).

AFRICAN AMERICANS BEGIN A NEW COALITION. Mayor Harold Washington (1983–87) had rallied an astonishing 73 percent of Blacks to vote in the primary of 1983 by promising to break the long-standing patronage and downtown development that kept Black (and Latino) neighborhoods at economic disadvantage. He had argued that two-fifths of the city was shortchanged by city services and funding, and it was their turn to take back city hall to begin the redistribution. His administration built a governing coalition of liberals, African Americans, and Latinos around a vision of a city in which development meant neighborhood empowerment and grass-roots groups had access to city hall. He brought a sense of hope to many who had become accustomed to hearing their city disparaged as a patronage-bloated, decaying part of the "rust belt," riven with racial and ethnic disparities (Mirel 1993).

Chicago's corporate leaders were ill-prepared for the first African-American mayor of Chicago. Most had refused to donate to his campaign, backing instead the son of their deceased friend, Richard J. Daley, who fared poorly in the primary debates but picked up the endorsement of the local papers anyway and came in third to Washington and Byrne (Shipps 1995).

Despite its lack of support for his candidacy, Mayor Washington knew that business had resources he would need to implement his vision. He reached out first to request business assistance in managing the city's finances, encouraging the creation of a Financial Research and Advisory Committee (FRAC) of loaned executives to guide it. With this small partnership begun, he approached business again in 1986 to help him create a version of the Boston Compact in which business guaranteed jobs for high school graduates in exchange for high graduation standards. A year-long summit of business and district leaders was to hammer out this agreement, but the effort was stillborn, largely because executives felt that Harold Washington's choice for superintendent, Manfred Byrd—the man they had passed over in 1980—resisted their plans (Shipps 1998).

By the fall of 1987, when the CTU began a strike that was to be its longest ever, frustrated business leaders were prepared to agree with community activists that the school system needed dramatic change. After discharging his duty as a reluctant labor negotiator, Mayor Washington gave them the opportunity. He reconvened the summit, authorizing it to devise a comprehensive school-reform plan, and backed it up by requiring both the board and the CTU to sign an agreement to participate, while adding 50 community members to the summit roster. Several weeks later he died—but the summit continued.

School reform engaged much of the city's political activity that otherwise would have been spent mourning the passing of a once-in-a-century opportunity to reshape Chicago politics. Yet, African-American activists were not so easily distracted. They bristled at the renewed criticism of the CPS "bureaucracy" and the teachers' union that the reform summit rhetoric engendered, and many were preoccupied with salvaging city hall for their community. In 1980 business had set the precedent of including Black leaders on the Board of Education and appointing African-American superintendents. In addition, the first African-American president of the CTU was elected. Moreover, by 1987 Black teachers and administrators outnumbered White teachers and administrators. Without mayoral support, they reasoned, this could all be threatened (Mirel 1993).

Although many African Americans acknowledged that the schools were not serving children well, they would have preferred that a solution come from within their community. Most of the problems White and Latino activists and business executives decried in the summit had existed during the 1970s when Whites controlled the system, without demands for a new governance structure. "Why not give us a chance?" was their question. The African-American president of the summit's Parent Community Council reasoned: "This system was messed up by them for a long period of time" (Lenz 1988).

The summit served as a useful outlet for community frustration, but it broke down by the spring of 1988 as separate factions vetoed one another's proposals. After one compromise bill drafted by business association staff and activists was rejected, Illinois House Leader Michael Madigan agreed to push through a rewritten version in the last days of the 1988 session.

AN OLDER ORDER REVIVES. Richard M. Daley, business's choice, was elected to serve out Harold Washington's term in a 1989 special election, after African-American Eugene Sawyer (1987–89) served briefly as acting mayor. The coalition that elected him included the city's White ethnics, wealthier lakefront residents and Latinos, but not African Americans. His coat-tails also brought the city its first Latino officeholders (Green 1991), one of whom would become the president of the school board when the 1995 law was passed.

The timing of this special mayoral election was crucial, because the 1988 law had given whoever was mayor the authority to appoint a seven-member interim board that would remain seated until after the first LSC elections and the SBNC could become organized. The business community wanted Richard Daley to make the selections for this powerful body (personal interviews during 1991).

Mayor Richard M. Daley (1989–present) selected an interim board that represented the major participants in the negotiation of the law, led by a trio of powerful business and political men: the president of a business group formed to help implement the law, Leadership Quality Education (LQE); the president of the Chicago Urban League; and a former Democratic alderman. This board negotiated a three-year teachers' contract that promised 7 percent raises for each year and hired another California African American, Ted Kimbrough, to be Chicago's next superintendent. In making these decisions, political and business leaders assumed they were purchasing labor peace, getting the school budget under control, and hiring a manager who would help them downsize and "restructure" the central office.

There was a fundamental mismatch between the 1988 law that Daley was empowered to implement and the resources and interests of his governing coalition. He reconstructed his father's governing coalition of corporate business and unions, expanding it to include opportunities for the city's fast-growing Latino population to enter the civic arena. This governing coalition had common interests in downtown development and the resources to see it happen. Daley specifically focused it on attracting the middle class and corporations back to the city (Shipps, Kahne, and Smylie 1999). These differences between his governing coalition and Washington's made it easy to find fault in the 1988 law.

Both business and the mayor questioned the new SBNC and the multiple and overlapping new governance structures. For many kinds of decisions, no one was sure where final authority lay. As one business leader put it: "This (school) board is . . . accountable to no one because it's accountable to everyone . . . there's no person or . . . group of people that this board has to answer to, not the mayor, not the city council, because it is a bottom-up board" (personal interview during 1991). Richard Daley sometimes sent back whole slates of candidates, refusing to appoint any of them. He and business agreed that civic elites frequently declined to serve on the board because the application process was too intrusive.

Even with increased powers, the SFA continued to be frustrated. Year after year it had refused to accept the system's budget and threatened to keep the schools closed until it was altered. At the same time, it rejected central-office restructuring plans, mandating its own plan that relied on outsourcing and downsizing. Neither threats nor mandates were successful. The chairman of the SFA analyzed the situation in grim management terms: "Across the board we had a central office that was failing, and we had fiscal crisis after fiscal crisis, and no sense of movement in [the] schools that weren't working" (personal interview during 1997). Daley was also troubled that principals answered to LSCs rather than to the central office.

Having been left out of decision-making by the 1988 law, the teachers' union also resisted the reform. One CTU leader reflected on the 1988 reform:

> It was a terrible experience and political trade-off which didn't include us.
> . . . The teachers were underrepresented. I think the first several years
> were about politics and governance; who's in charge of the council, who's
> in charge of the building, who's in charge of everything and not much got
> down to the teachers, outside of pressure. (personal interview during 1997)

As important, in early surveys, a majority of teachers reported no effect on their classroom practices (Easton et al. 1991).

Moreover, academic progress was difficult to document and uneven where it occurred. Only about one-third of the elementary principals and teachers reported that their schools had the procedural traits associated with the "effective schools" literature that White activists had relied on. Poor, predominantly African-American elementary schools fared worst on the process measures (Bryk et al. 1993). High schools across the city appeared unchanged, perhaps because their departmental structure and larger size made LSC governance less able to penetrate to the classroom (Sebring et al. 1995).

In the face of such continuing criticism, activists sought out the small opportunities of reform. Although interest in LSC elections had rapidly waned at the first elections (Shipps 1997), biennial elections gave community groups the most fruitful organizing opportunity they had seen in decades. The antipoverty money devolved to schools by the 1988 law leveraged a cottage industry of educational-improvement and community-organizing services that were greatly supplemented by foundation and business donations. By the 1990s more than a hundred nonprofit organizations were working with the schools (McKersie 1996). One small group of White activists committed to experimentation and LSC governance sought Annenberg Foundation support to keep their vision alive, and, in 1995, they attracted $50 million for five years. Ironically, the additional resources and national recognition came just as a new governance regime was taking over the school system (Shipps, Sconzert, and Swyers 1999).

Mayor Richard M. Daley Gets Control

When he ran for re-election in 1995 Richard Daley campaigned for the first time on school issues, fully aware that legislation was being drafted by a newly Republican legislature that would give him ultimate responsibility for the city's schools. Yet, the only common elements between his campaign platform and the new school law being drafted were the elimination of the SBNC and a concern for principal accountability. An aide to the mayor provided the reason:

> The politics of how this played out could not have been scripted better. It is one of the reasons why [New York] Mayor Giuliani can't get what Daley has . . . Albany doesn't want to give it to him. . . . [Daley] was very willing but had to play a little coy because of the Republican politics. The Republicans needed to have the "we're being tough on Chicago" stance, and the mayor needed to give them some of that.

A public-television journalist offered another explanation: "I think it is fair to say that the Republicans were much more inclined to give [the school system] to Daley than they would have been Harold Washington, because

I firmly believe that Richard M. Daley is a great Republican mayor" (personal interviews during 1997).

Rather than Daley, the primary impetus for the 1995 law came from Chicago's business community—this time joined by business-association leaders from state-wide, more conservative organizations. The key term used by all involved in drafting the 1995 law was "accountability," by which business leaders meant that "the mayor is accountable and he knows it. . . . We wanted [his] ownership here; we wanted somebody to take responsibility" (personal interview during 1997). When the 1994 election brought in a new Republican Speaker of the House and changed the chair of the House Education Committee, they saw an unprecedented window of opportunity. Their access to Republican lawmakers meant that executives would not have to rely on a compromise plan with any group represented by Democrats.

Consistently outvoted by Democrats when out of power, Republicans were determined to stop the financial hemorrhaging of the Chicago schools and curb the CTU in one blow. Predictably, the Illinois Manufacturers Association (IMA) took a strong anti-union stand and was backed by most of the other state-wide business associations. Local Chicago business associations, having spent a decade and a half trying to balance the school budget, sought an increase in funding in addition to management changes; but Republicans and the state-wide groups would have none of it (Civic Committee of the Commercial Club of Chicago 1995). No new funds were provided.

Most Chicago activists were not invited to the bill-drafting sessions, and some were unaware of them. The CTU was frozen out of the discussions. The lobbyist from the CTU attending some bill-drafting sessions told his colleagues: "I would go to the meeting on Tuesday morning and give our positions and would argue for our point of view and they would go out Tuesday afternoon or Wednesday and pass the exact opposite. No one had the slightest interest" (personal interview during 1997).

Those who wrote the 1995 law did not seek loyalty among the members of the CTU and the other 18 unions in the district, but Mayor Daley did. He knew that unionized civil-service workers could be more loyal than patronage employees, because they have both job security and regular raises. What Republican lawmakers and their business allies had constructed to punish unions for strikes and high salary demands, Daley used as a bargaining chip. He called the union heads into his office before the law was voted on to ask them not to fight it, because passage was virtually assured without Democratic votes. If they showed restraint, he promised to bargain back most of the offending restrictions after he was in control. He kept his promise. As one CTU leader put it: "Every right they took away, Daley gave them back in bargaining, every one of them" (personal interview during 1997).

Following the pattern of the interim board, Daley offered a four-year contract with 3 percent yearly raises. One year before this contract was to end in 1999 (and several months before Mayor Daley came up for a third term), a second four-year contract was ratified, again with 2–3 percent yearly raises. Union President Thomas Reese claimed that the second contract was "the most positive experience I have ever had" in 16 years of negotiating (Lawrence 1998).

Union officials also prefer to work with a management team that has, as one union lobbyist put it, "one purpose in mind: what can we do to make sure that we are going to continue labor peace in this city for the next few years?" He further explained:

> You go back to Harold Washington who tried to take a hands-off position even though he set up that [summit]. His basic position was to not involve himself. We did not find that tenable. It was too important, both to the city and to what we thought was the best for the student population and ourselves to be taking that kind of an attitude. (personal interview during 1997)

Although the CTU retained enough clout to defeat Republican and IMA plans, unorganized administrators had much less influence. After more than a decade of downsizing, the 1995 law further reduced the need for professional educators in the central office by simply replacing many of them with financial and business managers. With the unfettered ability to select the board of trustees and to appoint and determine the compensation for a CEO and his management team, Daley chose trusted city hall employees and business people for these posts. Gery Chico, his former chief of staff, was appointed president of the board of trustees, and Paul Vallas, his former budget director, became his CEO. Following these selections, about two dozen senior members of the school staff were to come from city hall and as many as 75 staff in less senior positions. As one senior manager proudly put it: "We came in two and three deep in each department" (personal interviews during 1997).

The titles (CEO, CFO, and so on), qualifications, and orientations of the management team underscore the corporate model that was being followed. The mayor's chief of staff explained why: "The mayor is a firm believer in strong management practices. . . . The expectation that an educator, for all their successes as educators, could suddenly step in and run a $3 billion operation isn't realistic." An executive was more direct: "The mayor is absolutely convinced that educators can't manage" (personal interviews during 1997).

To underscore this, new principals began to be screened and trained by privately managed corporate and MBA programs in 1998, even as CEO Vallas redefined their role as his managers in the schools. When schools are identified by the CEO as failing, principals are the first to be replaced, and management and financial assistance is the first to be offered. Principals continue to have some political accountability to LSC members, but that has been overshadowed by the new CEO's emphasis on strong and immediate sanctions for those schools that do not meet performance standards that he alone sets.

DALEY'S NEW AGENDA. When he took control of the system, Mayor Daley made it clear that the schools were to become part of his plans for Chicago's economic development. Success would be defined as the ability of the school system to attract middle-class families from the suburbs and maintain the confidence of corporate executives who might otherwise relocate (Kass 1995). A CTU leader put the mayor's thinking this way: "He said 'We want the middle class moving back into this city and they're not going to do it if the neighborhood schools aren't decent'" (personal interviews during 1997).

Incentives for middle-class families and options for them to have the full-service schooling they demand for their children have traditionally been scarce in Chicago's schools. A wide array of new educational options targeted to middle-class families with relatively high-achieving children has been created. In a speech given to the Chicago Retailers Association, CEO Vallas noted that many such initiatives—neighborhood enrollment set-asides for special schools in gentrifying areas and International Baccalaureate tracks and advanced-placement courses in high schools—could draw back a middle class whose eighth graders left the system at the rate of 49 percent in 1996 (Weissman 1997).

Key to his effort to attract the middle class is an ambitious capital renovation and rebuilding plan anticipated to cost more than $3 billion. Twenty-eight new elementary schools have been approved or built. As many as seven new college-prep or selective-enrollment magnet high schools are planned, the three most expensive of which (one cost $45,000 per student) are targeted for gentrifying areas in the north side. In some cases, these new college-prep schools are replacing existing vocational programs that serve poor and minority students. Aldermen agree that the process by which schools get fixed is political: "Almost all the schools I have are done already. If the (remaining) school councils and the principals were unhappy, they'd be over to see me" (Weissman 1998, 5). Then too, President Clinton claimed to be a "shameless advocate" of the CPS and open to appeals for federal assistance (Chicago Public Schools 2000a).

Just as important to the strategy of attracting the middle class are programs that promise to drain troublesome or slow-learning students from potentially middle-class schools and classrooms. "Transition centers" or "alternative" high schools for failing eighth graders, schools for students with severe discipline programs, and programs for dropouts all serve to ease the fears of middle-class parents worried that poor and undisciplined students might depress a school's reputation or hinder their child's progress (Shipps, Kahne, and Smylie 1999).

REGIME BENEFITS TO COALITION PARTNERS. Mayor Daley knew that the *sine qua non* for business was a balanced school budget. Benefiting greatly from the fiscal flexibility in the 1995 law, in its first two months his management team developed a balanced-budget plan that eliminated the immediate $105 million shortfall, and erased a projected four-year shortfall of $1.4 billion. Despite more than a decade of downsizing, another 200 central-office layoffs symbolically cut costs but were compensated for by higher salaries for their noneducational replacements. Daley reaped the rewards of these decisive gestures and became instantly identified with good management even among skeptics who doubted the numbers (Anderson 1998).

Big contracts to corporate businesses, institutions of higher education, and favored community groups encouraged in the 1995 law have also solidified financial and political ties between the district and other sectors of the city's economy. Although CEO Vallas no longer contends that contracting and outsourcing created fiscal savings, he argued that it is more efficient (presumably by externalizing transactions costs), and builds important support for the system (personal interviews during 1997; see also Wong et al. 2000).

Daley's political fortunes are more tightly linked to the public image of the school system that any of his predecessors, giving him an incentive to conduct a relentless "good news" media campaign that has been bolstered by the care that the mayor and the CEO take to speak with one voice. Reporters who routinely complained that previous superintendents did not return their phone calls are pleased. One even reported that there was no longer any need to research stories, since CEO Vallas called personally to provide one each week. A member of the senior management team spoke about the results:

> We have received little negative publicity over the past two years, which has changed the perspective and perception of the job that the Chicago public schools are doing in the eyes of the public. Because most people believe what they read, whether it's true or not. (personal interviews during 1997; see also Wong and Jain 1999)

REGIME EFFECTS. The new regime has many strengths: it has succeeded in improving the public image of the schools, achieved a balanced budget and labor peace, and begun a building program. However, the existing poor and minority students have suffered, and the long-term improvement in teaching and learning in most schools remains questionable. As one business-association leader dryly remarked about the mayor that he helped to put in power: "I wouldn't classify him right up there with John Dewey" (personal interviews during 1997).

Mayor Daley and CEO Vallas settled on standardized tests (the Iowa Test of Basic Skills [ITBS]) as their measure for low-achieving student progress. The 1995 law had not mentioned student consequences, but

Mayor Daley promoted high-stakes testing as the elimination of "social promotion" in Chicago's schools (Rossi and Speilman 1997). He has received widespread acclaim for acting decisively to retain at least 10,000 elementary students (14 percent) each year who did not achieve the target test scores set by Vallas (Moore 2000). As Daley himself put it: "Ending social promotions is one of the most important steps the Chicago public schools has taken" (Hardy 1998). Despite recent research that finds one-quarter to one-third of Chicago's students who fail the tests are inexplicably, and perhaps capriciously, "socially promoted" anyway, the program is widely promoted as a success because average test scores have risen each year (Roderick et al. 1999).

More troubling are findings that show that retained students do no better, and sometimes worse, than those with the same failing scores who were socially promoted. Failing African-American students are four-and-a-half times more likely than failing Whites to be retained (Latino bilingual students were exempted from the promotion policy until recently), and the vast majority of retained students come from low-income elementary schools. Those who fear a hidden dropout rate also point to the very low passing rates of eighth graders retained once, and a higher leave-rate among them (Moore 2000; Roderick et al. 1999). Such findings had limited impact on policy during Vallas's tenure (1995–01)—merely broadening the criteria that might be taken into account (e.g., attendance) when retention decisions are made.

Under the new regime, ITBS tests were also used to determine which schools are in need of the probation, remediation, and other school sanctions authorized by the 1995 law and amendments. This, too, had the mayor's blessing: "Probation is the most important step we have taken so far" (Daley 1997). Schools are put on probation based on the percentage of students who meet national test-score averages in reading and math. Initially, the threshold was set at 15 percent, but has been raised to 20 percent. This method of ranking schools netted 109 in 1996–97 and stands at 70 schools in 1999–00. Each year one or two dozen are eliminated from the list while others are added either because they improved or because they moved on to a more serious sanction (Chicago Public Schools 2000b, c; *Catalyst* 2000a).

Probation was the second step in an increasingly onerous takeover process that primarily triggered changes in the way the schools were governed. For instance, in probationary schools the CEO can dismiss principals and LSCs at will, while teachers can be dismissed under more serious levels of sanction. Even the curriculum can be prescribed. In 1998 CEO Vallas piloted standardized lesson plans for all grades in four academic subjects—9,360 plans in total—mandated for some sanctioned schools, optional for all (Duffrin 1998). The criteria ("significant progress") for getting off any sanction list, unlike those for being put on, are broadly defined and finally up to the discretion of the CEO and the mayor (*Catalyst* 2000b).

As in collective bargaining, the CTU has had some success in altering the school sanctions that affect teachers. In June 1997 seven of the initial 38 probationary high schools were identified for reconstitution based on their test scores. Of the approximately 700 faculty in these schools, 175 were told to seek another position or expect to leave the system (Martinez 1997). Two years later, only 40 were actually dismissed, but even this small number triggered a lawsuit by the CTU. It lost the suit but was able to get Daley to agree to an alternative to reconstitution, dubbed "re-engineering," in which teachers can opt for peer (rather than central-office) evaluation and are given more time to find another position in the system (*Catalyst* 2000a).

White and Latino community activists who feel betrayed by the turn of events in 1995 are skeptical about the mayor's plans for the schools. But the numbers alone suggest that African-American students and their community leaders are bearing most of the pain in this new school regime. Nearly every study of the system has shown that African-American children and especially those in "predominately" (over 85 percent) African-American and/or high-poverty schools (more than 90 percent low-income students) fare the worst. By their own report, LSCs in these schools are the most likely to be troubled with corruption, internal dissension, and unable to perform their duties (Ryan et al. 1997). Children in African-American or mixed minority (greater than 85 percent) schools as well as high-poverty schools receive by far the slowest instructional pacing, thus increasing the chances that these children will be retained because they were not given the opportunity to learn the material on which they are being tested (Smith, Smith, and Bryk 1998). Schools on probation fall disproportionately in the poorest (and therefore the most likely to be African-American) neighborhoods in Chicago (*Catalyst* 1998). Magnet and college-prep schools are least likely to be fully funded in predominately Black neighborhoods (Weissman 1998). These and many other differential effects raise troubling questions for this new school regime that have not yet been adequately addressed.

IMPLICATIONS OF REGIME THEORY APPLIED TO CHICAGO SCHOOLS

The new regime that has altered both the formal and informal patterns of governing the Chicago public schools is a direct reflection of Mayor Richard M. Daley's governing coalition. It is also a result of historical and contextual factors not easily duplicated elsewhere. The new regime is different from any before it. School governance under Richard J. Daley reflected his governing coalition that was heavily dependent on the Democratic machine and the appearance of disinterest in school affairs. He sought downtown development with the assistance of his business and union governing partners (Peterson 1981). Richard M. Daley also has downtown-development goals, but he is more dependent on the private-sector resources of his governing partners—also business and unions—because he does not have the political resources of his father's machine. In between the two Daley's, Harold Washington began to build a very different governing coalition, one which drew together the organized African-American community, corporate business, and a host of neighborhood groups. In the best of circumstances it was a difficult governing strategy. Without a mayor committed to coordinating the unequal resources of such governing partners and sustaining that vision, it was not viable. So how have these two mayors made a difference in the way the schools are governed?

How Mayors Make a Difference

When the mayor is in control of the schools, he or she draws upon a governing coalition to frame educational problems and determine which resources are needed to carry them out. How that coalition is formed determines in large part whose interests will be met. The clear contrast between Harold Washington's effort to create an inclusive, neighborhood-based process of school governance in 1987 and the current mayoral regime makes Chicago an especially enlightening case. Washington deliberately constructed a process (the reform summit) that put both poorly resourced community groups and well-resourced business groups around the same governing table, insisting that they come up with a consensus reform plan that would improve all the city's schools. This reflected his overall strategy for city governance: expanding opportunities for the lower classes. The school law that resulted also reflects his governing coalition. It built in governance roles for parents (LSCs and SBNC members), community organizations (as advisors to schools and as subdistrict council members), as well as for Latinos and African-American educators (as principals and central-office administrators). These structures helped to balance the role business held as "overseer" of the system, but relied on an unbalanced coalition for implementation.

When Mayor Daley inherited this system, his governing coalition was quite different, relying, like his father's, on business and the unions and aiming at downtown development. The law created by Washington's governing coalition was reinterpreted through Daley's coalition as fragmented, inefficient and potentially corrupt. Under Daley's watch, LSCs were described as ill-qualified for making large budgetary decisions, the overlapping authorities of the SFA, school board, and LSCs were seen as inefficient rather than as appropriate checks and balances, and the SBNC was regarded as hamstringing the mayor's ability to find good leaders for the system. These claims were all heavily influenced by a corporate model of decision-making, as was the 1995 law. Schools were re-envisioned as the engines of downtown economic development, to be governed by economic expertise rather than as the democratically governed, neighborhood-development institutions that undergirded Washington's conception.

Even so, Washington's coalition strategy left a political residue. When he put together business executives and community leaders, they learned to appreciate each other's positions, and, as important, parent and community voices were legitimized. Consequently, executives did not argue that LSCs should be disbanded in 1995, despite their reputed inefficiency and "bad" decisions. Despite flagging interest, LSC elections are still held. The central office has been given formal responsibilities that overlap with those of LSCs (e.g., firing the principal), creating jurisdictional problems, and informally their authority has been circumscribed, but this is quite different than the fate of the SBNC and the subdistrict councils.

If these are the lessons for Chicago from applying regime analysis, what are the implications for other cities?

History and Context Matter

Legal statutes that create new governing arrangements for schools are important enabling devices, but the informal ways that local political history and traditions of decision-making affect the implementation greatly determine their effects. The mayoralty in Chicago has a tradition of strong unilateral, often secretive decision-making and a long history of involvement in school policy. This tradition meant that Chicagoans in 1995 did not find it difficult to accept the withdrawal of even a minor check on the mayor's authority to select a school board. Although some community activists protested loudly, their concerns were ignored. It is likely that a city with the more common tradition of an elected school board could not sustain mayoral control in this way.

The informal history of Chicago's city hall governance arrangements has affected school policies in other ways. Rich Daley's relationship with the CTU has been heavily influenced by Dick Daley's efforts on its behalf two decades earlier. For instance, the teachers' union, which has long been a part of the mayor's governing coalition in the city, has been able to use its relationship with city hall to dampen the intended effects of the 1995 law. Republicans and downstate business interests had wanted to eliminate the union's power in school decisions and to break its bond with individual teachers by making them vulnerable to sanctions that the CTU could not mediate. The CTU was able to protect its members in spite of language in the law, because its special relationship with Mayor Daley enabled it to bargain back what the Republicans took away. Union bargaining with the mayor also forestalled even the relatively minor impact on its members from the test-based accountability standard. Cities where the teachers' union has no tradition of bargaining with city hall, and is not part of the mayor's governing coalition, must make quite different accommodations for a union role in governance.

Resources Matter More than Votes

Many education analysts assume that because parents and teachers have the most to lose from poor schooling, and count for many votes, their voices will be the loudest heard when decisions are made. Nevertheless, Chicago clarifies—as regime theory predicts—that those with the most resources to bring to city hall have the most influence on the decisions made. This is because the governing coalition a mayor needs to enact his or her policies rests on effectively mobilizing private-sector resources as much as it does on public-sector discipline and efficiency, and because a governing coalition need not be the same as an electoral coalition (Stone 1993).

When decisions about the local public schools leave the hands of a narrowly defined group of educational experts and come under mayoral control, those with resources to bring to the broader arena of city policy are privileged. Moving decision-making from educators to the wider arena of city-wide politics changes the rules of decision-making in such a way that those groups already privileged in other urban policy arenas (e.g., development, job growth, taxes) will also have more influence over school policy. The educators with the fewest resources to bear on city-wide politics are administrators, whose authority rests on professionalism.

The same argument holds true for most parents. The Chicago regime has a class bias in favor of middle-class parents. Despite their obvious role in electing the mayor, the working-class and poor majority do not have influence over school policies, because they remain unorganized and are easily pitted against each other when their children compete for test-score rankings. Moreover, poor and working-class parents have only voluntary resources to bring to the schools, and that makes them less valuable to the mayor's governing coalition. Lacking a city-wide impact, they have no real influence on the current school-governing regime.

On the other hand, business associations in Chicago (as in many cities) are highly organized. They have a great deal of management expertise and the wealth of large corporations behind their efforts and special access to the mayor by virtue of long-standing informal arrangements. This gives them a resource edge over other groups whose interests are more directly tied to the public schools. By using their common resources they will be more likely to prevail in negotiations over system-wide goals, and improvement strategies will be defined in ways that their expertise and resources can help resolve (Stone 1993).

In Chicago the business's resource "edge" was enhanced when banking executives stepped in to "fix" the schools in 1979. Their access to credit, loaned and retired executives with expertise in finance and management, and Mayor Byrne's dependence on them to maintain the city's bond ratings gave them the opportunity to redefine the district's problems—from racial integration to fiscal collapse (Moore 1988). The redefinition was accepted partly because fiscal collapse was a problem that business seemed prepared to solve—its readily available means helped to define the goals (Stone 1993, 12).

Less well-resourced civic organizations and social groups—Latino organizations, voucher advocates, school-reform groups, and the like— seek "small opportunities" to benefit from the new arrangements that emerge (Stone 1993, 11). But they can seldom have the level of influence over governance arrangements that better-resourced groups do, unless the mayor designs a process that actively requires their participation in decision-making. Although Daley's electoral coalition included Latinos, the relatively few resources they brought to the governing coalition meant that they had to be satisfied with city appointments and increased opportunities for employment in the schools, particularly as principals. African Americans were not part of either his electoral coalition or his governing coalition and were attempting to sustain a coalition around a very different agenda: desegregation and resource redistribution. They brought few resources to Daley's downtown-development agenda, since they had the city's largest proportion of poor citizens. Some found small opportunities for employment as well, but as a whole African Americans in Chicago have lost the agenda-setting position they briefly held and the formal authority they once had within the school hierarchy.

Implications

One consequence of regime theory applied to urban school governance is to reverse the relationship between state laws and city schools. Traditionally, educators have assumed that state legislators enact laws reflecting their ideas of what it takes to create good schools, and city districts implement those laws more or less faithfully. But the Chicago case shows how the laws that state legislatures create can be the product of a city's governing regime, reflecting the values and resources of local governing partners that the mayor has put together.

When mayors take control of schools, it is not so much their individual decisions about budgets or leadership that create a regime change but the informal arrangements that already characterize their governing coalitions. A mayor seeking only to maintain city services will need only a weak governing coalition and may generate little interference in professional school decision-making. No school regime change is likely to occur. On the other hand, a strong mayor who seeks economic development or social restructuring and has a governing coalition with the resources to deliver on those goals can change the regime by which schools are governed, altering not only which decisions are made but who makes them and how. Opportunities like this have been rare in urban public education—the last was nearly a century ago. If mayors take advantage of the political opening for increasing their authority that the current era provides, the benefits and costs—especially who is to be privileged and who forgotten—may be as long-lived and consequential as they were a hundred years ago.

ACKNOWLEDGMENT

The Spencer Foundation and the Annenberg Foundation funded portions of earlier research and the Carnegie Corporation of New York funded this synthesis.

◙   ◙   ◙

CHAPTER SEVEN

Implementation of an Accountability Agenda in High Schools

integrated governance in the Chicago public schools

KENNETH K. WONG, DOROTHEA ANAGNOSTOPOULOS,
STACEY RUTLEDGE, LAURENCE LYNN, ROBERT DREEBEN

IN 1995 THE ILLINOIS STATE LEGISLATURE ENACTED the Chicago School Reform Amendatory Act, granting the Chicago public schools the policy capacity to launch an ambitious educational-accountability agenda aimed at system-wide improvement in teaching and learning. The Act reversed the trend towards the decentralization of decision-making concerning school operations and integrated authority at the system-wide level. In our 1997 and 1998 reports on Chicago school reform, we identified this new governance framework as "integrated governance."[1] The major institutional features of integrated governance include the reduction of competing authorities, linkages among the school board, district administration, and city hall created through mayoral appointments, and system-wide authority to hold organizational actors accountable located in the office of the chief executive officer (CEO).

Under integrated governance, the School Reform Board of Trustees took several actions in attempts to strengthen the fiscal and political support for the school system. Using expanded powers over financial operations provided by the 1995 Act, the central administration improved capital funding, balanced the budget, and secured labor stability through a four-year contract with the teachers' union. The second four-year contract, approved in November 1998, took effect in the fall of 1999. The school board launched the first capital-improvement plan in decades to address the deterioration of the schools' physical plant. The administration also improved management efficiency by waging a very public battle against waste and corruption, down-sizing the central office, and contracting out several operations. These actions garnered the support of the business community and improved public confidence in the school system.[2] Building on these accomplishments, the district-level leadership moved to focus on the difficult task of improving the system's educational performance. Beginning in 1996, the CEO and School Reform Board of Trustees launched an educational-accountability agenda that focused on raising standards and improving performance outcomes.

This chapter first examines how the educational-accountability agenda formulated by the district under integrated governance has been implemented at the district, school, and classroom levels; and second, assesses its consequences for teaching. Though the agenda entails numerous initiatives aimed at different components of the system, we examine the implementation of the educational agenda at the high school level. In an introduction to the first draft of the district's *High School Redesign Plan*, CEO Paul Vallas noted the importance of improving high schools to the system as a whole:

> Whether we like it or not, the quality of our high schools will define the quality of our school system. While improvements at some elementary schools are remarkable, these improvements have not impacted our high schools or our finished product—high school graduates. Success in reforming education in Chicago hinges on our ability to solve the problems in our high schools.[3]

POLICY CONTEXT OF THE DISTRICT'S HIGH SCHOOL REDESIGN PROGRAM

The challenge of improving high school performance is clearly enormous. Table 7.1 indicates the persistence of low performance in high schools. The average percentage of students scoring at national norms in

TABLE 7.1

PERCENT OF STUDENTS AT NATIONAL NORMS IN DISTRICT HIGH SCHOOLS

Subject	1991	1992	1993	1994	1995	1996	1997	1998
Reading	23.35	20.24	21.00	17.65	19.49	16.92	20.92	23.10
Math	17.43	18.00	20.84	16.50	21.00	17.97	25.83	25.84

Source: Test of Achievement and Proficiency Reading and Math, 1991–1998. Chicago Public Schools, Department of Research, Assessment and Quality Review.

reading in the district's high schools during the past eight years ranges only from 17 to 24 percent. From 1991 to 1998, at the highest point, on average less than 30 percent of students in the district's high schools scored at the national norm on reading. The same holds true for math. In 1996, 38 out of the district's 62 nonspecialty high schools, or 58 percent, were placed on probation. In contrast, 71 of the 483 elementary schools, or 15 percent, were placed on probation. The district has reconstituted only high schools.

The district's educational agenda reflects a system-wide vision focused on improving high school performance. District policy is implemented, however, within a complex, multilayered organization. The central administration must rely upon principals, school administrators, teachers, and students to achieve the goals and objectives of its policies. These actors respond to district policies in ways that can support, limit, or undermine policy objectives.

Given this organizational reality, several questions arise concerning the implementation of the district's educational-accountability agenda. How do principals and teachers respond to district pressure for improved performance? How do these responses compare to school and teacher reactions to policies that rely more heavily on professional discretion? How do principals and teachers make use of district support? How do principals and teachers allocate their resources in response to the various types of district initiatives? And, most importantly, what effects do the responses of schools and teachers to district policies have on teachers' classroom practices?

RESEARCH DESIGN AND DATA COLLECTION

We address these questions by examining the implementation of district initiatives that are central to the administration's efforts to improve teaching and learning in the high schools. These initiatives are: probation and reconstitution; academic promotion; junior and senior academies; and student advisories. The district initiatives we examine entail different combinations of regulatory sanctions, district support, and school-level professional discretion. For analytical purposes, we identify how the central administration makes use of three types of leverage to raise school and student performance: *formal sanctions* against low performance applied to students and schools; *support* for low-performing students and schools; and *professional discretion* for school-level control over the design and implementation of improvement programs.

As table 7.2 suggests, the initiatives entail varying degrees of pressure, support, and professional discretion. Additionally, these can be targeted at more than one level of school organization. Probation/reconstitution is primarily a formal sanction, although it also involves support and some professional discretion. The district pressures schools to improve test

TABLE 7.2

DISTRICT-WIDE IMPROVEMENT STRATEGIES

	Strategies			
Types of policy leverage	Probation/ reconstitution	Academic promotion	Academies	Student advisories
Pressure	Threat of restaffing	Grade retention	Certificate of initial master, CASE	Required participation
Support	External partners, probation managers	Summer Bridge, developmental math and reading	Funds for common teacher-planning time, textbooks, and science labs	Teacher compensation, curriculum
Professional discretion	Principal selection of external partners	Promotion waivers; hiring teachers in Summer Bridge	Choice of organizational model	Choice of organizational model

scores through the threat of restaffing. The district also provides support to low-performing schools through external partners and probation managers, allowing principals some discretion in selecting external partners from a board-approved list. While probation/reconstitution targets low-performing schools, the district's academic-promotion policy is aimed at low-performing students. The district places pressure on students to improve test scores and course completion through the threat of grade retention. It also provides students who fail to meet these requirements with additional instructional time through the Summer Bridge Program and developmental math and reading courses.

In contrast to the mixture of sanctions and support that mark probation/reconstitution and academic promotion, the academies and student advisories allow for considerable discretion at the school level, along with formal sanctions applied to students. The district requires schools to have academies, yet schools determine how they structure them. The district also supports schools by providing funds for instructional resources and common teacher-planning time.

To examine the implementation of these initiatives and their consequences for teaching, we used several research strategies. Using semistructured questionnaires, we interviewed the chief executive officer, the chief education officer, the head of the accountability office, and other central-office staff responsible for developing and implementing programs in curriculum and instruction, professional development, and high school restructuring, as well as overseeing the implementation of probation and reconstitution. We also collected documentary materials from the board, including board policies, budget information, minutes of the Chicago School Reform Board of Trustees meetings, publications describing programs, and the district's new curriculum standards and frameworks.

To examine the effects of district policies on Chicago's high schools, we designed and administered a survey of principals in nonspecialty high schools. The goal of the survey was to identify how principals have responded to various district policies and the types of district support the principals have received. Forty-one of the district's 62 nonspecialty high school principals, or 66 percent, completed and returned the questionnaire. Principals were asked to identify their school's approximate enrollment and demographics. They provided information regarding teacher recruitment and retention; they also answered questions about the implementation of the Chicago public schools' high school restructuring efforts, student promotion and enrollment, and program development. If their schools were on probation or being reconstituted, principals were asked to identify the type of services the district provided them. They were also asked to rate the helpfulness of these services to their school-improvement efforts.

The survey provides a system-wide perspective that augments the case studies we have conducted in four Chicago high schools. The schools represent the range of district-initiated interventions. Of these schools, one is reconstituted, one has been on probation for two years, one was removed from probation after one year, and the fourth is under no district intervention. We began collecting data in two of the schools during the 1996–97 school year and continued during the 1997–98 school year, adding the other two schools that year. At each school, we interviewed the principals, administrators, and English and mathematics teachers.

In each of the schools we conducted classroom observations of ninth- and eleventh-grade regular English and math courses. The district's criteria for probation and reconstitution center on the percentage of ninth and eleventh graders who score at national norms on the Test of Achievement and Proficiency (TAP) math and reading tests. Ninth and eleventh grades represent the "high stakes" grades for schools. The district also targets ninth graders with its promotion policies, described below, and initiated high school restructuring efforts in the ninth grade. If district policies such as probation/reconstitution and the academies have an effect on schools and teachers, we should see them most clearly at these grades. Given the district's emphasis on math and reading scores, we observed math and English classes, again, because they should most clearly reflect school- and teacher-level responses to district policy. In total, we collected over 200 hours of classroom observations.

Table 7.3 reports the basic demographics of the case-study high schools and indicates their performance on the TAP. School A has never been on probation. It has been in our case study since July 1997. School B was on probation for one year, 1997–98. School B has been in our case

TABLE 7.3

CHARACTERISTICS OF CASE-STUDY HIGH SCHOOLS

School*	Status	Enrollment, 1997–98	% racial and ethnic minority, 1997–98	% LEP	% low-income	% of students at national norm on TAP, 1997–98: reading	math
A	Non-Prob.	≥2,000	100	0	80	35	40
B	Former Prob.	1,500–2,000	75	30	100	30	30
C	Prob.	≥2,000	90	30	80	10	30
D	Reconst.	1,000–1,500	100	0	90	5	10

To protect the anonymity of the case-study schools, percentages have been rounded to the nearest multiple of five.

study since June 1996. School C was on probation for both years of our study. Our research in school C began in January 1998. School D was on probation during the 1996–97 school year. In June 1997 it was reconstituted, and it remains in reconstitution to this date. School D has been a case-study school since June 1996.

FORMAL SANCTIONS AND SUPPORT

Since taking leadership of the district in 1995, the central administration has applied increasing pressure upon students and schools to improve students' academic performance through the creation of formal sanctions. The academic promotion policy requires students in the third, sixth, eighth, and ninth grades to score at district benchmarks on standardized tests or risk being retained a grade. Provisions outlined in the 1995 law give the Board of Trustees and the CEO the authority to identify low-performing schools and place them on probation or reconstitution. The district's probation policy also holds principals and teachers accountable for student achievement as measured by standardized test scores. Schools with less than 15 percent of their students scoring at national norms are placed on probation. Schools need to increase the percentage of their students scoring at national norms to 20 percent in order to be removed from probation. Continued low scores place schools under the threat of reconstitution, under which principals and teachers can be dismissed.

Probation and Reconstitution

In all of the case-study high schools we found that school-level responses to probation and reconstitution place increasing constraints on teachers' instructional decisions. All three schools that faced probation and/or reconstitution mandated that teachers implement several types of activities. Schools varied in the degree to which they coordinated and monitored these efforts. School D created several coordinator positions charged with developing and overseeing the implementation of school-mandated test-practice and test-skills-development activities. Teachers submitted students' work on these activities to the relevant coordinators. In school B, a Reading Task Force coordinated teachers' use of reading strategies through a monthly calendar that identified the day of the week teachers in each department were expected to use a specific strategy. Administrators and external partners (discussed further below) monitored teachers' use of the strategies in their classrooms. School C initiated school-wide test-skills-development activities on a more experimental basis. Although the principal resisted direct classroom monitoring of these activities, teachers were still expected to implement various types of activities such as silent sustained reading and test-preparation activities. Even in school A, which was never on probation, teachers were expected to teach test-taking skills in student advisory periods and within their classrooms as the test date approached.

In order to assess how teachers responded to these school-level mandates, we analyzed the amount of instructional time teachers devoted to test-preparation activities. We classified classroom activities into three categories: *test-taking, test-skills development,* and *other instruction. Test-taking* activities simulate test materials and conditions. Students work individually on materials formatted like the TAP and the IGAP (Illinois Goals Assessment Program). Teachers do not provide coaching and may or may not time students during these activities. *Test-skills development* includes two types of activities. The first involves teachers leading students through test-preparation materials. These materials are typically provided to teachers by subject-matter department chairs and/or school administrators. Teachers elicit answers from students and discuss why these answers are correct. The second type are activities specifically aimed at developing skills required on the test but with broader applications. These activities must be mandated at the school level to be classified as test-skills development. They are direct school responses to the district's emphasis on improving reading test scores, although they have broader applications and also seek to improve reading and math instruction across the school. *Other instruction* activities include those under teacher discretion that do not directly relate to test-taking preparation, but, rather, represent what many teachers in our study call the "real" curriculum. Although they most likely develop skills required on the TAP and IGAP, these activities are aimed more at meeting curriculum objectives than at raising students' test scores *per se.*

Our analysis of classroom observations in the case-study high schools indicates that teachers accommodated to the district's use of test scores as the criteria for probation and reconstitution. This was particularly true for English teachers. English teachers in the three case-study high schools that had been on probation or reconstitution allocated over one-fifth of their

TABLE 7.4

ENGLISH TEACHER ALLOCATION OF TIME 1997–98 (IN MINUTES)

School	Semester	Test practice	Test-skills development	Other	Total minutes observed
B	First	68	35	841	944
	percentage of total	7	4	89	100
	Second	252	313	353	918
	percentage of total	27	34	38	100
	Total	320	348	1,194	1,862
	percentage of total for year	17	19	64	100
D	First	0	580	209	789
	percentage of total	0	74	27	100
	Second	59	477	429	965
	percentage of total	6	49	45	100
	Total	59	1,057	638	1,754
	percentage of total for year	3	60	36	100
C	Second	19	180	687	886
	percentage of total	2	20	78	100
A	Second	0	0	880	880
	percentage of total	0	0	100	100
	Total minutes observed	398	1,585	3,399	5,382
	% of total minutes observed	7	29	63	100

instructional time to test-taking and test-skills-development activities. In the first year of our case studies, 1996–97, English teachers in school B spent 25 percent of observed instructional time on test-taking and test-skills development, while in school D they spent 36 percent of observed time on the same types of activities (see table 7.4). During 1997–98, English teachers in school B allocated 36 percent of their instructional time to test-taking and test-skills development. English teachers in school D devoted 63 percent of instructional time to test-related activities. In school C, English teachers spent 22 percent of observed time on test-related activities. Math teachers tended to allocate less time to test-practice and test-skills-development activities than did English teachers (see table 7.5).

Probation also affected teachers' allocative decisions in school A. Although school A was never on probation, in the four weeks preceding the administration of the TAP, both English and math teachers reported that they would begin test-practice and test-skills development. Since this occurred after our classroom observations, this is not reflected in our analyses. Teachers in school A did allocate instructional time to test-

TABLE 7.5

MATH TEACHER ALLOCATION OF TIME 1997–98 (IN MINUTES)

School	Semester	Test practice	Test-skills development	Other	Total minutes observed
B	First	0	33	639	672
	percentage of total	0	5	96	100
	Second	73	168	652	893
	percentage of total	8	18	73	100
	Total	73	201	1,291	1,565
	percentage of total for year	5	13	82	100
D	First	62	64	387	513
	percentage of total	12	12.5	75.5	100
	Second	215	0	801	1,016
	percentage of total	21	0	79	100
	Total	277	64	1,188	1,529
	percentage of total for year	18	4	78	100
C	Second	0	12	698	710
	percentage of total	0	2	98	100
A	Second	0	40	590	630
	percentage of total	0	6	94	100
	Total minutes observed	350	317	3,767	4,434
	% of total minutes observed	8	7	85	100

related activities in response to the probation policy, even though the school had never been placed on probation.

Our classroom observations suggest that teachers integrated test-skills-development activities into the curriculum. In schools B and D, English teachers increased the amount of time they allocated to test-skills development since the district instituted the probation/reconstitution policy. School B was removed from probation after a year. Yet English teachers in the school allocated more instructional time to test-taking and test-skills development *after* probation than while *on* probation. In addition, during 1997–98, English teachers in school B adopted textbooks with a reading focus and devoted 15 weeks to the Scholastic Reading Achievement (SRA) kits. In school B, then, the probation policy prompted English teachers to refocus the curriculum onto reading and test-taking skills.

Like English teachers in school B, English teachers in school D increased the amount of time they spent on test-skills-development activities over the two years of the probation policy. During the first year of reconstitution, English teachers devoted a full 60 percent of their observed instructional time to test-skills development. While English teachers in the other case-study high schools allocated the majority of classroom time to the standard curriculum, English teachers in school D, while under reconstitution, devoted the majority of class time to test-related activities. In effect, test-related activities displaced the standard curriculum in school D—the school under the most severe district pressure.

While our analysis of instructional time indicates that teachers respond to the probation policy's focus on test scores, our case studies also suggest that some conflict within schools has emerged as a result of the policy focus. This conflict manifests itself in several ways. First, given the probation's emphasis on reading scores, English teachers appeared to feel the most pressure to allocate time to include test-related activities. Interviews with English teachers in schools B, C, and D reflected their ambivalence about the policy's effect on the English curriculum. Teachers in all three schools referred to the test-taking and test-skills-development activities as "suspending the curriculum," or as interruptions to the "real curriculum." English teachers in school C expressed this ambivalence more directly. Although we have seen an increasing integration of a reading focus and test-skills development into the English curriculum in schools B and D, teachers in school C were much more likely to express frustration with the idea of teaching discrete reading skills. Most teachers maintained that the English curriculum should focus on literature and that reading should be taught through literature as opposed to workbooks and test-like selections.

In sum, schools have responded to probation/reconstitution by mandating that teachers implement various test-preparation and skills-development activities. These school-level mandates constrain teachers' use of instructional time. As district pressure on schools increase, school-level mandates place increasing constraints on teachers' instructional decisions. Teachers express ambivalence about allocating instructional time to test-related activities. In addition, some conflict has emerged among teachers along subject-matter lines as a result of the emphasis on reading scores.

District Support: External Partners and Probation Managers

The district provides several types of support to the schools on probation and reconstitution. The district required each school on probation to work with a probation manager and an external partner. The external partners and probation managers act as external consultants, providing the school with the resources it needs to meet the School Improvement Plan (SIPAAA). Probation managers are current or former high school principals whose role is to oversee the development and implementation of the school-improvement plan and to monitor the school-improvement process. The district pays for probation managers. External partners are teams of support personnel from national reform groups and local universities who are chosen by schools from a board-approved list. During the first year of probation, the district pays for the external partners. The schools are expected to pick up one-quarter of the cost during each subsequent year of probation. In sum, the external partners bear the most responsibility for driving the school-improvement process.

The survey of principals indicates that the external partners and probation managers provide various services to schools on probation. The majority of principals surveyed, 72 percent, report that they meet with their external partners from one to five times a week. In contrast, less than 30 percent of the principals surveyed indicate that they meet with their probation managers weekly. Sixty-one percent of the principals report that they meet with their probation managers once or twice a month. A large portion of the principals, 83 percent, use the external partners for professional development, while 72 percent use the partners for curriculum development and 56 percent use them for the purpose of monitoring teachers in the classroom. Half of the principals said that the external partners assisted in developing the SIPAAA.

Principal and teacher responses to external partners, as indicated by the survey of principals and our case studies, contrast sharply. The survey indicates that principals felt the external partners to be helpful. The principals also indicated that their effectiveness remained quite stable over the two years of probation. During the 1996–97 school year, 13 percent of the principals reported that the external partners were not helpful, while 67 percent said that they were helpful or very helpful. By the 1997–98 school year, 69 percent reported that the external partners were helpful or very helpful; only one principal expressed frustration with the external partners.

In contrast, teachers in our case-study high schools reported little contact with external partners and, in at least two cases, considerable conflict. The majority of teachers in schools B, C, and D who, because of probation and/or reconstitution, have had external partners at their schools for two years, reported that external partners have had no effect on their teaching. In school B, after two years (1997–98) with the same external partner, seven English and two math teachers said that the external partners provided them classroom assistance.

In schools C and D, teachers similarly reported that the external partners have had little effect on teaching; in addition, these teachers reported conflict with the external partners. During the second year of probation in school C, only one English teacher said that the external partners had positive effects on his teaching; no math teachers reported positive effects. Eight English teachers and six math teachers expressed considerable dissatisfaction with the external partners.

During the year of probation, teachers in school D reported "miscommunication" between the external partners and teachers. Some teachers refused to allow the partners into their classrooms, and many said that they were dissatisfied with the quality of the services the external partners provided. The principal expressed similar dissatisfaction and "fired" these partners at the end of the first year of probation. In interviews during the first year of reconstitution, 80 percent of the teachers reported that the new external partners had no effect on their instruction, and 87 percent said that they had had no effect on curriculum. No teacher indicated external-partner involvement in their classroom instruction, such as observations or evaluations.

In short, while results from the survey of principals indicate that the majority of external partners had considerable interaction with teachers and that principals rated them as helpful, teachers in our case study either had no contact with the external partners or found them unhelpful. Teachers' frustration with the external partners appears to revolve around two issues. First, teachers reported that they resent what they see as the external partners asserting authority over instructional practices. The fact that the majority of principals report using external partners to monitor classrooms suggests that teachers are responding to the evaluative role external partners have been given by principals. In schools B and D, this role led to conflict during the first year of probation. Teachers in school D refused to let external partners into their classrooms, while those in school B balked at the external partners' classroom checklist, saying that it was too evaluative and not supportive enough.

The second source of conflict arises from the contradictions between the district's stated objectives for the external partners and the goal of probation and reconstitution. For schools on probation and reconstitution, the central goal is raising test scores. Principals and teachers are held directly accountable for improvements in standardized test scores. In contrast, the district has charged the external partners with whole-school improvement. This long-term vision of school improvement may run counter to the immediate focus on raising test scores.

At the school level, this conflict manifests itself in what teachers see as a lack of focus on the part of external partners. When asked, teachers in school B could not identify the external partners' goals. In school C, the external partners focused their work around their own standards. The standards promoted by the external partners were in sharp contrast to the types of skills required of students by the TAP tests. The reading standard entailed three components: 1) students will read 25 books over the course of the school year; 2) students will "go deep" into at least one area of interest; and 3) students will read informative material and "produce written and oral work that summarizes information, relates new information to prior knowledge, and extends ideas and makes connections to related topics or information."[4] Fulfilling these standards could involve students employing skills required on the TAP test such as making generalizations and inferences and identifying cause-and-effect sequences and main ideas. However, the standards offered teachers few strategies and materials to improve students' reading scores on the TAP. Because teachers bore the

major responsibility of improving student achievement, the lack of corre-
spondence between external partners' goals and methods and the demands of the probation/reconstitution policy gave rise to teachers' dissatisfaction with the external partners.

In sum, there appears to be a mismatch between the long-term goals
the district established for the external partners and the immediate pressures of the probation policy. As the schools place more constraints on
teachers' instructional time (as indicated above), teachers feel these pressures keenly. When the external partners provide little support to address
the immediate concern of improving test scores, teachers find them unhelpful at best—and at worst resent their intrusion.

The Challenge of Enrollment Fluctuation

Probation and reconstitution have had mixed effects on teacher recruitment and student enrollment.[5] One unintended consequence of the
district's probation and reconstitution policy may be a reallocation of
teachers and students away from low-performing schools. Although enrollment declines often predate probation, the district policy may be reinforcing an existing trend. These fluctuations may create new challenges
for the district and probation/reconstituted schools as the latter struggle
to maintain resource stability.

Our survey of principals shows a reallocation in enrollment. We asked
principals to indicate if ninth-grade enrollment in their schools declined,
stayed the same, or increased during the 1995–96, 1996–97, and 1997–98
school years. Of the 17 principals of schools on probation during 1996–97
who responded to the question, 41 percent said that their enrollment declined during all three years. The same percentage said that enrollment
stayed the same during all three years. Only three of the 17, or 18 percent,
said that their enrollment increased. In contrast, only three, or 17 percent,
of principals of nonprobationary schools reported enrollment declines during the same time period. Fifty percent of these principals reported enrollment stability, and an additional 33 percent noted enrollment increases.

Our case-study schools fit this pattern: the greater the intervention due
to low performance, the greater the challenge of retaining students and
faculty. While school A—the nonprobation school—reported enrollment
and faculty stability, the three case-study schools on probation or reconstitution experienced enrollment and faculty fluctuations.

Since being taken off probation, school B has attracted both students
and teachers to the school. The school hired eight new English teachers for
the 1997–98 school year. Four had been student teachers at school B in the
spring of 1997. Three were drawn to the school because of its reputation
and had experience teaching in the district. The school's enrollment also increased from 1,712 students in September 1997 to 1,804 a year later. Administrators attributed this to the school's improved reputation.

School C's enrollment, in contrast, dropped after being placed on probation. In September 1997 the school had 2,094 students; a year later this had dropped to 1,781. Teachers and administrators attributed this decrease to elementary schools advising their students to enroll in other nonprobation high schools and to competition among high schools in the region for students. The school anticipated losing teaching positions due to the drop in enrollment.

School D, the reconstituted school, experienced a great deal of faculty and enrollment instability with reconstitution. Under the terms of reconstitution, the principal was given the authority to rehire the entire staff. When the school reopened in August 1997, 40 percent of the faculty had been replaced with many new to teaching. Ten percent of the retained teachers left school D before the 1998–99 school year to take positions in nonsanctioned schools. Roughly 30 percent of the faculty at the school were teaching outside of their certification.

Enrollment decline has worsened since reconstitution in school D. According to one school administrator, in October 1996 the high school had over 1,400 students. By September 1997 the school had dropped to 1,100 students. It opened the 1998–99 school year with 900 students. The principal attributed the 32 percent decrease in two years to the stigma of reconstitution.

The case-study schools adopted various strategies to cope with the competition for students and faculty to which probation may contribute. All of the schools in the study implemented programs intended to attract higher-performing students. School A initiated a pilot International Baccalaureate (IB) program in the summer of 1997, in addition to its 20-year-old magnet program. School A also implemented its own summer school transition program for all incoming ninth graders. Students could not enroll in the school unless they had participated in this program. Through this summer program, school A added enrichment activities for incoming students. Schools B and C also implemented IB programs, although they had yet to be admitted into the formal IB organization. School D implemented an entirely new organizational structure centered on small schools.

These findings suggest that as the public becomes more informed about the schools' test achievements, market-like competition among schools may emerge. The use of test scores to determine a school's probationary status may contribute to various patterns of student enrollment, which include, among others, decreasing enrollment at probation and reconstituted schools and increasing enrollment at nonprobationary schools. All of our case-study schools have responded to this market-like pressure by implementing specialty programs in order to attract higher-performing students.

ACADEMIC PROMOTION

In the spring of 1996 the district declared that it would end social promotion and announced a new academic-promotion policy. The policy tied student promotion from the third, sixth, eighth, and ninth grades to both course credit and standardized test scores. According to the policy, third, sixth, eighth, and ninth graders could be retained a grade if they failed to score at the district benchmark on nationally normed tests, the Iowa Test of Basic Skills (ITBS) or TAP for ninth graders. The district set the benchmark at approximately one grade-level below the national norm to pass to the next grade. Students who failed to post adequate scores were required to attend a Summer Bridge remediation program. In addition, the policy also required third, sixth, and eighth graders to receive passing grades in reading and mathematics and to have no more than 20 unexcused absences. Ninth graders were required to earn at least five course credits during their freshmen year and have no more than 20 unexcused absences.

Summer Bridge Program: An Example of Support and Teacher Discretion

The Summer Bridge program for low-scoring students was a central component of the district's promotion policy. The board provided Bridge teachers with scripted lesson plans that identified lesson objectives and materials, the order of activities, how the teachers should present the material, and the instructional format teachers should use. At the end of the seven-week program, students took the ITBS or TAP again. If they met or exceeded the district benchmark, they were promoted to the next grade. If they failed, they were retained. Eighth graders who were 15 or over were placed in district transition schools.

In 1997 the district's Summer Bridge program included third, sixth, and ninth graders. According to district figures, 40,949 students, or 35 percent of the district's students in those grades, were required to enroll in Summer Bridge based on their spring 1997 test scores. Of those, 34,052, or 83 percent, were tested at the end of the program. The district reported that 14,491 students posted scores at or above the district cutoff score. This represented 43 percent of the students tested and 35 percent of the total number of students required to take the program. Due to waivers that the district granted students for promotion, 49 percent of the students who attended the Summer Bridge program were promoted to the next grade. For ninth graders, of the 14,287 students who should have been in the program, 9,610, or 67 percent, were tested at the end of it. Of that number, 3,696, or 38 percent, met the cutoff score.[6]

In 1998, according to district figures, 27,797 third, sixth, and eighth graders should have attended the program based on test scores. Of that number, 24,619 students, or 89 percent of the eligible students, were tested at the end of the summer. Of the students tested, 9,924, or 40 percent, posted the required scores. In 1998 11,458 ninth graders should have attended Summer Bridge. Of those students, 6,698, or 58 percent, took the TAP test at the end of the summer, with 3,501, or 52 percent, passing. In total, 31 percent of the ninth graders who should have attended Summer Bridge met the promotional requirements by the end of the program.[7]

In 1997 the district hailed the program as a triumph. Gery Chico, who was the School Reform Board of Trustees president, attributed the program's success to "high standards, high expectations, accountability and a structured curriculum,"[8] and Mayor Daley said that the results showed "that every child can learn, we just need to work with every child."[9]

However, confusion arose and continues surrounding the degree of success of the Summer Bridge program. It centers on how to distinguish students promoted due to passing test scores at the end of the program from those promoted because they received waivers. In part, this lack of clarity stems from the multiple criteria used to determine whether students meet the academic-promotion standards. Altogether, there are 22 different combinations of these conditions with different consequences.[10] The central office aggregates student data in its reports on the Summer Bridge program and promotion rates, thus obscuring these distinctions.

Teacher Implementation of the Summer Bridge Curriculum: Teacher Discretion and District Directives

In order to examine the implementation of the Summer Bridge program at the high school level, in 1997 we interviewed and observed the classrooms of five teachers involved in the TAP remediation program at school A, for a total of 1,350 minutes of classroom observations. In 1998 we interviewed and observed eight teachers for two days teaching in Summer Bridge programs at schools A and C—for a total of 1,440 minutes of classroom observations. Although one should not hastily generalize from our findings given the small scope of our sample, our intensive data collection and analysis does provide insight into how teachers cope with the demands and objectives of the Summer Bridge program and the district's curricular and instructional directives.

A key component of the Summer Bridge program was the board's "scripted" curriculum. The board provided all Summer Bridge teachers with a curriculum guide that included detailed daily lesson plans. The lesson plans identified the lesson objectives, the materials to be used, how teachers should use the materials, instructional formats, and the sequence of activities. Teachers reported that district officials stressed adherence to both the content and pace of the curriculum through emphasizing compliance in mandated in-services and monitoring classrooms.

Teachers expressed general satisfaction with the quality of the curricular materials. However, they complained that the pace was unrealistic. Teachers felt that they needed to slow the pace in order to address students' learning needs According to one central staff member, the administration was aware of teachers' complaints but maintained that the pace was appropriate:

Teachers complained about the pace and difficulty of the materials. Many schools were used to using materials not at grade level. The teachers were not accustomed to teaching at grade level. If we don't bring children up to grade level they are never going to improve. . . . It was a shock in Year One. Teachers said "These are eighth grade materials!" We said, "We know."

Our analysis of the Summer Bridge program focuses on how teachers resolved competing demands stemming from what they perceive their students' learning needs to be versus board pressure for curriculum adherence. We compared the types of activities mandated by the board curriculum with the types of activities teachers implemented in their classrooms. In addition, in order to assess how teachers addressed the issue of instructional pace, we analyzed the amount of time teachers spent on each type of activity.

We categorized the types of activities mandated in the board's ninth-grade Summer Bridge curriculum[11] and then analyzed classroom observations to ascertain the types of activity teachers complied with, modified, or omitted. We considered activities to be modified if teachers maintained the overall lesson objective but used materials different than those assigned in the curriculum and/or used a different instructional format. For example, teachers frequently maintained the lesson objectives for workbook activities but substituted different workbook pages. Teachers may also have maintained objectives and materials but placed students in groups or pairs, thus modifying the activity format.

Even with district pressure for compliance, teachers maintained a high degree of discretion over the choice of activities they taught. It should be noted that teachers did not create their own activities and lessons. Although they modified the board curriculum, the materials and activities they taught came from the scripted curriculum. Table 7.6 shows that during the summers of 1997 and 1998 math teachers assigned only 25 percent

TABLE 7.6

SUMMER BRIDGE CURRICULUM ANALYSIS: PERCENTAGE OF BOARD ACTIVITIES TEACHERS COMPLIED WITH, MODIFIED, OR OMITTED (SUMMERS 1997 AND 1998)

Subject	*Total curricular activities assigned by board*	*Board activities teachers complied with as % of total*	*Board activities teachers modified as % of total*	*Board activities teachers omitted as % of total*
Math	$n = 51$	25 ($n = 13$)	24 ($n = 12$)	51 ($n = 26$)
Reading	$n = 85$	35 ($n = 29$)	9 ($n = 8$)	56 ($n = 48$)

of the activities in the district curriculum, while reading teachers assigned 35 percent. Math teachers modified 24 percent of the assignments and omitted 51 percent. Reading teachers modified 9 percent of the assignments and omitted 56 percent.

Teachers interviewed stressed their belief that Summer Bridge students had particular learning needs that required them to slow the pace of instruction and focus on basic skills. The high percentage of activities teachers omitted indicates that they did slow the pace of instruction considerably. In order to understand how teachers attempted to address students' learning needs, we analyzed classroom observations to examine the amount of time teachers allocated to different types of activities.

We classified the math activities included in the board curriculum into six categories.[12] *Demonstration/explanation* involves teachers demonstrating mathematical processes and/or explaining math concepts and their application. *Manipulative* involves students using real-life objects to understand math concepts and processes. *Drill* refers to worksheet activities that typically involve computation problems, although they may also include word problems. Teachers may lead discussions on these activities, which typically involve teachers asking students for answers, then correcting these answers or showing students how to do the problems. These discussions differ from *demonstration/explanation* in that teachers show students how to do individual problems as opposed to providing explanations, followed by students applying the explanations to solve problems. *Tests* typically involve chapter reviews and/or a series of math problems from the workbooks. Some assignments call for teachers to create their own tests. *Calculator* activities require students to use calculators and to learn calculator functions. *Group* work involves students working with one or more students to solve assigned problems. These problems can be either computational or conceptual.

In reading, we classified activities into five categories. *Workbook* activities involve the teacher leading the class through pages in the workbook and/or students completing workbook pages alone while seated. When students are assigned workbook activities as seatwork, the board curriculum generally calls for teachers to follow up with class discussion. The SRA requires students to work individually on Scholastic Reading Achievement kits. These assignments involve students in reading and answering questions on short reading passages. Students progress through the kits at their own pace. *Story* involves students working with longer reading selections, typically from the district-assigned multicultural or science-fiction readers. These selections are significantly longer than those found in workbooks. Although this work could provide students with more latitude for interpretation, board activities assigned with the stories typically focused on outlining story structure and short-answer questions. *Group* work involves students working with one or more of their peers to complete an assignment. *Timed readings* are assignments that simulate test-taking condi-

TABLE 7.7

Summer Bridge Activity Analysis: Reading
(Summers 1997 and 1998)

	TYPE OF ACTIVITY				
	Workbook	*Timed readings*	*SRA*	*Story discussion*	*Group*
Total number of activites assigned by board	24 100%	18 100%	16 100%	21 100%	6 100%
Number of board activities teachers assigned	18 75%	6 33%	1 6%	3 14%	1 17%
Number of board activities teachers modified	4 17%	2 11%	0 0%	2 9%	0 0%
Number of board activities teachers omitted	2 8%	10 56%	15 94%	16 76%	5 83%

tions. They are activities from district-assigned workbooks that require students to read and answer multiple-choice questions on test-like passages within a certain time period.

Tables 7.7 and 7.8 show the percentage of activities within each category that English and math teachers assigned, modified, or omitted during the summers of 1997 and 1998. Table 7.7 indicates that English teachers assigned the majority, 75 percent, of the workbook activities mandated by the board curriculum. They tended, however, to omit most of the other types of activities. Table 7.8 shows that math teachers made similar decisions. Math teachers tended to assign and/or modify *demonstration/explanation* and *drill* activities from the board curriculum. In short, both math and English teachers chose to implement activities that focused on discrete skills and enabled them to lead students through highly defined materials. In contrast, both math and English teachers tended to omit activities that involved individualized or small-group instructional formats that may allow students more control over the pace and focus of learning. They also eliminated activities that could require students to grapple with concepts or interpretation. In math, teachers modified or eliminated 100 percent of the manipulative activities mandated by the board, while English teachers eliminated 76 percent of the story activities.

Our analysis of teachers' use of instructional time generally confirms the findings of our activity analysis. Table 7.9 indicates that reading teachers spent the majority of the time during 1997 and 1998, 48 percent, on

TABLE 7.8

SUMMER BRIDGE ACTIVITY ANALYSIS: MATH
(SUMMERS 1997 AND 1998)

			TYPE OF ACTIVITY				
	Drill	*Test*	*Demon-stration/expla-nation*	*Group*	*Manipu-latives*	*Calcu-lator*	*Chalk-board*
Total number of activites assigned by board	15 100%	8 100%	9 100%	4 100%	6 100%	3 100%	6 100%
Number of board activities teachers assigned	4 27%	2 25%	5 56%	0 0%	2 33%	0 0%	0 0%
Number of board activities teachers modified	7 47%	1 13%	0 0%	1 25%	1 17%	0 0%	2 33%
Number of board activities teachers omitted	4 27%	5 63%	4 44%	3 75%	3 50%	3 100%	4 67%

workbook activities. Similarly, math teachers spent 46 percent of their time on *drill* activities. In addition, math teachers spent 25 percent of their instructional time on *demonstration/explanation*. While reading teachers spent 22 percent of their time on *story* activities, it should be noted that they still eliminated 76 percent of these types of activities assigned by the board.

In sum, teachers' instructional decisions suggest that they responded to the objective of the Summer Bridge program—raising standardized test scores—by focusing on discrete skills. While the board curriculum contains activities and materials intended to enrich students' understanding of math concepts and reading skills, teachers tended to eliminate these types of activities. Teachers were presented with several types of constraints that influence their instructional decisions. In interviews, teachers mentioned two constraints in particular: *time* and *student ability* as measured by test scores. Teachers coped with these constraints by modifying the board curriculum to focus more narrowly on the program's testing objective and what they perceived to be their students' learning needs. Although teachers' decisions appeared to conflict with central-office imperatives to adhere to the board curriculum, they indicate that teachers did indeed align their instructional decisions to the program's objective.

Given the high degree of discretion teachers in our study exerted over instructional time, pace, and materials, teacher assignment to the Summer

TABLE 7.9

TEACHER TIME ALLOCATION, SUMMER BRIDGE (1997 AND 1998)

	Type of activity	No. of minutes allocated to activity	% of total minutes observed
MATH	Drill	494	46
	Demonstration/explanation	275	25
	Test	111	10
	Group	80	7
	Manipulative	11	1
	Calculator	0	0
	Management	61	6
	Nontask	48	4
	TOTAL	1,080	99%[*]
ENGLISH	Workbook	824	48
	Story	370	22
	Timed readings	104	6
	Group	108	6
	SRA	45	3
	Management	64	4
	Nontask	80	5
	TOTAL	1,710	94%[†]

[*]Difference from 100 percent due to rounding.
[†]Six percent of observed time (115 minutes) was spent on newspaper activities and social discussion in two teachers' classrooms.

Bridge program should be carefully considered. The selection of teachers for the program has been based on a volunteer rather than a certification basis. At the two schools we observed, three of the six teachers teaching math were certified math teachers. While various subject areas involve teaching reading, two of the eight reading teachers had certificates in English. The scripted curriculum provided by the board is intended to provide a minimum level of competency. The scripted curriculum does not, however, negate the highly autonomous nature of teaching. Assigning teachers that may lack the requisite content and pedagogic knowledge needed to teach students with difficulties may undermine remediation efforts.

While teachers report difficulties balancing demands to adhere to district materials versus student learning needs, there appears to be little teacher resistance to the Summer Bridge program. In contrast, considerable confusion about the practical implications of the program for student placement in the case-study high schools persists. Administrators in these schools report that it is unclear what low test scores for ninth graders actually mean. Schools place low-scoring students, along with students who do not meet the course credit requirements and/or have excessive absences, in "demote" divisions, or homerooms. Because there are no prerequisites for any sophomore course but geometry, these students still enroll in sophomore-level courses. In the ninth grade, then, the sanctions associated with the academic promotion policy are largely social and symbolic. Students are told that they are in a demote division, but other formal sanctions are not apparent.

PROFESSIONAL DISCRETION AND RESTRUCTURING HIGH SCHOOLS: ACADEMIES AND STUDENT ADVISORIES

The district's High School Redesign Plan, first drafted in December 1996, seeks to restructure all aspects of high school operations. High schools must implement the following eight components of the plan: 1) a core curriculum driven by district standards and assessments; 2) junior and senior academies; 3) student advisories; 4) community-service learning requirements for students; 5) support and recovery programs for failing students; 6) expanded academic- and career-specialty programs; 7) restructured time schedules; and 8) improved professional development for principals and teachers. Schools have the flexibility to determine the models they will use to implement each of these elements.

The evolution of the High School Redesign Plan over the course of three years reflects efforts by the central administration to negotiate often-competing demands that arise from various constituencies and demands associated with organizational problems and realities. During the first year of his administration, CEO Vallas initiated the high school restructuring effort in response to concerns about high schools identified by university and reform groups. For example, one study highlighted the high rates of student failure and attrition at the high school level.[13] After meeting with superintendents and principals from successful public, Catholic, and private high schools across the state, the central administration created a steering committee and seven task forces to develop a plan in response to this failure. The task forces mobilized broad political support and represent an attempt by the central administration to build consensus. In addition to members of the central office and principals and teachers in the system, the 130 members of the task forces include representatives from foundations and businesses as well as school reformers, local school-council members, and university representatives. Many of the participants had been part of the previous governance reform and hence were highly suspicious of the 1995 integrated governance reform.

The first version of the redesign plan, drafted and publicly disseminated through a series of hearings held in December 1996, provided schools with a high degree of autonomy as advocated by pro-decentralization reformers. The revised plan, issued in March 1997,[14] retained the themes of increased "academic press" and "personalization" advocated by pro-decentralization reformers and presented an action plan for implementing several of the task forces' recommendations. Again, schools maintained discretion over the choice of models and the organization of programs associated with the plan.

The High School Redesign Plan,[15] issued by the central administration in April 1998, reflected the administration's comprehensive efforts to transform high schools through uniform academic standards and the creation of more career- and academic-specialty programs. This document highlighted "school enhancements" and enrollment concerns. It identified the increasing number of schools that had or planned to implement advanced academic programs such as Advanced Placement (AP) courses, a CPS Scholars program, and International Baccalaureate programs. It also highlighted district policies concerned with maintaining neighborhood school boundaries, with curtailing midyear transfers, and with setting aside 30 percent of magnet-school-enrollment openings for neighborhood students. It maintained flexibility for local schools in the selection of restructuring models; its commitment to advanced academic programs and bolstering neighborhood schools reflects district responses to concerns about the schools' relation to the overall strength of the city.

The evolution of the High School Redesign Plan reflects the administration's efforts to address various constituencies and develop broad support for what it considers one of its central initiatives. The administration focused on two components of the Redesign Plan—academies and student advisories. Data from our survey of principals and case studies indicate that the implementation of the two initiatives has given rise to very different patterns of conflict and accommodation. Schools largely accepted the academy initiative, while teachers mounted considerable resistance to the student advisories.

The Junior/Senior Academy Initiative

The junior/senior academy initiative provided the organizational framework for changes in the high school curriculum and students' progression through and graduation from high school. Students in the junior academy enrolled in courses focused on a common core curriculum. Students were required to earn course credit in the core subject areas and pass the Chicago Academic Standards Exam (CASE) in order to be promoted to the senior academy wherein they could enroll in focused career and academic programs. Students stayed in the junior academy until they completed these requirements.

In the 1997 High School Redesign Plan, the academies fell under initiatives aimed at restructuring "organization and time." It was grouped with initiatives such as four-year career academies and vocational-education programs, student information-systems reforms, and alternative scheduling. District materials did not specify how schools should structure their academies. Instead, district documents specified the mission and goals of the academies. According to the revised March 1997 High School Redesign Plan,[16] the mission of the junior academy was "to establish a sound foundation in the core curricular subject areas while providing a smaller, more personalized environment.[17] The goals of the junior academy are stated as follows: 1) reducing the number of course failures; 2) improving attendance patterns; and 3) maintaining support networks for academic and social needs."[18] The district relied upon professional discretion at the school level in the design and implementation of the academies in each high school. Unlike probation and academic promotion, there were few formal sanctions attached to the academies initiative.

Analysis of our survey of principals and case studies indicates that schools have accommodated to the district's academies initiative to a high degree. A full 98 percent of the principals surveyed reported that their schools had junior academies during the 1997–98 school year. In those 40 schools, all ninth graders were enrolled in the academy, while 35, or 88 percent, of the academies enrolled all tenth graders. Survey responses also indicate a high degree of compliance with the stated policy objectives. Eighty percent of the principals surveyed reported that a primary focus of the academies was to improve academics; 56 percent reported that counseling was a central focus; and 54 percent reported that improving attendance was a primary goal.

This pattern of accommodation in enrollment and goals also appears in our case studies. Three of the four high schools had either a freshmen or junior academy during 1997–98. Schools A and C had similar organizational models that reflected district goals of providing students with academic and social support by organizing teachers into teams or "pods." School D developed a freshman academy that enrolled all ninth graders. Teachers at school D did not formally coordinate their curriculum, but were expected to provide student support through advisories rather than through a team or pod approach.

Unlike the other schools, school B did not officially have an academy. During the 1997–98 school year, a group of teachers initiated a small program for incoming freshmen focused on an environmental theme. The program represented a school-within-a-school model and involved six teachers and approximately 140 freshmen. The goals of this program were to integrate the curriculum across disciplines and to provide students with more personalized relations with teachers and more enrichment opportunities such as field trips and assemblies. Students moved from class to class as groups in an effort to develop supportive relationships. In 1997–98 students with low reading scores constituted the majority of the students in the pod.

Although the academy structures differ across the case-study schools, in large part they reflected the district goals of improving attendance and providing students with increased academic and social support. Teachers in schools A and C felt that student attendance and behavior improved because of the pod structure. In both schools they reported that the team approach fostered collegial relationships that enabled teachers to identify student problems and intervene more effectively than before.

The survey of principals indicates that principals also attributed improvement in student attendance and discipline to the academies. Seventy-eight percent of them reported that they observed an improvement in student attendance since the implementation of the academies. Seventy-one percent attributed improvements in testing to the academies, and 63 percent reported improvement in discipline. The survey and our case studies thus suggest that teachers and principals believe that the academies are achieving the goal of improving attendance patterns and providing students with social support.

Curriculum Standardization in Core Subject Areas

A central component of the academy initiative was to standardize curriculum and assessment. The 1995 Reform Act expanded the power of the central administration over curriculum; the district responded by making efforts to standardize the curriculum across the system. These curriculum standards—a joint effort of the board, the Chicago Teachers' Union (CTU), and various university-based consultants—were aligned with the state goals and provide broad objectives for each subject area. During the 1997–98 school year the district created and disseminated programs of studies that were aligned with the standards for ninth- and tenth-grade core-subject-area courses. These programs of study specify the skills to be developed and the materials to be covered in each course.

The district developed and implemented district-wide final exams, or CASE, aligned with the standards. The district piloted the CASE in ninth-grade algebra, English, and science courses in June 1998. Central-office officials reported that 75.8 percent of the ninth graders passed the English CASE, 42.7 percent passed the history exams, 35.5 percent passed the biology test, and 25 percent passed the algebra exam.[19] In order to pass, a student needed to answer correctly at least 50 percent of the questions. The district planned to implement CASE exams at the tenth, eleventh, and twelfth grades by the school year 2001–02. One central-office administrator said that the CASE would be factored into student grades, and the High School Redesign Plan indicates that the CASE will be one criterion used to determine students' promotion from the junior to senior academies.

At the high school level, the standardization of the curriculum was accompanied by focusing the ninth- and tenth-grade curriculum on core subjects. The district increased the high school graduation requirements in math from two to three years, and in science from one to three years. The district also eliminated pre-algebra courses and mandated that low-scoring students enroll in developmental math classes concurrent to their enrollment in algebra. Students who posted low scores in reading enrolled in development reading courses, further reducing course options. The district also split the physical-education requirement into two years of physical education and two years of career education. Finally, it added two years of foreign-language study to the required courses and a community-service requirement.[20]

While district efforts to standardize the curriculum played a crucial role in the implementation of the academies and of the High School Redesign Plan in general, they represented just one constraint on curricular decisions made by teachers. Actors at different levels of the school organization placed pressure upon schools and teachers to align their curriculum with various standards and objectives. Schools and teachers had to deal with state goals and assessments as well as subject-matter standards promoted by professional associations. These factors competed with the district emphasis on the TAP and CASE.

In order to assess how district initiatives influence teachers' curricular decisions, we asked teachers how the curriculum was developed for the courses they teach and how they made use of the state assessment, IGAP, TAP, CASE, and the subject-matter department. Table 7.10 shows the number of teachers by subject matter in each of our case-study high schools who reported that their curricular decisions were influenced by the state goals, IGAP, TAP, their subject-matter department, and the CPS Standards. Teachers could report that none, one, or all of the factors influenced their curricular decisions. There could be a total of 16 reports in each category in school A, 45 reports in school B, 25 reports in school C, and 37 reports in school D. In total, there could be 123 reports in each category.

Subject-matter departments play a key role in the coordination and standardization of the curriculum. Teachers mentioned that they coordinated the curriculum with departmental colleagues 68 times. In contrast, they reported that they aligned their curriculum with the CPS Standards 34 times, and that they aligned their curriculum with the state goals 32 times. In our case studies, the department appeared to be more influential in English teachers' curricular decisions than in those of math teachers. Out of a possible 56 reports, English teachers said that they coordinated their curriculum within their department 32 times, while of the 51 possible reports in math, teachers reported departmental coordination 21 times.

Although the department appeared to play a key role in curricular standardization for many teachers, there was wide variation across and within schools. A good example of this was at school B. During the first year of probation, English teachers in school B reported aligning their curriculum with state goals as well as within the department, but during 1997–98, the year following probation, English teachers reported only departmental

TABLE 7.10

CURRICULUM STANDARDIZATION: NUMBER OF TEACHERS BY SCHOOL AND DEPARTMENT WHO REPORT HOW CURRICULUM IS STANDARDIZED

School	Department	Year	State goals	IGAP	TAP	Department	CPS standards
A	English (n = 8)	1997–98	5	0	2	6	7
	Math (n = 8)	1997–98	2	1	2	4	6
B	English (n = 12)	1996–97	4	4	1	7	1
	Math (n = 10)	1996–97	4	2	1	5	0
	English (n = 13)	1997–98	0	1	1	8	0
	Math (n = 10)	1997–98	1	4	4	2	1
C	English (n = 14)	1997–98	1	7	7	3	6
	Math (n = 11)	1997–98	0	9	6	4	6
D	English (n = 9)	1996–97	1	5	2	8	0
	Math (n = 12)	1996–97	4	5	2	6	3
	English (n = 8)	1997–98	5	3	5	7	5
	Math (n = 8)	1997–98	5	3	4	8	5
	TOTAL REPORTS:		**32**	**44**	**37**	**68**	**40**

Note: The total number of teacher interviews was 123.

coordination. The increased importance of the department stems in large part from the principal's efforts to strengthen the department as noted above.

The importance of the department in the coordination of the English curriculum in school B contrasts with the apparent lack of coordination in the math department in that same school. Although the principal of school B, in response to a report by a district probation-assessment team, pushed for standardization of the curriculum within courses and promoted departmental exams, math teachers seldom mentioned that they coordinated their curriculum within the department. During 1996–97, the first year of probation, 50 percent of the math teachers reported departmental curricular coordination. After probation, only 20 percent reported departmental coordination.

The second most-reported influences on curricular standardization were the IGAP and TAP tests. There were 44 reports of IGAP influence, and 37 reports of TAP influence. While the tests promoted curricular standardization, they did so in rather superficial ways. Teachers reported implementing test-preparation activities, but referred to these activities as a "suspension" of the regular curriculum or "taking time out" of the curriculum. Thus, while the tests *did* prompt teachers to coordinate test-preparation activities, they tended not to consider these efforts as part of developing the "real" curriculum.

Our case studies indicate that district efforts to standardize the curriculum have given rise to conflict, particularly in relation to the academies initiative. This conflict emerges at the intersections of district policies. Different district policies place often-competing curricular demands upon schools and teachers. The conflict primarily surfaces among English rather than math teachers and arises in the implementation of the district's standards and assessments, the goals of the academies, and the use of the TAP as the main criterion for placing schools on probation or reconstitution.

As noted above, the district created programs of study and CASE exams aligned with the Chicago Academic Standards. The programs and CASE place pressure upon teachers within subject matters to teach specific materials and objectives. In contrast, one of the goals of the academies was to encourage curricular integration across subject matters. In our case studies, teachers resolved this conflict by shifting their curriculum to fulfill the requirements of the CASE rather than the academies. Teachers in school C's junior academy reported that they developed an integrated math/science and English/history curriculum during the summer of 1997. When they returned to school in August of that year, the district informed teachers that they would be required to follow the programs of study and that the CASE would be piloted in the spring of 1998. Although teachers said that they did not receive the programs of study until later in the school year, they threw out their integrated curriculum to follow the district frameworks. In a school already under pressure by probation, teachers responded to the policy with the clearest form of accountability. The CASE can measure not only student performance but can also, to a limited degree, indicate teacher compliance with the programs of study. In contrast, there are no district measures to enforce the integrated curriculum.

Conflict also arose because teachers had to simultaneously deal with demands placed upon them by the CASE as well as the threat of probation and possible reconstitution that accompanies the TAP. This conflict was most prominent in school D, which faced the greatest district pressure under reconstitution. Teachers in school D expressed anxiety about the CASE exams in the weeks prior to the test. One English teacher said that once the TAP was over, she would start to review elements of poetry for the CASE. Another said in May, "I've already said we've blown that [the CASE], since my students are not going to pass or fail on that, since the school is not being judged, I didn't put emphasis on this." Teachers at school D had focused so much of their instructional time on TAP preparation that they had not completed much of the curriculum that would be assessed by the CASE.

Although the majority of principals identified academics as the primary focus of the academies, their responses suggest that the academies have had a greater effect on students' social behavior and test performance than on curricular and instructional practices. Teacher comments in our case-study high schools generally confirm this. While teachers in both schools A and C—the two schools most positive about the academies— reported that the team approach improved student attendance, many also said that they seldom collaborated on the curriculum. One teacher in school A provided examples of how his team worked to help students but said that interdisciplinary teaching remained at an informal level, with teachers discussing lessons rather than coordinating them. Teachers in school C reported that their efforts to coordinate interdisciplinary lessons were undermined by the board's programs of study. With the implementation of the programs, the teachers coordinated assignments within subject matters *across* pods rather than *within* pods. The math and English teachers in school B's pod reported that they did not have adequate time to integrate their curriculum across subjects. In light of this, the teachers followed their department curriculum. In short, while teachers and principals credit academies for improvement in student attendance and discipline, the effects of the academies on the curriculum and instruction remain unclear.

Student Advisories

During 1997–98 the CPS initiated the student-advisory program as part of its high school restructuring plan. The CPS expected schools to implement an advisory period in students' schedules. In a summary of the goals, a CPS document states: "Small groups foster a sense of family, collaboration, connection, and caring among students and staff."[21] The initiative called for each student to be assigned a teacher/advisor who would play a supportive role by acting as a liaison between parents and the school, keeping track of advisees' progress, and guiding students during the school year. The CPS also expected teachers to implement a curriculum of study skills, life skills, and career education. To facilitate the curriculum, the district distributed two books of recommended activities. These included activities centered on career and vocational goals, academic goals, and social goals and concerns. While the program was mandated for freshmen and sophomores, schools were free to implement it school-wide.

In contrast to the academies initiative, the advisory program met with considerable teacher resistance. Conflict arose between the board and the CTU over teacher compensation in the spring of 1997, when the board first introduced the program. The union viewed the program as an additional preparation, but the board refused to provide extra compensation. The conflict remained unresolved throughout the 1997–98 school year. This resulted in tensions between teachers and principals at the school level. One central-office staff said this about the implementation of the program:

> Teachers said it's an extra function we don't get paid for and we're not doing it. . . . Another problem has been the CTU contract. If a school wants a variation from the contracted 50-minute periods they have to have 50 percent plus one vote to get a waiver. Even when it's no more than 15 or 20 minutes, the principals still have to get the vote. Many principals lost the vote about advisories. In deference to grieving, at two or three schools the faculty members groaned and they don't have advisories. . . . We'd like to have had the advisory implemented this year and next year but the system didn't provide the support for the principals to get this done.

The unresolved conflict between the CTU and the board concerning advisories resulted in varying commitment to the program at the school level. While school D allotted 25 minutes each day for division (or homeroom) and advisories at all grade levels, school C held advisories one day a week only for ninth and tenth graders, and school D held advisories during long divisions scheduled at the end of each quarterly marking period during 1997–98. Teachers in schools B and C reported that the marginalization of the advisories indicated by the scheduling left the program fragmented.

In addition to conflict over compensation, in case-study schools B, C, and D teacher interviews suggest that they felt uncomfortable with the expansion of their role inherent in the advisory goals. One teacher in school B felt that the board curriculum touched on subjects that teachers were not trained to handle and posed risks to students. Most teachers reported that they seldom used the board curriculum. When they did, many said that they merely distributed the materials and discussed them briefly. Teachers preferred to develop informal relationships with their students and most often reported that they used the advisory as a study hall, providing students with academic tutoring and test-preparation activities. This suggests that teachers in the three schools rejected the counseling aspects of the program and limited the policy objectives to providing informal social and academic support for students.

Teachers in schools B, C, and D also reported frustration with the lack of incentives and sanctions for students associated with the program. Teachers across the three schools reported that students did not receive credit for attending the advisories and that there were no penalties for absences. As one teacher in school C said about the lack of student commitment, "No carrot—no stick." The lack of formal guidelines for students placed an even greater emphasis on teachers' commitment to the program, something that our case studies suggest varies considerably and tends to be low.

School A's advisory program differed from the program in schools B, C, and D in that it was more school-based. During 1997–98 the school devoted 45-minute class periods four days a week, and a 10-minute class period one day a week, to advisories. Rather than relying on the board curriculum, the school delineated the types of activities for each day. These activities included reading, math, personal development, and journal writing. Teachers were expected to hand-in weekly lesson plans with their intended activities. Teachers at school A were generally positive about the advisories, although their commitment varied. In addition, the principal complained that he lacked the authority over teachers who elected not to use the school's advisory lesson plans.

The implementation of the academies and the student advisories has given rise to different patterns of conflict and accommodation. Our survey of principals and case studies suggests that little conflict has arisen in association with the academies. An overwhelming majority of the schools have implemented some form of a junior academy, and the majority of principals attributed improvements in student behavior and attendance to them. In addition, principals reported receiving support from the central office for the academies. Our case studies suggest, however, that the academies' impact on instructional processes remains unclear. Further, efforts to standardize and focus the curriculum on the core subjects are in conflict with the academy goal of integrating the curriculum across subject matters. Teachers were required to negotiate these competing goals. Our case studies suggest that they do so in ways that reinforce subject-matter distinctions.

In contrast, the implementation of the student-advisory program has been severely limited due to conflict surrounding issues of teacher compensation and the expansion of the teachers' role. While some schools have restructured their schedules to develop advisories, some have implemented only a few advisory periods throughout the year, or none at all. These decisions relate to the level of teacher resistance to the program.

Further, student advisories rely much more heavily upon teachers' voluntary commitment to develop personal relationships with their students than do the academy initiatives.

Conclusion

Integrated governance has enabled Chicago's district leadership to focus on system-wide efforts to improve student and school performance. The administration's educational-accountability agenda tried to leverage improvement in performance outcomes by establishing and enforcing system-wide standards. The four initiatives we studied—academic promotion, probation/reconstitution, academies, and student advisories—illustrate the different types of leverage employed by the district. The initiatives entail different mixtures of formal sanctions, support, and professional discretion. Our findings suggest that diverse patterns of accommodation and conflict arose as schools and teachers responded to the various types of leverage. These patterns of accommodation and conflict exerted different effects on teaching within schools and classrooms.

The district launched numerous initiatives in its efforts to improve teaching and learning in high schools. Our study indicates that these initiatives had some impact on how schools and teachers allocate instructional resources. While district efforts began to show some progress during the period of our research, the district must confront several key challenges in order to encourage and maintain more sustained, long-term improvement.

The district's educational agenda revolved around the use of formal sanctions, support, and professional discretion. A key challenge for the district is to strike a balance among these different policy levers in order to support sustained improvement in the high schools. This is most crucial in schools that remain on probation and under reconstitution. These schools, on the whole, were making only slight improvements as measured by standardized test scores, even with the support of external partners and probation managers. In addition, the stigma attached to schools under probation and reconstitution may impede efforts at faculty and student recruitment that could provide the necessary resources for long-term school improvement.

It is crucial, then, for the district to reconsider how it supports these low-performing schools. It needs to assess how key resources, including funds, district and school staff, and university support, can be better utilized. The district has several options in this case. First, it can maintain its current support system but reconsider the responsibilities it assigns to external partners. The district needs to reconsider the goals it sets for the partners with the central objective of probation/reconstitution—namely, the immediate improvement of test scores. With a mission focused specifically on improving reading and math instruction, external partners can provide targeted support to schools. At the same time, partners and schools need to ensure that this is not at cross-purposes with long-term change.

Second, the district can reorganize its support system and rebuild the district's own capacity for providing schools with technical support. In this regard, the advisory system developed by the Birmingham Local Education Authority, Chicago's sister district, can serve as a model. The Birmingham Advisory and Support Service (BASS) is staffed with 30 "teacher advisers" who provide teachers with training in classroom practices, and with another 35 "link advisers" who assist schools in dealing with issues that affect the entire school organization. BASS staff assesses each school on the improvement it has made in terms of gains in scores on the national exam. The advisers target their assistance to the schools based on these assessments. School staff is integrally involved in establishing the improvement plans.

Third, the use of local universities to create an innovative teacher recruitment/induction program may result in more long-term, district-wide instructional improvements. School B's principal in our case study established strong connections with teacher-education programs and used student-teaching positions as a means to recruit and assess new teachers. The district can work more closely with not only teacher-education programs, but also arts and science programs within universities to establish these ties in more high schools and to develop an induction period that would greatly enhance the effectiveness of its current recruitment and monitoring programs.

District efforts to direct instruction are greatly circumscribed by the high degree of professional discretion inherent in the teaching task. Although the district has created several mechanisms by which to evaluate teachers, the organization of instruction at the time this research was undertaken made evaluation difficult and limited its effect on improving instruction. Given this reality, the district should consider ways of supporting evaluations and professional development that draw upon the strengths of school faculty. The successful schools in our study have sustained professional development that draws upon both external experts and school staff and teachers. In addition, teachers within departments coordinate the curriculum. By providing schools with funds and technical support for teachers to collaborate, observe, and evaluate one another, the district could support more sustained instructional improvements than efforts to control instruction through a scripted curriculum.

Finally, district policies appeared to be contributing to a movement of faculty and students away from probationary schools. This redistribution will drain resources needed for improvement away from these schools and may result in overcrowding in other schools, thus undermining improvement efforts in general. The district needs to examine both how its own policies contribute to this redistribution, and how demographic changes within the city affect enrollment patterns. It is the responsibility of the district to coordinate supply and demand; no other level of school organization is equipped to address these issues. In this regard, the district needs to consider how it will deal with schools that are undersubscribed and oversubscribed for a sustained period of time. The central concern for the district is to ensure that students in both types of schools receive adequate resources and opportunities.

NOTES

1. Kenneth K. Wong, Robert Dreeben, Laurence Lynn, Jr., and Gail Sunderman, "Education Policy: Integrated Governance as a Reform Strategy in Schools" (*International Journal of Economic Development 2*, no. 2 [2000]: 218–55). Kenneth K. Wong, "Integrated Governance in Chicago and Birmingham (UK)," chapter 5 (pp. 161–212) in M. C. Wang and H. J. Walberg, eds., *School Choice or Best Systems: What Improves Education?* Mahwah, NJ: Lawrence Erlbaum Associates, 2001.

2. Kenneth K. Wong and Mark Moulton, "Developing Institutional Performance Indicators for Chicago Schools: Conceptual and Methodological Issues Considered," pp. 57–92 in Kenneth K. Wong, ed., *Advances in Educational Policy*, vol. 2: *Rethinking School Reform in Chicago*. Greenwich, CT: JAI Press, 1996. Kenneth K. Wong and Pushpam Jain, "Newspapers as Policy Actors in Urban School Systems: The Chicago Story" (*Urban Affairs Review 35*, no. 2 [1999]: 210–46).

3. Chicago Public Schools, *High School Redesign Project: Draft for Discussion and Input*. December 1996.

4. National Center on Education and the Economy, *New Standards: Performance Standards*, vol. 3: *High School*. NCEE and The University of Pittsburgh, 1997.

5. Resource-allocation literature suggests that teacher skill and student aptitude constitute key instructional resources. Distribution of these resources at the various organizational levels of schools bear significant consequences for teaching and learning. Adam Gamoran and Robert Dreeben, "Coupling and Control in Educational Organizations" (*Administrative Science Quarterly 31*, no. 4 [1986]: 612–32). Rebecca Barr and Robert Dreeben, *How Schools Work* (Chicago: University of Chicago Press, 1983).

6. Chicago Public Schools, *1997 Summer Bridge Program Pass and Failure Rates, Preliminary Results*.

7. Chicago Public Schools, *1998 Summer Bridge Program Pass and Failure Rates, Preliminary Results*.

8. Chicago Public Schools, *Eighth-Graders Master Promotion Criteria: Students at All Levels Showed Growth*. Chicago Public Schools, Office of Communications, August 14, 1997.

9. Chicago Public Schools, *Summer Bridge Program Triumphs: Preliminary Test Scores Spell Success*. Chicago Public Schools, Office of Communications, August 13, 1997.

10. Chicago Public Schools, *Guidelines for Promotion in the Chicago Public Schools, 1997–1998*.

11. Chicago Public Schools, *Building a Bridge to the 21st Century: Teacher Handbook, Summer Bridge Program '98, Grade 9.*

12. Our categorization of activities is based on our interpretation of the objectives and procedures of the activities found in the board's Summer Bridge curriculum for ninth grade. We did not use skill taxonomies to distinguish between high- and low-order activities, because our focus is on how teachers interpret and cope with district policy demands and directives rather than on assessing the district's curriculum *per se.*

13. Consortium on Chicago School Research, *Charting Reform in Chicago: The Students Speak.* July 1996.

14. Chicago Public Schools, *Design for High Schools.* March 1997.

15. Chicago Public Schools, *Design for High Schools: Update.* April 1998.

16. Chicago Public Schools, *Design for High Schools.* March 1997.

17. Ibid., p. 8.

18. Ibid., p. 73.

19. *Chicago Tribune,* September 3, 1998.

20. Chicago School Reform Board Meeting, February 26, 1997, report no. 97-0226-MO1.

21. Chicago Public Schools, *Student Advisories.* CPS Webpage: <www.cps.k12.il.us>.

■   ■   ■

PART THREE

External Intervention to Improve Urban School Systems

State and Federal Intervention to Improve Baltimore and Washington, D.C.'s Public Schools

JAMES G. CIBULKA

T HE PERCEIVED INADEQUACIES of urban school systems in the United States have been a preoccupation of citizen reformers and policy-makers for at least four decades. Yet the persistence of urban education as a policy "problem" suggests that there has been little consensus as to what the problem means, much less how to solve it. A variety of reform nostrums have competed for dominance, often in succession as earlier reforms proved inadequate or lost favor.

A complicating factor in the reform of urban education has been the politics surrounding urban education. These politics have been characterized by high levels of racial and social conflict, unstable alliances, bureaucratic unresponsiveness and institutional rigidity, high leadership turnover, and intergovernmental intrusiveness. The governance system is itself an object of dispute in these politics. This is because the governance system is viewed by protagonists as embracing core values and interests. These key values and interests serve a *legitimating function* for any political regime that embraces them. In the case of urban education, at least four principles have been in conflict. These principles often operate in tension, much like core values such as freedom, equality, and efficiency.

THE PRINCIPLES OF GOVERNANCE

Representativeness

Political actors have sought to assure that urban school systems represent local needs through formal structures of policy-making such as school boards. This value reflects the long tradition of local control in American education. However, representativeness is a multifaceted concept and has meant different things at different points in our political history. In the nineteenth century, school boards were large and represented local schools. At times they have represented wards or other subjurisdictions. Progressives favored small boards elected at-large in order to attract "qualified" candidates; such individuals were to take a city-wide perspective on issues rather than representing narrow, parochial interests (Kaufman 1956). *Descriptiveness* is another embodiment of representativeness (Pitkin 1967). It focuses on the likeness between the public and their representatives on obvious traits such as race or ethnicity. School boards have been deemed representative at various times depending on their likeness with their constituents, regardless of their actions. A corruption of this idea of representativeness, which grows out of the descriptive perspective, is the tendency to evaluate employees according to the same criteria. It is a corruption of representativeness, because the employee has an inherent conflict of interest between representing his or her personal interests and the broader interests of that racial or ethnic group with whom he or she shares a likeness. Moreover, descriptiveness has no standard for judging the individual's behavior apart from the traits shared. Nonetheless, urban school systems have become employment regimes for the Irish, Jews, Italians, African Americans, and others, particularly if these groups are excluded from other opportunity structures in the city.

Election of school boards has fluctuated between representation of city-wide districts and from wards or subdistricts of the city, depending on which coalition of reformers was able to mount a successful argument. Since there is no settled wisdom on which approach to representativeness is superior, the pendulum has swung back and forth. Elsewhere, the idea of representativeness never was associated with elections. Instead, school boards were appointed by mayors or governors using any number of different representative criteria discussed above—experts who were to be trustees, members of geographic regions, representatives of constituencies who might have a vital interest in the school system (such as the teachers' union or other labor groups), or members of racial or ethnic groups. Implicit in the appointed model, however, is the idea, or certainly the reality, that the mayor or governor appointing school board members will be able to influence their actions.

Accountability (Governance Oversight)

In a democratic polity, one of the legitimating principles of any political regime is that it is accountable to external authorities to prevent abuses of power by either a majority or minority. Thus oversight can be provided in numerous ways. General-purpose governments can have jurisdiction over special-purpose governments; thus city governments under the leadership of mayors and city councils can run schools. There can be a hierarchical ordering of authority between subordinated and subordinate government units; for example, one unit of government can be dependent on another to raise money and authorize expenditures. Authority can be shared among levels of government in a federal system; for example, cooperative federalism. Separate branches of government can operate within a system of checks and balances. Populist techniques such as bond referenda or voter overrides may be employed to authorize certain kinds of expenditures.

In times where the competence or integrity of individuals responsible for an institution is questioned, extraordinary oversight measures may be employed. The courts may step in and take over operations through a special master, or a superordinate government may take over the operation. A "control board" may be created. The administrative structure may be reformed with a redistribution of authority. Finally, nontraditional authorities with special skills may be recruited to address the perceived problems.

Urban school systems have been subject to many of these provisions, both as permanent reforms and as temporary measures. In cases where they lack independent taxing authority, they are dependent on a mayor and/or common council to determine their budgets and to raise revenue. Since school systems depend also on state revenues, particularly urban ones, to fund a significant portion of their budget, they are held accountable by state officials for the performance of their pupils. In 1979, when the Chicago public schools experienced financial cutbacks and were accused of financial mismanagement, a School Finance Authority was created by the Illinois legislature to oversee the school system's budgets. A similar provision occurred in New York City in 1975, with general oversight of all city expenditures. For many decades the Seattle public school system was subject to voter approval of its annual budgets in order to comply with a state law.

Executive Leadership and Competence

One perspective on governance is that institutions run more effectively if they are staffed and led by highly competent individuals. There are many perspectives, however, on what kind of leadership skills an institution needs. The standard criterion in organizations that perform specialized or highly critical functions is whether the institution recruits and retains technically trained professionals to undertake nonroutine tasks, and particularly to lead the organization. Traditionally, the desired qualifications for prospective superintendents emphasized an advanced degree such as a doctorate, alongside relevant experience. However, when the institution is discredited, candidates with nontraditional resumes are desired. The public looks to business persons with expertise in running a large organization. They believe a lawyer may be able to negotiate the tricky relationships with employee organizations, advocacy groups, and other stakeholders. Politicians such as former governors and mayors are presumed to be expert in constituency management and charismatic leadership, qualities that may better enable them to navigate the hyper-politicized world of urban education. Here the approach to restoring legitimacy is personified. In this personalized view of leadership effectiveness, the new executive may be given an opportunity to bring in a "new team."

Those who favor executive leadership also turn to new institutional arrangements that arguably favor the exercise of strong executive authority. This may include stronger authority over budgets, greater power in recruitment and evaluation of personnel, and related prerogatives. It may also mean unconventional leadership arrangements where two leaders split responsibilities in order to make the leadership task manageable and workable.

Market Choice

More recently, market efficiency and consumer sovereignty as organizing principles have won favor. The causes of this revival of faith in markets have been discussed widely elsewhere and need no elaboration here. Generally, those who favor more of a reliance on markets point to two major benefits ostensibly associated with markets: first, greater technical efficiency in the use of resources to produce products or services (quite apart from the allocative efficiency of such a system), resulting in alleged improved student outcomes (productivity); and second, greater responsiveness to the customer or client, resulting in improved satisfaction. There are a number of variations in the forms market mechanisms can take, such as charters, vouchers, and private contracting. All rely on some combination of market exchanges, bureaucratic organization, and patterns of external accountability. For market enthusiasts, however, these differences are not so significant as the organizing principle itself—that consumers should have choices and that producers should operate within a competitive market that makes them accountable for the outcomes they produce. This approach then is very different from those discussed above.

In both Baltimore and Washington, D.C. the story of school reform has been a tale of competition among these key principles. A governance system high on representativeness was discredited in both cities, leading to external intervention. However, the reform strategies employed were dramatically different, leading to attempts to reassert mayoral leadership in Washington, D.C., while in Baltimore the mayor's role in school affairs was sharply reduced as a result of state intervention. Market reforms have proven a popular alternative in the District, while in Baltimore they have been discredited.

Challenges to Executive Leadership/Competence

Mayor Marion Barry's lack of leadership precipitated a loss of public confidence in the management of the District of Columbia municipal government. In 1995 a Republican Congress and Democratic President Bill Clinton stepped in to temporarily revoke the District's home-rule charter and appoint a financial control board (officially known as the "D.C. Financial Responsibility and Management Assistance Authority") to oversee the District's finances. Mayor Barry had acknowledged earlier that the city government structure had become unworkable. He had invited federal authorities to gradually take over various municipal responsibilities, including running the city's prison, its mental hospital, and its largest welfare programs (*Washington Post* 1995). The city recorded a record $335 million deficit in 1994 due to overspending. Wall Street creditors dropped the District's credit rating to "junk bond" status in February 1995. The General Accounting Office (GAO) declared the District "insolvent" in the same month.

To be sure, the economic recession of the early 1990s had hurt the District's economy. Yet the philosophy of Barry, and a major reason for his popularity with the city's largely poor, African-American population, was that city government should help the city's neediest residents through tough times, many of whom depend on the District government for a livelihood. Critics charged fraud and mismanagement on a grand scale. Previously, 12 District officials, including two deputy mayors, had been sent to jail, and Barry himself had been caught in a highly publicized sting operation using cocaine in 1990 (Jaffe and Sherwood 1994). Indeed, a national public opinion poll ranked Washington, D.C. as the most poorly run city in the nation.

Given the combination of fiscal exigency and poor confidence, Congressional officials (including key supporters of the District such as Rep. Eleanor Holmes Norton [Dem., District of Columbia] and Rep. Julian Dixon [Dem., Calif.]) and the president agreed that drastic measures were required to avoid total collapse. There was a price to be paid for a $146.7 million bailout loan by the federal treasury to help the District meet its bills and dodge total insolvency. It was Norton's proposal to set up a temporary financial control board, which eventually was adopted. Eventually this financial control board took over the city's personnel, procurement, technology, and property-management offices, along with the city's nine largest departments. It also assumed control of labor union negotiations. The only more drastic option under consideration and favored by "hardcore" District critics in Congress was replacing Barry with a federally appointed receiver. The law gave the control board the authority to reject budgets proposed by the mayor and the council and to impose spending plans of its own (Wise and Schneider 1995).

If poor executive leadership was viewed as a primary cause of the District's municipal problems, the federal government's external oversight appeared to remedy that problem. One of the most important developments in helping restore confidence in the District was the election of a new mayor associated with reform. The takeover legislation had created a new role of chief financial officer, who Barry acknowledged would have more "responsibility" than the mayor. The mayor's choice for the powerful post, which included authority to revamp the District's financial management, was Anthony A. Williams, a brilliant, no-nonsense graduate of Yale, Harvard Law School, and Harvard's Kennedy School of Government, who had headed community development and housing departments in Boston and St. Louis and had served as chief financial officer in the U.S. Agriculture Department in the Clinton administration. Williams's aggressive leadership soon put him at odds with Barry over spending cuts. The reputation Williams built for restoring the city's financial credibility on Capitol Hill and Wall Street, despite making enemies in the labor movement, laid the foundation for his decision to seek the mayoralship in 1998 when Barry chose not to run for another term.

Williams's election as Washington's mayor in November 1998 restored credibility to the office. He demonstrated his ability to work effectively with the members of the financial control board and thus provided a perfect role model for those concerned about the need for strong and competent executive leadership of the District. By January 2001 the District had amassed a surplus of $241 million, in sharp contrast to the low point in 1996 when its deficit had been $518.2 million. For the fourth consecutive year the District had balanced its budget, and Williams could take credit for much of this "billion dollar bounce." Officials planned to request bond-rating agencies to upgrade the city's borrowing status. Williams had accomplished this turnaround by creating a broad-based coalition that was very different from that of his predecessor. He won by a better than two-to-one margin against Republican council member Carol Schwartz, a popular veteran politician. Still, he carried all eight wards. Indeed, the mayoral race had transcended the usual racial polarization of the District's politics, with both Williams and his White opponent attracting support that cut across racial lines.

Representativeness as a Factor in School Reform

Initially, the overall crisis in District finances and the mayor's role in creating it had been the focus of the financial control board's actions. However, within a year it turned its attention to the public schools. The school system was in undeniable decline. Its performance was by nearly all accounts dismal. Student achievement was deplorably low and declining, with rising dropout rates and mounting school violence. School spending was criticized as being too high at $7,665 per pupil in 1994–95, which was 26 percent above the national average and $2,000 higher than neighboring Baltimore. Employee morale was sagging, and school admin-istrators were unable even to provide an accurate count of the number of students in the school system. Middle-income residents, both Black and White, responded to this mess by moving to suburban communities, and Washington, D.C.'s population continued to hemorrhage. Since 1970 it had lost at least 66,000 students, reducing its enrollment to 88,000. Moreover, buildings were decrepit and disgracefully maintained. Several schools were delayed in opening in the fall of 1996 due to safety concerns. From the inception of the city's financial crisis, school officials were implicated in overspending and mismanagement. For example, a GAO study alleged that District school officials diverted $50 million from required fire-code repairs to pay staff salaries. Then-Superintendent Franklin Smith admitted spending only $2 million on maintenance annually despite a $211 million fire-code problem. Also, the 11-member board was deeply divided along ideological lines, unable to agree on privatization proposals or whether to fire Smith.

The control board's first response to this perceived crisis, in the sum-mer of 1996, was to sweep away Smith's financial oversight powers amid reports of financial improprieties involving school contracts and the diver-sion of $12.3 million budgeted for school-lunch programs, as well as main-tenance funds to pay staff salaries. Further, the board consolidated his budget authority under a chief financial officer for the schools, who answered directly to Anthony Williams. Faced with further evidence of Smith's recalcitrance, the control board replaced him summarily. It also reduced the authority of the school board to advisory status and trans-ferred control of the school system to a new, nine-member panel that it ap-pointed (aka the "Emergency Transitional Board of Trustees"). The con-trol board also appointed Julius W. Beckton, a former university president, Reagan appointee, and retired three-star Army general, to replace Smith as head of the system.

One of the most sensitive issues for residents of the nation's capital is their dependence upon the federal government and their limited powers to govern themselves, especially in a city whose population has included large numbers of African Americans. The legacy of slavery and racial injustice present throughout American society inevitably is especially troubling when the federal government itself is in control. Consequently, the federal government's takeover of the city government had been unpopular, prompt-ing one minister to characterize the relationship of the new control board to the District as that "of master to servant" (Schneider and Wise 1995).

From the beginning, the control board's intervention in school affairs was under attack. For many of the District's residents, preserving their in-fluence over their public school system was even more significant than protecting a voice in municipal affairs. For example, before the federal takeover, even the mayor was given only limited control over the public schools, prompting Marion Barry to complain: "It's depressing to think what the schools are not doing, and it doesn't have anything to do with money. It has to do with leadership" (Sanchez 1990). While Eleanor Holmes Norton had played a pivotal role in supporting the District's take-over, she described the school takeover as a slap at home rule. The move also was widely opposed by community groups.

This public resistance to the control was undoubtedly a factor contrib-uting to the short, unsuccessful tenure of Julius Beckton as superintendent. He had fed the flames of resentment by reminding District residents that he worked for the control board rather than the school board. Without signif-icant support from District leaders and residents, Beckton soon found him-self mired in many of the same controversies that consumed his predeces-sor—budgetary deficits, controversy over proposed school closings, a lawsuit over unsafe school buildings, and spending improprieties. Beckton resigned 17 months into his term, citing exhaustion.

Even Tony Williams encountered resistance when he sought more influence over school policy-making. To increase his authority, he favored replacing the 11-member elected school board with one appointed by him-self. City council members argued for a smaller, elected board, citing the need for electoral representation and the principle of home rule. Williams settled on a compromise proposal from the council, brokered by the finan-cial control board, to create a hybrid nine-member board: four members selected by the mayor, four elected from newly drawn districts, and a pres-ident elected in a city-wide ballot. The referendum also provided that after four years the District council, without another referendum, would decide whether to keep the structure or move to some other governance model.

The referendum held in June 2000 was extremely close (19,643 for and 18,795 against). Unlike the mayor's election two years earlier, this one divided sharply on racial lines. Many Black voters were unhappy that under the redrawn districts, which combined wards, their voice was reduced. "They didn't give east of the [Anacostia] river [a predominantly Black area of the city] any consideration," one resident complained. An-other warned that this would be giving the mayor too much power (Blum and Cottman 2000).

Given the opposition to greater mayoral influence, it could be ex-pected that the mayor's appointments to the board would be criticized. For his appointments, he tapped people with credentials—an education professor, a facilities-management expert, and two nationally known aca-demics. Critics on the council wanted geographic representation and grass-roots leaders. "He's got the Ivy Leaguer types," complained one council member (Pierre 2000).

In short, if the federal government's intervention could be said to have restored public confidence in District government largely by embracing a new managerial approach to mayoral authority, for the District's public schools that same strategy largely failed politically.

Growing Interest in School Choice

While mayoral influence over the schools has been viewed skeptically by many, there has been a growing interest in school choice as an alternative reform strategy. The growth of charter schools in the District has been prodigious. At a time when the overall enrollment in the school system continued to fall to approximately 67,000 in the 2001 year, down 2,700 pupils from the previous one, charter-school enrollment surged to an estimated 10,819 students. This was about 16 percent of enrollments in the traditional school system. These developments have not been accidental. Congressional Republicans had repeatedly tried to use their influence over the District's public schools to install voucher schemes, without success. The federal takeover proved to be an opportunity to establish charter schools, and a special board was created to authorize such innovations. While some of the charter schools have proven controversial, particularly those created in the early years by the school board rather than the new chartering board, they have proven popular both with middle-class parents and among poor parents seeking an alternative to failing neighborhood schools.

In short, if federal oversight of the District's public schools remains controversial, ironically it has facilitated parental interest in market choice as an alternative to a school system that has resisted fundamental reforms.

STATE INTERVENTION IN BALTIMORE'S PUBLIC SCHOOLS

A Challenge to Mayoral Authority

In 1997 Maryland state officials succeeded in largely reversing a long institutional history dating back to 1898 in which Baltimore's mayors had held authority and responsibility for the city's public school system.[1] This dismantling of mayoral authority was accomplished in the name of improving educational opportunities and outcomes for the city's impoverished and largely African-American schoolchildren. A new city–state partnership was created to overhaul the school system's management and governance. The partnership was bitterly opposed not only by employees of the school system, whose resistance might be expected, but also by many segments of Baltimore's community, in an atmosphere characterized by racial conflict with civic leaders and state officials. Yet this realignment also was accomplished with the reluctant acquiescence of the city's African-American mayor, Kurt Schmoke, whose election a decade earlier had been heralded as an opportunity to reform Baltimore's beleaguered and resource-poor public school system. While he had made education reform a top priority and used his considerable leadership talents and political resources in pursuit of that goal, in the end the mayor was seen as part of the problem rather than the solution to the steady decline of the Baltimore City Public School System (BCPSS).

The Baltimore case provides an unusually vivid demonstration of the conflict between the competing principles of executive leadership and representativeness. To understand the roots of this conflict in recent decades, we must look at least as far back as the regime of William Donald Schaefer, who served as mayor from 1971 until his election as governor in 1986, and how he learned this lesson. Schaefer's public controversy with the city's first Black superintendent became an intensely racial dispute between community activists and the majority White school board, which sensitized him to the political costs of becoming too engaged in school affairs. A teachers' strike in 1974, in which Schaefer had taken a strong stand against the teachers, also became intensely racial. Thereafter, Schaefer allowed the school system's administrative, teaching, janitorial, secretarial, and paraprofessional jobs to shift to Black control, even as he maintained White control over jobs at city hall. According to Orr (1999, 58), the mayor used the school system as a source of patronage. Appointing supporters allowed him to maintain control as mayor even as the city's population turned 59 percent Black by 1980. (The school population had turned majority Black between 1960 and 1970.) Moreover, it was a strategy that removed race as a visible and volatile issue in school affairs. Schaefer focused instead on economic redevelopment of the city's downtown, paying little attention to public school issues. So evident was this that the *Baltimore 2000* report issued in 1986 criticized him and admonished future mayors to provide stronger leadership to reform BCPSS.

In this respect, Black control of jobs became a form of representativeness. If city residents could not elect their school board members, at least they could have people *like* them in positions of authority. The conduit for this employment regime was the mayor himself, working through a network of ministers and members of the city council. Whereas in Washington, D.C. elected board members fulfilled this brokering role, in Baltimore the system of patronage led directly to the mayor's office. Of course, it would be an overstatement to blame Schaefer totally for the larger demographic trends in Baltimore's population and the resulting problems this occasioned for BCPSS. Yet shifts in the racial makeup of the city were not in and of themselves problematic. Rather, it was the loss of White residents as well as the flight of middle-class residents, both White and Black, which proved problematic. Under Schaefer's watch, BCPSS became an overwhelmingly poor school system, signaling the loss of a middle-class population and tax base in the city as residents fled to suburbs. Even those who remained in the city increasingly chose to send their children to private schools. Arguably, more assertive mayoral leadership might have stemmed these trends.

By the late 1980s, however, a new breed of urban mayors such as Kurt L. Schmoke was emerging, who saw the improvement of their city's school systems as inextricably linked to the fate of their cities, and ultimately, their own success. Schmoke also seemed to represent a new generation of African-American leadership, having been raised in the city yet a graduate of Yale University and Harvard Law School, as well as a Rhodes Scholar. His election in 1987 emphasized public education and downtown redevelopment. Schmoke had argued that the school system needed dramatic improvement and promised a "renaissance in public education." Indeed, Schmoke's education-reform agenda appeared to have wide political support and had helped him defeat the incumbent African-American mayor Clarence "Du" Burns. The new mayor's reform agenda resonated with renewed attention to school reform by the Greater Baltimore Committee, whose corporate leadership had focused mainly on downtown redevelopment since the 1950s. Schmoke's election encouraged local organizations to place a higher priority on school reform (Orr 1999). Baltimoreans United in Leadership Development (BUILD), a coalition of 55 Black churches and labor organizations (including the Baltimore Teachers' Union [BTU]), had been active in antipoverty issues and in school reform since 1983. Schmoke had endorsed BUILD's agenda and embraced it as a close ally after he was elected.

Despite much initial consensus on the need for school reform among key organizations supporting Schmoke, the new mayor became embroiled in controversy on a variety of education issues. The debate over site-based management (SBM) beginning in 1988 was one example. Schmoke sided with a proposal drafted by BUILD that was heavily influenced by the BTU, an important political ally. This was in direct opposition to a plan that had been developed by the superintendent at the time, Alice Pinderhughes, whom he forced to retire. Yet Schmoke's handpicked replacement of Superintendent Pinderhughes, Richard Hunter, rejected the SBM plan the mayor had endorsed, and the mayor found himself in an increasingly awkward position as political groups drew up sides in favor of or against the plan.

In 1989 the mayor and superintendent differed openly on a proposal favored by Schmoke and endorsed by the locally influential Abell Foundation, to permit the Barclay School to adopt a curriculum used at the Calvert School, an exclusive, prestigious private school in the city. Superintendent Hunter became an object of controversy. Schmoke became embroiled in this conflict and eventually engineered Hunter's removal.

However, Schmoke's choice to replace Hunter, Walter Amprey, proved just as controversial not only among local activists and civic leaders, but among key state legislators. Delegate Pete Rawlings had commissioned a report, the *CRESAP Study* (Associated Black Charities 1992), which had recommended the phase-in of enterprise schools—another term for SBM. Amprey declared in the spring of 1994 that all city schools would henceforth be enterprise schools, with no planning or phase-in, and not surprisingly his pronouncements were accompanied by little change, as documented by a 1995 study commissioned by the legislature at Rawlings's behest. This controversy became one of the major political elements undergirding demands for reform of the governance of BCPSS. Schmoke also had suffered a severe erosion of trust owing to the controversy between 1992 and 1994 over his endorsement of the Tesseract project in 15 elementary schools, a private-management experiment by Educational Alternatives, Inc. (EAI), discussed below. Thus, despite much promise and high expectations, Schmoke encountered one controversy and setback after another in his efforts to reform BCPSS.

While Schmoke's education leadership was disappointing to many who had held high expectations for him, the responsibility for many of the problems confronting BCPSS in the 1980s and '90s could be traced to the policies of Schaefer. Indeed, by the time Schmoke mounted a campaign to create a renaissance in Baltimore's schools in the late 1980s and '90s, the political and financial base supporting the Baltimore school system had narrowed, even as its educational problems mounted.

Converging Factors Propelling State Intervention

If mayoral leadership was discredited, the question was, what authority would step in to provide a new governance solution, and what would that be? The perception that Baltimore's political power structure was incapable of reforming the school system provided the underpinning for state intervention. There were essentially three parallel tracks of events that eventually converged and led to the emergence of the partnership proposal.

POOR EDUCATIONAL PERFORMANCE IN BCPSS. First, the state's efforts to promote a new state-wide accountability system for schools inevitably shed a spotlight on the low student performance in Baltimore. In 1989 a gubernatorially appointed state "Commission on School Performance" had concluded that there was little evidence of how well Maryland students were prepared by its public school system to function in the new economy (Maryland State Department of Education 1989). The commission recommended creating an accountability system to provide these data. Most of these recommendations were adopted by Maryland's powerful State Board of Education, without the necessity of legislative action. Maryland became one of the first states to adopt high-stakes testing, accountability reporting, and a program of intervention in low-performing schools. The annual reporting of school scores in core subjects in grades 3, 5, and 8 on the Maryland School Performance Assessment Program (MSPAP) began in 1992. Beginning in 1994, the state declared low-performing schools "reconstitution-eligible" and set in place regulatory requirements to assure improvements. Not surprisingly, these state reforms were not popular in Baltimore. While the idea of taking over failing schools had been endorsed in 1991 by the Greater Baltimore Committee, the state teachers' union had seen it as a plot to privatize the schools, raising themes similar to those in the controversy over EAI. Also, MSPAP was staunchly opposed by community, civic, and political leaders in Baltimore as being likely to single-out unfairly the city's poor children. The assessments were designed to be rigorous criterion-referenced exams, linked to standards. Whether MSPAP is unfair is a matter still being debated, but the fears of Baltimore leaders proved to be accurate. While performance state-wide on the new assessments was low, a large percentage of BCPSS schools performed miserably on the state assessments.

MSPAP thus provided a policy framework within which state officials could identify large numbers of low-performing schools in BCPSS (over 80 by the late 1990s) and measure specific progress or lack thereof both in the system as a whole and in the reconstitution-eligible schools. Locally, the state's actions were viewed as a euphemism for state takeover. Teachers' unions portrayed the state's motives, and the local response to the state, as a privatization scheme and a thinly veiled attempt to shift the blame for school failure from the state to teachers and schools. However halting the support for the program initially, the powerful state board did not back off the regulation. As more and more schools were designated for possible reconstitution, however, the state began to reexamine its policy, which was premised on the idea that failing *schools* are the problem. Yet if so many schools in one school system fail to meet state standards, it is the *system* that is failing. The state was coming to the realization that attacking failure on a school-by-school basis, while it might work in many counties, was an incorrect strategy for Baltimore City.

ARGUMENTS OVER STATE AID. Second, the dispute over school spending and mismanagement led by Del. Pete Rawlings, a powerful state legislator, led to a direct confrontation with Schmoke and his local supporters. The reconstitution provision also provided a rationale for arguing that the city's school-performance deficiencies were not just a matter of providing more money, but were systemic problems. The state found this an appealing argument because it was on the defensive. Baltimore had agitated for years that it was not receiving its fair share of state aid. In 1979 then-Mayor William Schaefer had mounted an unsuccessful lawsuit, arguing that the city suffered from overburdens caused by educational needs, costs, and municipal-funding requirements. In 1986 a local civic organization had mounted an unsuccessful campaign in the state legislature. After Kurt Schmoke was elected mayor in 1987 he threatened lawsuits, and in 1992 nearly joined the American Civil Liberties Union (ACLU) in a suit. He had been dissuaded by a sympathetic Donald Schaefer, who was now governor, that a state-appointed commission could rectify the problem. However, the state legislature ignored the recommendations of the "Governor's Commission on School Funding," prompting the ACLU to file suit in 1994. The city filed its own suit in 1995.

However, the aggressive posture of the city in its negotiations with the state legislature was risky, because it allowed state officials to point to the poor management of the school system as the cause of its financial problems and to argue that additional state aid would be wasted. An important factor in highlighting the issue of managerial incompetence was the leadership of Del. Rawlings in the Maryland General Assembly. Rawlings, who represents a Black district in the city, chairs the powerful Appropriations Committee in the Maryland House of Delegates. He forged an alliance with another key legislator, Senator Barbara Hoffman, and with State Superintendent Nancy Grasmick. Working together in sponsorship of a study (MGT of America 1995), they placed the spotlight on failure to implement managerial reforms in the school system recommended in the *CRESAP Study*. The state legislature then withheld state aid pending improvements (Shatzkin and Bowler 1995). The lack of progress led Rawlings to support state intervention and to face down Black legislators in Baltimore who wished to protect the city from the state's demands for reform.

DISABILITY LAWSUIT. State education officials also lost confidence in the fiscal management of the city school system. These concerns arose out of a long and bitterly contested lawsuit (*Vaughn G., et al. v. Amprey, et al.*) brought against BCPSS in 1984 by a disability-rights organization, the Maryland Disability Law Center. The plaintiffs argued that special-education students were not receiving services to which they were entitled under state and federal laws. The federal court ordered protections for special-education children and removed operating authority for these programs from BCPSS, placing the programs under direct supervision of the court. The inability of the school system to develop an adequate management system, or to spend special-education dollars effectively, proved to be a long-term problem and contributed to the perception that BCPSS was a dysfunctional bureaucracy. Initially, the state threatened to withhold $43 million in state and federal special-education funds. Later, Nancy Grasmick, the state superintendent, decided to join the plaintiffs in successfully requesting that a court-appointed oversight team be permitted to review Baltimore Superintendent Walter Amprey's appointments above the rank of teacher. This action led to sharply deteriorating relationships between the two parties, and the inability to resolve the legal dispute to the satisfaction of plaintiffs and the state contributed directly to the state's decision to expand its external oversight of BCPSS.

These converging forces created a political climate in 1997 allowing state officials to intervene to reform the governance structure of the city school system. An out-of-court consent decree (Thompson and Siegel 1996) and subsequent legislative enactment, which were described as a city–state "partnership," had three basic components: an overhaul of the governance structure; a dramatic restructuring of BCPSS's management; and additional state funds in exchange for continuing oversight by the state.[2] A new nine-member board of commissioners was appointed jointly by the mayor and governor, based on a nominating slate provided by the State Board of Education. The kinds of affiliations and expertise required for these members were enumerated. The new board was given authority to hire a chief executive officer (CEO). The CEO, subject to board approval, appoints a chief academic officer, responsible for system-wide curriculum and instruction, and a chief financial officer. Both these officers also have contracts that are contingent upon effective performance of their duties. Further, the state agreed to provide $230 million in additional state aid over a five-year period plus additional monies for school construction. The monies were to be targeted on improving educational performance for schools.

Market Reform

Unlike Washington, D.C., Baltimore experimented with one version of market reform earlier than many cities. That experiment was deemed a failure, and it has colored all subsequent discussion of this alternative. In 1992 Baltimore contracted with Education Alternatives, Inc. (EAI) to operate nine elementary schools for five years. EAI was at that time the largest company of its kind. The move reflected the frustration of Mayor Schmoke with efforts to reform his city's public school system after five years of efforts, and he had the support of Superintendent Amprey. The contract had been urged by Robert Embry, president of the influential Abell Foundation and former head of the State Board of Education. It was backed by the Greater Baltimore Committee and the *Baltimore Sun*. The teachers' union was impressed by the firm's programs in Minnesota and Miami, Florida.

While the story of the experiment and the reasons for its failure are complicated, the contributing causes were both educational and political. Initially, the program was well-received by parents, teachers, and students. The experiment encountered considerable opposition from community leaders and ministerial leaders, who spoke against handing education over to a firm whose major motive was making a profit. These organizations were not only philosophically opposed, but they were concerned about loss of jobs and Black racial dominance of BCPSS. The BTU also had a change of heart after initially supporting the experiment.

The firm reluctantly agreed to launch its experiment without a planning period, owing to pressure from the mayor. There were no accountability and performance standards in the contract. Community opponents turned to the city council, where the project received withering criticism, particularly from mayoral aspirant Mary Pat Clarke, propelled by BTU protests against Amprey's plans to expand the EAI contract. In the end, EAI was done in by a test-score controversy in which EAI was accused by the *Sun* of overstating test-score gains. The following year an external evaluation found that there were no achievement gains at the EAI schools compared to counterparts elsewhere in the city. The contract was not renewed.

Earlier efforts to introduce elements of even modest privatization encountered fierce opposition in Baltimore, such as the Barclay Public School controversy mentioned earlier. Efforts by Superintendent Amprey to introduce private contracting at low-performing schools also proved unsuccessful. Still, contracting out low-performing schools by the state remains an issue. The state board's decision to reconstitute several schools in 2000 and turn them over to the Edison Corporation was opposed by many in the community. The following year, however, there was less opposition to the state board's decision to permit the Baltimore city schools to reconstitute a failing school with a private contractor. Nonetheless, school choice is not viewed as a strong alternative path to reform in Baltimore.

CONCLUSION

The two cases analyzed in this chapter illustrate the complexity of external intervention strategies for reforming urban school systems. I have interpreted the events in both cities as the product of competing governance values and the interests that attach themselves to disputes over values. Essentially, the American political culture is rather unsettled about which of these values should have priority—a confusion complicated by the fact that any system of school governance is likely to honor some combination of them. We have seen how representativeness remains a cherished value in both cities, strongly identified with African-American control. Throughout the 1970s and '80s representativeness was closely associated with mayoral leadership. But as the school-reform movement took hold this alliance became discredited, and both mayoral leadership and perceived excess representativeness (either through elected school boards or descriptively representative employees) fell out of fashion. External oversight brought with it a concern for restoring competence to school governance and management. In Washington, D.C. this brought the heavy hand of federal power as a temporary arrangement in both the city's municipal government as well as its public schools. When it comes to education, however, Washingtonians remain deeply divided over handing more authority over to the city's chief executive, jealously guarding their prerogatives to have an elected school board. The current system is a compromise.

In Baltimore, external oversight led to a clearer rejection of the old system of representativeness. The city–state partnership limits the mayoral role to having a voice in the appointment of school board members, who are chosen as much for their competence as their representativeness. The partnership also created a politically independent management system strongly influenced by business values of efficiency.

What improvements have resulted from these externally induced reforms?[3] There are at least four criteria one might use to answer that question. One is whether the system has led to greater stability in the executive leadership of the school systems. Superintendent turnover has been a major problem in most cities, and both Baltimore and Washington, D.C. had been plagued by leadership turnover and controversy in the years prior to the reforms. In both cities, however, this problem has continued after the external intervention. Baltimore has now its third superintendent since 1997. Carmen Russo was appointed in 2000 after an interim superintendent, Robert Schiller, and a short tenure by Robert Booker. In the District, Julius Beckton's brief term was succeeded by Arlene Ackerman, and more recently by Paul Vance. At the moment both Russo and Vance appear to enjoy broad support, but the political climate surrounding both is subject to change.

Another criterion is whether the financial management of the system has improved, inasmuch as this was an issue prompting federal and state intervention. Both school systems have continued to be plagued by financial mismanagement. In Baltimore, contract scandals involving top officials contributed to Booker's resignation. In the District, Superintendent Vance has been embarrassed by surprising cost overruns, which were criticized by the mayor and city council (Strauss 2001).

A third criterion to judge the interventions' success is whether the reforms have broadened public support for the school systems. There is little evidence of this in Washington, despite respect for Vance's leadership. The school system continues to lose enrollments, and the mayor's involvement has not yet galvanized renewed civic and political support for the schools. In Baltimore, the city's long-standing funding disputes with the state legislature suggest the limits of political support for redressing historic funding inequities facing the city's school system. The system has been in repeated disputes with the state since the partnership began over whether the state has delivered on its funding promises.[4] In addition, the mayor's disengagement from the schools, as provided for in the partnership agreement, may prove to be an impediment, although the newly constituted Board of School Commissioners enjoys widespread respect and may therefore compensate for mayoral involvement. The school system recently was able to attract $8 million in local foundation support and $12 million from other foundations to fund improvements in the city's high schools.

Finally, the bottom line usually asked in judging school reforms is whether student achievement is rising. In Baltimore, elementary test scores have risen for several years consecutively, leading to favorable media comment and growing public confidence (Bowie and Niedowski 2001). The scores still remain lowest among Maryland's 24 jurisdictions, but the school system has been closing the gap. Middle and high school achievement remains largely unchanged. In the District, despite some modest improvements in tests cores under Ackerman's superintendency, there has been little change since, and SAT scores actually have fallen.

When these four criteria of effectiveness are considered together, then, they do not offer a picture of dramatic progress. Institutional reforms do not often lend themselves to quick turnarounds, despite the expectations they evoke. The governance and management reforms discussed here have not reversed many of the impediments to fundamental reform of urban schools, such racial and class interests limiting support for reform, poor neighborhoods and public services, workplace inequality, a limited supply of qualified teachers and administrators for urban schools, the challenges of motivating students from impoverished backgrounds, and the difficulties of engaging parents to support their children's education.

Perhaps the major unanswered question is whether choice will supplant the reigning principles that have organized school governance for nearly a century. This seems unlikely in Baltimore for the near future. In Washington, D.C. market reform has slipped in through the back door in the form of charter schools and continues to provide an antidote for frustrated parents.

NOTES

1. A more complete analysis of the Baltimore case, with extensive reference citations, can be found in Cibulka (2003).

2. In addition, certain legal issues were resolved relating to the lawsuits. Court supervision of the special-education programs of BCPSS was reduced. Continuation of the court monitor's function was left contingent on further negotiation, depending on school system progress. However, other provisions of the prior court orders in *Vaughn G., et al. v. Amprey, et al.* remained intact.

3. Findings of a state-mandated evaluation of Baltimore's city–state partnership conducted by WESTAT can be found at <http://www.bcps.k12.md.us/admin/westat/index.html>.

4. In April 2002 the state legislature approved a new funding proposal based on the recommendations of a state Commission on Education Finance, Equity, and Excellence (known as the "Thornton Commission," because it was led by former Prince George's County School Board Chairman Alvin Thornton). The new plan would raise state aid to school districts over a six-year period by $1.3 billion, or 35 percent. The commission sought to eliminate disparities between rich and poor school districts, but its proposal was changed to accommodate complaints from Montgomery County officials, who claimed that despite being the state's wealthiest jurisdiction, it had large numbers of poor and limited-English-speaking children. Because the legislative action was a compromise, it was unclear how much Baltimore City and other needy jurisdictions would actually benefit from this new formula (see Montgomery 2002).

◨   ◨   ◨

CHAPTER NINE

The Role of Sanctions for Improving Persistently Low-Performing Urban Schools

early findings of policy effects on
teacher motivation in
the Maryland accountability system

HEINRICH MINTROP

ACCOUNTABILITY SYSTEMS DIFFER widely with respect to measurements (i.e., standards, performance assessments, indicators), expectations (i.e., top performance benchmarks, average performance, growth increments), incentives (i.e., rewards and sanctions, criteria for entry into and exit from probation), and interventions (i.e., oversight, regulation, assistance). For example, some accountability systems combine quantitative with qualitative performance measures and indicators, such as the city of San Francisco used to do (Goldstein, Kelemen, and Koski 1998), some are purely quantitative. Some have very high goals, such as in Virginia (Portner 1999), some peg their expectations to average student performance, such as in Texas (Sandham 2000). Some systems are tough on sanctions, such as in the city of Chicago (Chicago Public Schools 1997; Wong et al. 1997), while others strongly emphasize support for teachers, such as in New York (Ascher, Ikeda, and Fruchter 1997). Some identify rock-bottom performers as probationary schools, such as in Maryland, while others target growth deficits on all performance levels, such as in Kentucky (Guskey 1994; Petrosko 1996).

These policy-design differences will slant educators' responses to accountability and the imposition of sanctions (Elmore, Abelmann, and

Fuhrman 1996). Thus, it is necessary to be specific about design features that structure the accountability environment for educators. The Maryland accountability system that is examined in this chapter is classified as follows: the state provides a broad framework that lays out learning standards. The weighty core of the assessment system for elementary and middle schools is an intricate performance-based test, the Maryland State Performance Assessment Program (MSPAP), that challenges traditional teachers to change their instruction towards increased writing, group work, and problem-solving activities. Performance goals are high. The state proclaimed a rate of 70 percent of a school's student body passing the MSPAP with "satisfactory." Acceptable performance benchmarks have been attained by only the best schools in the state.

The state identifies schools as "reconstitution-eligible" (RE) (the term Maryland uses for probation) that are performing in the bottom range and that have declined in previous years (Maryland State Department of Education 1997). Seven years after the inception of probation, the state has thus identified about a hundred schools, most of them located in the state's largest city, Baltimore. The repercussions of this situation for the Baltimore City school district are examined by James Cibulka in chapter 8 of this volume. In 1998 the mean percentages of students passing the MSPAP with satisfactory performance in schools identified as RE until 1998 are 8.9 percent in math and 8.7 percent in reading among RE elementary schools, and 10.9 percent in math and 7.6 percent in reading among RE middle schools. To date, only one school has exited the system successfully, and only three schools were actually taken over by the state and passed on to private vendors, the ultimate sanction so far. In shorthand, we classify the Maryland case as a design with *high goals, low stakes, and hard cases.*

High-stakes accountability systems are rarely pure incentive designs in reality. Particularly in dealing with persistently low-performing schools, incentives are often imposed in conjunction with process controls and compensatory funding. For example, in Maryland, state or local governments grant a limited amount of additional funding and mandate schools on probation to submit a school-improvement plan. At the same time, the state refrained from extensive assistance features akin to the original Kentucky "Distinguished Educator" program installed by the state for its "schools in decline." State monitors are part of the Maryland policy design, but their role is restricted to being the "eyes and ears" of the State Department of Education. Capacity-building measures are left to districts. Districts have mandated schools to participate in specified professional development, to follow an approved curriculum, to implement new instructional programs, and to accept oversight by state or local monitors. Lately, some districts have begun to mandate schools to contract the services of comprehensive school-reform models.

Thus, when we interpret educators' responses to accountability, two limitations obtain. First, identified patterns in the data have to be understood in the context of a specific accountability system and cannot be generalized to accountability in general. Second, we cannot study the effect of the "incentive" of probation in isolation from all the other levers external agencies simultaneously use to encourage and structure performance behavior at school sites. To take the Maryland example, the actual imposition of sanctions may pale in comparison to all the process controls put in place that are justified by the school's status.

This chapter concentrates on educators as individual actors. It explores how teachers and administrators respond to the imposition of probation on their schools. Organizational responses of schools to probation (e.g., internal dynamics of faculties, principal leadership, selected strategies, external supports, performance outcomes) are not considered here. Data on organizational responses are in the process of analysis. The focus on educators' individual-performance motivation is warranted by the centrality of incentives and sanctions in high-stakes accountability systems. By their very nature, such systems rely on the motivational effect of incentives and sanctions. One could argue that for persistently low-performing schools, the connection between sanctions and workers' motivation is the linchpin of an effective accountability design. Without this connection, without a surge in individual educators' willingness to engage in school improvement as a result of sanctions, accountability systems seriously atrophy.

THE CENTRALITY OF INCENTIVES AND SANCTIONS IN HIGH-STAKES ACCOUNTABILITY SYSTEMS

In a purely economistic conception of high-stakes accountability policies, the imposition of sanctions is seen as a means to increase the performance motivation of putatively under-performing employees. High-stakes accountability, in this conception, is resource-neutral; that is, improvements occur as a result of changed orientations and dispositions towards work effort. According to Hanushek et al. (1994), past school-reform attempts have not improved student performance and have encouraged waste of human and financial resources, because schools and educators lacked clear performance incentives. A good incentive system is tightly linked to student performance. It specifies goals and leaves it up to educators to decide how to achieve them so that schools can pursue solutions that best fit their unique needs. Since the link between resources and inputs on the one hand and student outputs on the other is weak and not clearly understood, a good incentive system balances "flexibility in the means of education" with "crystalline clarity regarding the desired ends" (Hanushek et al. 1994, 88). "Performance incentive systems are intended to attract and retain the best teachers and administrators and to focus their energies and abilities" (p. 90) on student learning. Performance categories are mainly calculated on the basis of student-achievement tests. High performance triggers a reward and low performance a penalty.

Not all conceptions of high-stakes accountability are as agnostic about process inputs as the above-cited economists' approach. O'Day and Smith, reflecting on the use of systemic reform policies to address educational inequalities, postulate a combination of outcome-based performance measurements with opportunity-to-learn or input standards when evaluating a school's performance. But in their conception as well, incentives and sanctions are hypothesized to do a good part of the job. According to O'Day and Smith, when low performers prove nonreceptive to performance information, intensity of sanctions should increase. For under-performing schools on probation that fail to undertake self-correcting actions, reconstitution (i.e., the reconfiguration of the whole-school organization by means of zero-based staffing or takeover) may be imposed. "*High stakes* in theory will increase motivation and performance" (O'Day and Smith 1993, 286 [italics in original]). While high-stakes accountability systems have been proliferating in many states as a means to effect a productivity boost in schools state-wide, they are particularly popular in urban systems as a means to address the highly publicized issue of "failing schools" (Price 1997; Riley 1997). Lately, the federal government as well has announced plans to attach accountability provisions to its redistributive Title I program. Not surprisingly, a large number of schools on probation in our study are urban schools.

Policies intended to induce change are designed with a specific theory of failure and a theory of action in mind. That is, they make often implicit assumptions about their target problem and anticipate a way that policy recipients will change their behavior. Redistributive policies (Peterson, Rabe, and Wong 1991) were guided by the assumption that under-performance was substantively a result of under-resourced learning environments; a high frequency of low-performing students in particular schools was evidence for the schools' needs for additional resources. Incentive policies, on the other hand, place the burden of responsibility for poor performance on the employees' work effort. Under-performance becomes associated with failing teachers and administrators. In its pure form, incentive policies direct new funds in the form of rewards to schools only *after* they have already turned the corner and have posted improvements. Without this lag time, poor performance would be rewarded and the effect of incentives—positive as well as negative ones—would be lost. In theory, an organization in free-fall that was unable to halt declining test scores would be left alone until it crashes. In a pure incentive scheme, sanctions would intensify to a point at which site employees finally muster the energy to enact improvement strategies.

Thus, high-stakes accountability systems largely bank on the power of incentives to motivate. In practice, districts and states tend to intervene much earlier with the infusion of new funds and technical assistance; and the recent re-emphasis on capacity-building among educational scholars and policy-makers (Massell 1998) may echo, or signal, a turning away from pure incentive policies. Nevertheless, the effectiveness of incentive policies hinges upon their motivational force in raising educators' work performance without large new infusions of resources and capacity-building measures. Is this trust in the motivational force of incentive policies warranted?

MODELS OF PERFORMANCE MOTIVATION

In the field of educational research, little work has been done on the effect of sanctions on school performance. Firestone and Pennel's (1993) review of the literature on incentives, teacher motivation, and job performance highlights the connection among performance incentives, commitment, and job design. The issue of sanctions is touched upon very sparingly. Likewise, the literature on high-involvement management (Mohrman, Lawler, and Mohrman 1992; Mohrman, Mohrman, and Odden 1996) looks at teacher work motivation in relationship to workplace structures and positive rewards for high performance. The latter is true as well for the literature on merit pay as performance incentive for teachers (Conley and Odden 1995). The role of sanctions is largely left unexamined. An exception in this regard is Malen (1999).

Although sanctions may cause discomfort and diminish satisfaction, they may not necessarily translate into diminished job performance. Studies in the tradition of behaviorist industrial psychology have not found a clear relationship between job satisfaction and job performance (Lawler 1973, 82). While job satisfaction is seen as being related to commitment expressed in phenomena such as turnover and absenteeism, performance motivation is often conceptualized in relationship to a sense of efficacy (Ashton and Webb 1986), control (Weiner 1986), clear goal-setting (Locke 1968), and rewards (Lawler 1973). These varied though related sources of motivation (Rowan, Chiang, and Miller 1997) are assumed to increase performance. In the classical behaviorist formulation (Vroom, cited in Lawler [1973]), the combination of clear goals (i.e., measured growth targets), rewards for achievement, and penalties for failure affects work performance positively if the employees see their work as having strong instrumentality towards achieving rewards and averting penalties and if expectancy and valence of rewards are high. In other words, if teachers believe that the task of meeting external performance targets is in their control and they have the requisite competence for its execution, if they see a connection between individual effort and expected reward, if they deem the attainment of the reward likely, and if they value the expected reward itself or the aversion of penalties, the motivational model underlying high-stakes accountability systems would predict teachers to increase their performance. Thus, teachers strive for goals that are clear, specific, worthwhile, and attainable (Kelley and Protsik 1997).

Kelley and Protsik use these models to explain teachers' responses to the Kentucky accountability system and its incentive program, which included pay awards for successful schools and the threat of drastic sanctions for persistently failing schools. In their sample of six schools that successfully improved performance, they found evidence for the motivating influence of the Kentucky incentives. Interviewed teachers saw their school's target score on the performance-based test—the Kentucky Instructional Results Information System (KIRIS)—as a clear goal and with attainment within their control (Kelley and Protsik 1997, 486). However, lack of control over student achievement over time was a particularly salient issue in schools with high student mobility. Teachers said they had changed their practice so that test and instructional formats would better match. Not surprisingly perhaps, teachers in these award-winning schools felt able and competent to achieve their goal. Interestingly, despite their schools' performance success, they were more motivated by fear of sanctions than reception of monetary rewards.

In their comparison of the high-stakes Maryland accountability system with the low-stakes Maine accountability system, Firestone and colleagues (1997) found a similar fear of sanctions among Maryland educators, even through probation and reconstitution were distant threats for study participants. None of these studies were conducted in schools that have already encountered sanctions. For those schools, however, fear of the unknown has transmuted into a known quality.

Behaviorist models of work motivation have been criticized as being inadequate for educators. Shamir, in an insightful theoretical synthesis of research on motivation, criticizes motivation theories that view the individual as a "rational maximizer of personal utility" (Shamir 1991, 406) on the grounds that these theories are not sensitive to the situation of educators at schools. In Shamir's view, expectancy and goal-setting models of motivation presuppose "strong situations," namely, situations structured by clear and specific goals, reward expectancies, and clearly identifiable relationships among increased effort, performance, and reward. In "weak situations" where rewards are less abundant, where there is less tendency to differentiate among individuals on the basis of work performance because of collective orientations, or where links between performance and rewards are more difficult to construct, "point of action" theories of motivation, as he calls them, are less adequate. These models of motivation are useful in predicting discrete task behavior, but they are less powerful in explaining a "diffuse and open-ended concept of commitment" (Shamir 1991, 408) that refers to a "shifting number and range of rather ill-delineated performances rather than to ironclad and numerically constant behaviors having clearly defined parameters that everyone knows" (p. 408).

For educators, a model of motivation based on the idea of "self-concept" and the moral and expressive side of human nature might be more appropriate. Central to Shamir's model is the idea that work instills "meaning" into individuals as it "connects the individual to the concerns that transcend his own limited personal existence" (1991, 409). Individuals are motivated to maintain and enhance their self-esteem and self-worth. Self-worth is tied to a sense of virtue and moral worth and is grounded in norms, values, and moral obligations concerning conduct. Much work conduct, according to Shamir, is explained by internal standards and self-evaluative action. Self-concept is not always related to clear expectations, immediate and specific goals, and rewards received. Shamir's model is echoed in studies that ascertain the importance of intrinsic motivation and psychic rewards for teachers' work motivation (Johnson 1990; Lortie 1975), as well as in the literature on teacher burnout in urban schools (Le-Compte and Dworkin 1991).

Our research does not aim at testing the veracity of various models of teachers' work motivation. Rather, the models serve to formulate categories that guide instrument development and data analysis. In the interviews, we searched for clues indicating both reward-calculus and needs-expression models of motivation. The categories, introduced in the findings section, help us explore our central question: How does the imposition of probation influence the performance motivation of teachers working in schools on probation? In exploring this question, we address a cardinal claim of incentive policies—namely, that the imposition of sanctions will make educators at school sites pro-active participants in school improvement, steered by outcomes, acting autonomously in search for the means.

THE DATA

Findings for this chapter are derived from case studies of seven schools in two urban districts. Each case database consists of a minimum of 21 formal, semi-structured interviews and many more informal ones, though not all interviews speak to the issue of performance motivation. The protocol for 105 interviews explicitly addressed performance motivation. Each school was visited numerous times over a two-year period. At least four meetings at each school were formally observed, though the researchers participated in a number of additional meetings as they pursued their ethnographic inquiry at the sites. A minimum of six lessons at each site were observed and subsequently debriefed with the teachers. The quantitative data component, a survey questionnaire, is not analyzed here. In addition, we interviewed district officials who were responsible for programs in schools on probation, as well as state officials and monitors. All interviews were transcribed, entered into a qualitative database manager (NUDIST), and coded. While interpretation of the data was pre-structured by theoretical hypotheses, some patterns and categories emerged directly from the data.

The seven urban schools were selected according to a number of criteria, such as school type, duration in the program, district, educational load, and performance history. Four of the schools are middle schools, three are elementary schools. Four are located in district A, a large urban school district, three in district B, a suburban district with strongly urban characteristics. Two of the schools, one elementary and one middle school, are probation veterans. They were identified in 1993 soon after the policy was enacted. Four of the schools were newly identified when the study began in 1998. One middle school was added to the selection in 1999 as a school with a decidedly positive performance record. With the exception of the latter, percentages of free- and reduced-lunch-meal recipients range from 50 percent to 100 percent. The racial composition of student bodies is at least 90 percent African American in all schools. Interviews conducted in the four newly identified schools reflect educators' incipient experience with probation.

TEACHERS' RESPONSES

The data presented in this section have to do with teachers as individuals. To understand their reactions to probation, we need to analyze at first the strength of the signal of probation. Only when teachers are aware of the probationary status of their school and when they know what this status entails will they be moved to act. Secondly, we want to know if probation induces in teachers the willingness to act on their own; that is, to increase performance as a self-directed activity. Self-directedness may be indicated by teachers telling us in the interviews that they adjusted their expectation of students', or their own, performance to the high expectations of the accountability agency, work harder generally, work at learning new skills, or changed instructional practices in accordance with performance assessments (in the case of Maryland with performance-based student-learning assessments).

To recapitulate briefly, performance motivation can be framed as a function of the probability with which teachers expect to meet the performance goals of the accountability agency, the value teachers place on reaching performance rewards (here primarily increasing test scores and averting sanctions and stigma), and finally teachers' sense of their own role in influencing performance outcomes. Alternatively, performance motivation could be found in the personal meaning teachers attach to their work, the internalized standards with which they judge themselves that are derived from these meanings, and the congruence of these standards with the external criteria of the accountability agency. Teachers according to this model not only gauge the value of potential rewards based on these standards, but also the fairness of external assessment criteria and the worthiness of the goals.

Presumably, if teachers are aware of probation and know what it entails, if they deem the accountability criteria with which they are judged as fair, if they value external student achievement and behavior goals and the reward of exiting probationary status highly, either extrinsically or intrinsically, and if they see themselves as central actors and in substantial control in meeting performance goals, then one could expect the signal of probation to trigger self-directed activities on the part of teachers, at least within the realm of teachers' autonomous classroom space. The following section summarizes the patterns that were identified in the analysis of interviews. The summary presented here will be brief. The long version of this analysis can be found in the technical report.

Awareness

Generally speaking, the level of awareness of RE varies among teachers in the seven schools. Two schools in our case-study selection had been on probation for three years at the time of data collection. In these two schools, particularly in the larger middle school, we found quite a number of teachers who were not aware at all of the policy, or knew very little about it. But even for more veteran teachers, RE did not feature highly on their attention screen. In newly identified schools, probation is initially of high concern for teachers, but the effect wears off rapidly when public attention wanes and the feared repercussions, due to lack of parental attention and indifference among colleagues outside of the school, seem manageable. In district A, half of all schools carry the RE label. Over the years, teachers have learned to live with it. In district B, "being RE" is still a noticeable badge of poor performance and "getting off the list" is more strongly desired. Because of high teacher turnover, large numbers of new teachers entering the school subsequent to identification are either not at all or only vaguely aware of what it means to be in an RE school, or, if they are aware, they feel they do not own the problem, since they were not present during the decline. For most new hires we interviewed, RE did not figure into their decision to accept a position at the school.

Threat

In none of our interviews did teachers indicate that they feel threatened by the status of RE. Three reasons are given, and one reason can be inferred. First, in times of teacher shortage, a job at another school can always be found: "There is always a job for a good teacher." Second, teachers at RE schools for the most part feel they are indispensable in the difficult task of educating socially challenging students. Many feel they have a special competence in surviving and making the best of the difficult socioeconomic environment of their students. Some teachers, third, would welcome state takeover, because that would free them from the inadequacies of the local district administration. State takeover would bring in another force that would have to take responsibility for the affairs of the school. Last, for many teachers, ties to the specific school are weak, and many respondents admitted in the interviews of considering moving or transferring elsewhere, not necessarily due to the school's RE status but more to immediate adversities at the site or for personal reasons. The hope is expressed that RE status is not meant to be punitive. Particularly in district B, with few schools on probation, RE is associated with more funds, personnel, and resources—said to be sorely needed for the school to be successful.

Fairness

Interviewed teachers in the seven schools hold contradictory views on the accountability system. Being held accountable for performance is widely accepted. It is the right of the state to utilize an external test to measure school performance, and since the state chose to select these specific tests, it behooves teachers to pay attention to them. But, at the same time, the accountability system as presently designed and carried out is seen as unfair to teachers in schools that educate such a large number of challenging students. Knowing where one stands vis-à-vis the rest of the state is seen as a useful feature, but increasing test scores to the high levels demanded by the state is a low priority for many respondents, though all teachers express the desire to help increase the test scores of their school. The diagnostic function of the tests is seen as valid, but goals are seen as unrealistically ambitious. Most teachers in these troubled schools reject the view that the low test scores are a reflection on their own performance, though the school's shortcomings in student performance are, at times shamefully, acknowledged. Some acknowledge that reconstitution was a wake-up call well-deserved by the district and the school. Thus the rightfulness and authority of the accountability system are accepted on general principle, while their applicability is refuted for the specific case due to the extraordinary social challenges of the student population.

Conflicting Goals

MSPAP, the state's performance-based assessment tool and centerpiece of the accountability system for elementary and middle schools, is accepted as a fact. Many teachers describe how the MSPAP has become the overwhelming preoccupation of the school, though less so in nontesting grades. A smaller number of teachers equate the test with good teaching; that is, the performance-based activities on the test reflect the kind of classroom they aspire to, prominently featuring teamwork and higher-order thinking skills. But at the same time, many informants point to a lack of fit between the test format and the needs of their students, which presumably lie in the area of basic skill development and often range far below the grade level the test is geared to. Teachers repeatedly bemoan that the MSPAP is "too hard" for their students, leaving both students and teachers at a loss as to what to do. None of the teachers report that as a result of MSPAP they reevaluated or upgraded their own expectations of students.

Goal conflicts are common and are produced by the difficult task of balancing perceived student-learning needs with tests that emphasize both basic skills (MFT [Maryland Functional Tests], CTBS) and higher-order thinking and social skills (MSPAP)—the latter on a highly ambitious achievement level. In middle schools, one reported way of coping with the two distinct test formats is an emphasis on basic skills in the fall when the MFT is given, and on performance-based tasks in the spring when the MSPAP is given.

Expectation of Success

Most of our interview partners in the seven schools are avowed optimists when asked to voice their expectation of the school's success in either increasing test scores or exiting probation. But this optimism is laced with a pessimistic undertone. Overall, interviewed teachers are skeptical as to reaching the external quantitative-performance goals but find growth in small increments possible, though a number of them are unclear whether these envisioned increments would "get them off the list." For the few teachers who actually muse in their interview about this topic, ways to get off the list seem elusive. At the time the interviews were conducted, no school had ever exited probation. Yet, despite skepticism, optimism is the only option in this situation for many. In many instances this optimism is based on the teacher's strong "belief" in a positive outcome. A less faith-based and more reasoned optimism links performance hopes for improvements to the new funds RE schools receive, new personnel the school has on board, new instructional programs the districts have acquired, and new technology that has been installed. In schools that experienced test-score increases in years prior to the decline that led to probation, some teachers voice confidence that past performance may be repeated.

Optimism is only infrequently linked to classroom conditions. A minority of teachers state that they simply work harder, and in a few instances teachers point to the visibly beneficial effects of new programs in their classrooms (perhaps because of the timing of the interviews, evaluation of these new initiatives could not have been expected at this time). It seems safe to say, however, that for the majority of informants, expectations of success tend to be linked to classroom-external events and conditions beyond their control. Changes in their own classrooms that instill optimism revolve around strategies to "inundate students with MSPAP."

Control

This orientation towards the external environment reappears when teachers are asked to explain the low performance of their school. The *school's* low scores are almost always translated into low *student* performance, which, in the view of our interview partners, is mostly due to the challenging living circumstances of the students: poverty, unstable families, drugs, and the like. Parents are often mentioned as not being constructive participants in their children's education. In addition, high student mobility, the failure of feeder schools in the case of middle schools, deteriorating neighborhoods, teacher turnover, and, last, the large number of inexperienced teachers in the school are cited as causes for low performance. In light of numerous external causes, it is especially irritating for teachers that, in elementary and middle school, teachers alone carry the burden of accountability, since they are the only ones for whom the tests are high-stakes. Thus in their eyes, school accountability is not a shared responsibility among all participants of the educational process. This diminishes the fairness of the accountability system, as it exposes teachers to the socially irresponsible behavior of families without recourse—for example, when the school "desperately" tries to compel parents to send their children to school on MSPAP days in order to avoid the zero-point penalty for no-shows.

A number of teachers and administrators find themselves at a loss to explain what leads to the fluctuations in test scores that many schools experienced in the past. While they believe that the school continuously worked hard, they do not see this reflected in the test scores. As a result, they either discount the reliability of the test or express helplessness as to what strategies might have the desired effects on the scores. Rather than being in control of the situation, they become exposed to the vagaries of a system whose fairness they doubt.

Two coping strategies were observed in response to this situation. Some teachers, mainly senior teachers, insist on doing what has worked for them regardless of the talk of "failure." They have learned to control students, compel them to work consistently, and survive the stress involved in teaching these challenging students. These are teachers who affirm that politicians and administrators are too far removed from the classroom and the social milieu of their students to know what works. They dare "the state to come in and show us how to do it better." Another group of teachers, however, is less confident. Although doubting the fairness of the probation verdict, they concede that something has to be done to improve the low performance of their *students* and they express willingness to try out strategies, programs, and models that have proven effective in other schools. Probation increases their willingness to give up classroom autonomy and do what they are told will work. The rationale goes that if the state knows that the school is failing, why don't "they" tell the school how to do it better, why don't "they" give the school the model of a successful school.

In most respondents' eyes, teachers are already doing "the best they can." Most interview partners see themselves as highly involved and committed to the school's success, though a number of them, particularly in the newly identified schools in district B, concede that after the school received RE status, things tightened up. "Getting off the list" is the avowed goal of all respondents, but many teachers' own contribution in reaching this goal remains opaque.

Internal Standards

The tendency of our interview partners to externalize both causes and remedies for low performance *as defined by the accountability system* does not mean, however, that they deflect all criticism or deny all blemish as far as their teaching is concerned. Many of them judge themselves, quite conscientiously at times, but the criteria used are different from the ones promulgated by the accountability agency, notwithstanding the ground-swell of institutional legitimacy and authority on which the state can count in general principle. The most frequently mentioned *raison d'etre* for the teacher at school is the progress he or she is able to induce in individual students. The most frequent reward cited is the occasional appreciation he or she is accorded by these students. This orientation towards the individual student is coupled with a sense of mission for the community. Many of the interviewed teachers are African American and feel a sense of affiliation with the African-American communities that surround the selected RE schools. Some interview partners say they chose to dedicate them-selves to this particularly needy group of at-risk students. Yet they are not quite sure how long they will stay, especially if they are novices, whereas the more seasoned teachers voice a sense of pride in having found a way to master this difficult and challenging teaching assignment.

Common to many of these teachers is an emphasis on citizenship and basic skills—said to be needed by students to secure later employment. Basic skills and disciplined conduct substantiate the goals of the educational process and the criteria to judge ones's teaching effort. Modeling appropriate social behavior and work habits and transmitting basic knowledge looms as an arduous task, in the face of which concerns for MSPAP scores become a secondary concern. Conflicts with individual students, the inability to control one's classes or to compel students to work, not reaching one's lowest-achieving students at all, or not making any progress despite repeated attempts at re-teaching are grounds for our interview partners to doubt their effectiveness as teachers, in the face of which data-driven diagnostics pale in their significance. Many stories from classrooms are related with a tinge of frustration, sometimes helplessness or even victimhood—for example, in the case of the teachers in one RE school who prayed together in the morning for strength to make it through the day. Particularly novice teachers, represented in large numbers in most RE schools, are preoccupied with day-to-day survival in the classroom. But such preoccupation is not restricted to that group.

External Rewards

Although teachers in the interviews affirm that theirs is a stressful and challenging yet meaningful job, they doubt that parents, the wider public, and the distant state authorities appreciate their toil. Teaching under the circumstances in which many RE schools find themselves, many interviewees hold, is short on external rewards; the abysmally low salaries are a symptom of society's disrespect for teaching, and particularly teaching in poor communities where salaries are even lower. With this experience in mind, one has to refrain from expecting too much in terms of external rewards. Being identified as reconstitution-eligible confirms low external-reward expectations.

Subgroups

While commonalities among teachers across the interviews are striking, suggesting to us that there exists a ground-swell of consensus on many issues among teachers in schools on probation, two subgroups are distinct. First, there is the group of novice teachers. Although numerous at the school sites, they are actually under-represented in our interview sample. Not surprisingly, novice teachers tend to be preoccupied with the day-to-day challenges of classroom management and daily lesson plans against which concerns for the whole school, such as probation, pale. Some novice teachers were told up-front that their new assignment was in a RE school, but not too many of them either paid attention or knew the relevance of this designation.

Second, there is the small group of activists. This group often consists of career teachers—namely, teachers that strive to move up in the school-system hierarchy. Frequently, these career teachers are at least partially released from the classroom. In many schools, career teachers and activists expend an enormous amount of energy on school improvement. Though often in agreement with their less-involved colleagues in viewing the accountability system as unfair to the school, they more readily deem the MSPAP as a measure of "good teaching," are willing to answer the wake-up call, and accept the challenge of increasing test scores. What RE schools do with the status of probation depends very much on the interaction of this group with their less-involved colleagues and the administration at the site.

The situation of principals under conditions of probation is quite different from that of teachers. The 13 principals we interviewed in the seven schools are well aware that prospects of keeping their position depend on their ability to raise the school's performance scores. Since many RE schools (including the seven selected schools) improved only marginally or not at all after identification, punitive transfers of principals are frequent. In four of the seven schools in our selection, the RE designation was accompanied with an immediate change of the principal. Two of the four new principals did not survive their first year after RE designation, and one was transferred after his second year. One school has had a new principal every year for the three years since we began data collection. In three schools, the long-term principals survived the RE designation but they felt highly uncertain of their tenure. One of them subsequently lost her job and chose early retirement, leaving only two principals who survived RE designation in their assignments. One of those two retained his job against the explicit wish of the state department to remove him.

For principals, probation is high stakes. In the interviews with principals, performance indicators of the accountability system are a central concern that guide chosen actions and strategies for the site. The centrality of test scores, however, is tempered by a number of factors. First, not unlike many teachers, principals in these seven schools as well feel buffeted by the ups and downs of test scores, rather than in control of them. Even in schools that posted gains, principals are not sure what strategies, of all the ones they tried, were actually the ones that caused success. Second, the principals are aware of the districts' inclination to move them swiftly when short-term test-score gains are not forthcoming. Hence they calculated their chances of success with a tone of resignation. Third, districts customarily rotate principals for a variety of reasons regardless of schools' performance scores, making transfers less punitive and more a fact of life for principals. Fourth, concern about test scores are an added burden to the principal's already overflowing daily agenda. Nevertheless, more than any other actor at the school site, it is the principal who feels the pressure of accountability and who in many instances reacts to probation with more determined leadership. While in theory the accountability agency holds whole organizations accountable for performance and is geared to provide incentives for individual teachers to improve instruction, in actuality it reaches the principal as the sole responsible actor who is made to stand for the performance of the organization and vicariously experiences the imposition of sanctions that personally hurt. High-stakes school accountability in the Maryland system is in essence high-stakes principal accountability.

I will briefly touch upon principals' actions here, though a more detailed analysis is left for a future report on organizational responses to probation. Because of the weak motivational force of probation on classroom teachers, the fate of internal school-improvement processes rests on the shoulders of the school leadership. District and state mandates, availability of additional resources, principals' role concept and leadership skills shape their response to probation. First and foremost, principals treat district and state mandates—for example, the external performance goals for the school, tests and other performance indicators, and district-adopted programs and behavioral expectations—as givens, not up for debate. In none of the seven schools did probation elicit a lively debate on the meaning, the fairness, or the appropriateness of the new status. Although principals themselves are in many instances not convinced of the wisdom of the accountability system, they either appeal to their faculties to accept reconstitution as a fact, or they present their measures as indisputable external demands.

Principals in the seven schools described themselves in the interviews as managers in charge of the organization. In all likelihood, this role concept has a long tradition independently of the reconstitution status of the school, but it seems that probation reinforces principals' roles as managers. Enforcing strategies and behaviors becomes their foremost concern. According to staff comments about the few principals that survived the RE designation in their schools, accountability has made their principals into more vigilant managers, overriding the paternalistic style with which administrators and staff traditionally accommodated each other.

CONCLUSION

In theory, the threat of sanctions and the status of probation are to provide an incentive for teachers and administrators to increase their work performance. As for classroom teachers, we asked whether performance improvement becomes a self-directed activity as a result of probation. Since teachers are fairly autonomous actors in their classrooms, this quality of self-directedness is of great importance for the potential sustainability of instructional improvement. On the basis of evidence from the interviews, the motivational effect of probation in the seven selected RE schools in Maryland is in all likelihood fairly weak.

Whether one follows a more behaviorist model of performance motivation or one that emphasizes intrinsic self-actualization needs, probation, as constructed in the Maryland accountability design, comes up short as a motivator. Apart from the fact that the signal rapidly wears off until it is habitualized in the daily affairs of long-term RE schools, probation is not perceived as a threat nor is the stigma of great concern for a long time, especially in districts such as A where half the schools are so identified. Therefore the low-stakes character of reconstitution diminishes the urgency for performance changes. Although a continuous increase in performance scores is desired by virtually all, the value placed on performance targets and the accountability system overall is lessened due to the perceived unfairness of the system and to goal conflicts. These conflicts arise from multiple indicators and the gap between the goals of the system and the reality of classrooms. While a great majority of respondents expect to see school improvement in the future, much of that success expectation is presented as an article of faith or is linked to new external resources, rather than being characterized as an unleashing of internal performance potentials. Causes of decline and remedies for improvement tend to be located externally; thus the sense of control of the performance situation seems feebly developed.

Teachers' internal performance standards are not congruent with the external standards of the accountability agency. Many teachers' self-concept eschews the image of the score maximizer in favor of the image of an educator beholden to the intellectual and social growth of individual students and committed to the needs of the local community. Likewise, rewards are derived from encounters with individual students or learning groups and from psychic satisfaction, contrasted with the dearth of rewards that can be derived from the external environment of the school. Thus the needs for actualizing their internal norms and standards of teaching would lead many of our interview partners away from the accountability system. Hence a fairly weak motivational effect of probation seems likely whether one applies a reward calculus or a needs-fulfillment model. On the other hand, as a tool of the state, the accountability system is accepted as a fact of life, and low *student* performance is accepted as a valid concern of the state. Hence probation seems to be associated with a more pronounced disposition to comply on the part of educators who lost confidence in knowing what to do.

While the motivational effect of Maryland's design of probation on "ordinary" teachers is weak, probation triggers heightened concern in all principals and a determination in some to tighten-up administration and take an assertive leadership role. Whether this surge of energy translates into actual success depends on the skill of the leader. Furthermore, at some sites more than others, probation provides the vehicle for a small cadre of career teachers to profile their competence through active participation in school-improvement activities, oftentimes far exceeding the regular duties of the workday.

The motivational impetus of probation in the seven schools can be summarized as follows: Probation has a low motivational effect on regular classroom teachers and produces a widespread disposition among them to comply with external measures and "solutions"; it has a high motivational effect on principals as figureheads of the organization; and it serves as a career vehicle for a small cadre of activists. The result of this pattern is a managerial dynamic of school improvement that is primarily composed of principal leadership, the skill of the career teachers at the sites, the quality of the externally prescribed measures and programs, and a compliant though fairly unmoved teaching majority.

PART FOUR

Conclusion

◨   ◨   ◨

CHAPTER TEN

Urban Education-Reform Strategies

comparative analysis and conclusions

JAMES G. CIBULKA

WILLIAM LOWE BOYD

I N THE INTRODUCTION we indicated that three governance-reform strate-gies tend to dominate discussions of urban school reform: *systems reform, strong mayoral roles,* and *external intervention.* To varying degrees, each of these strategies is linked to the principle of accountabil-ity, which we define as responsiveness to external authority and control. Each strategy makes somewhat different assumptions about how account-ability forces will improve urban school systems.

We noted, however, that in practice, policy-makers tend to mix strate-gies.[1] All of the urban school systems we know of—certainly the ones dis-cussed in this book—are experimenting with some combination of these approaches. The convergence of reform efforts around a relatively finite set of strategies reflects the emergence of school reform as a national problem that has engaged the public, policy experts, civic elites, the media, and politicians. Because policy discussions have taken on a national character, on the surface, the language of reform used across the cities looks quite similar. Yet once one moves beyond a superficial rhetor-ical level, the experiences of each city with reform are quite variable. The social, political, and institutional contexts of the cities have led to many different approaches to these strategies.

Recognizing that each city is in some respects unique, in this chapter we try to look for common threads and generalizations. We see our task here as employing the cases to provide evidence of the respective strengths and weaknesses of systems reform, mayoral control, and external intervention strategies. As we discuss each strategy, we will draw on a variety of insights from the various chapters and not confine ourselves to the classification of cities under each section of the book. Chicago, for example, is not only mayoral control (part 2) but also systems reform (part 1).

We will present a general framework for summarizing and generalizing from the lessons to be found in these individual chapters. Of course, a comparative case analysis, as a method, cannot provide conclusive proof of the generalizations drawn from it. Such lessons must be tested on a larger number of cases. Yet we do believe that the insights to be drawn from this framework suggest in broad outline the directions future policy must take if urban school reform is to be effective. Our discussion follows the order in which these strategies, and the cases linked to them, were presented in the book.

SYSTEMS REFORM

As we indicated in the book's introduction, *systems reform* is a loose cluster of policy ideas and strategies aimed at changing systemic features of urban schooling. Systems reform theorists reject the idea that significant improvements can be made in urban schools without addressing the interdependent aspects of the policy system in which they are embedded. They view programmatic initiatives as flawed because they are limited in impact—they may affect a limited number of children and schools. But they may fail to set in place all the policy and resource requirements for making those programs work effectively at the implementation stage. Systems reformers invoke themes such as policy alignment and policy coherence. They seek to influence the motivations of students and educational professionals by altering incentives and sanctions. For example, this strand of education reform seeks to alter student and teacher performance by setting curricular standards and assessments. When systems reformers talk of making financial commitments to urban schools, their language tends to be couched in terms that emphasize strategic financial investments such as early childhood initiatives or increasing resources designed to improve student literacy. Moreover, for systems reformers, the unit of intervention, as we said at the outset, is the entire policy system as it bears on student performance. Thus, a range of policy supports that are antecedent and complementary to schools is stressed, such as the availability of high-quality child-care and strengthening support systems to create healthy families. Many elements of not only local education policy, but also policies of state and federal governments receive attention. For example, it is said that teacher-education programs and programs to prepare school leaders, as well as professional-development priorities, must be aligned with state curricular standards and assessments.

What are the potential advantages and disadvantages of this general approach to reform? The primary advantages of the systemic approach are that it attempts to grasp what has been called the "policy puzzle" (David 1990) in a comprehensive way. Unlike many policy efforts to fix schools, the systemic approach tries to be proactive rather than merely a reaction to discrete symptomatic aspects of student and school failure. Like many other planning approaches, systems reform focuses on means–ends relationships. It is an attempt to gain consensus on the multiple causes of student and school failure and the policy requirements for achieving success. A second strength of the systemic approach is that it emphasizes reduction of fragmentation within the policy system. Wong and colleagues, who refer to "integrated governance" in Chicago as an effort to strengthen the fiscal and political support for the school system, strike this particular theme in their chapter (chapter 7). An educational-accountability agenda has been an essential part of that integrated governance strategy, with a multitude of initiatives aimed at different components of the educational system.

The chapter on Los Angeles (chapter 1) by Kerchner and Menefee-Libey illustrates the need for a systemic approach. Reflecting on decades of efforts to reform the Los Angeles Unified School District (LAUSD), they employ the metaphor of improvisational theater sketches to capture the lack of coherence in these reform efforts, when viewed over time. Each sketch has been appealing at the moment, but they have added up to nothing coherent. Some reforms led to subsequent problems. In the 1970s and '80s reformers challenged authority in a manner that led to loss of political control over education policy-making to the courts and the state legislature, and to the rise of racial and ethnic politics. In other cases, the reforms dealt with discrete aspects of LAUSD's needs, such as finance, district reorganization, and so on. The involvement of Mayor Richard Riordan represented still another effort to address a lack of priorities in the school system and the micromanagement practices of its school board, but his efforts were impeded by lack of authority and other factors. Kerchner and Menefee-Libey blame permanent "institutional patterns and incentive systems that encourage improvisational policy-making." These are rooted in fragmented authority shared among many governments. In speculating on the future, the authors set forth a best-case scenario that they view as unlikely. It would require a coherent program of systemic reform, sufficient influence to be successful, and a broad coalition to sustain these reforms. In short, they present LAUSD as a "negative case" of what occurs when systems reform is missing.

Cooper and Bloomfield's chapter (chapter 3) offers an optimistic picture of what systemic reform—in this instance a new statute passed by the New York State Legislature in 1996—can accomplish to improve the performance of the New York City public school system. As Cooper and Bloomfield explain, the Act weakened the authority of the decentralized community school districts and the district superintendents. It recentralized the school system in important respects by giving new authority to the chancellor. Yet, they believe that the Act was more than "just another round in the centralization–decentralization effort," and they reject the familiar metaphor of a pendulum to describe the impulse underlying this governance shift. They characterize strategic management as a significant departure from either traditional top-down or bottom-up reform-governance strategies. For example, they point out that both the chancellor and school-site leaders have new control over resources. Here again, they strike a theme often found in the systems reform literature: the need to realign the educational-governance system so that it is more flexible and performance-driven. Yet they do not deal with the political turbulence that led to a change in superintendents in the nation's largest school system. Whether the reforms they describe are well-enough institutionalized to survive regime changes in a school system is unclear.

Whatever the merits of systemic reform, it does seem clear that this approach to reform also has serious limitations. Its potential advantages, as discussed above, as well as its disadvantages are summarized in table 10.1. First, systemic reform is complex and not easily understood except by technically informed policy experts. While it is easy to wrap the pieces together rhetorically as an effort to make students and schools more accountable, the details of the reforms often prove to be unclear and confusing, particularly to teachers and administrators. Because of this complexity, a second problem often arises: systemic reform encounters significant implementation challenges. Unforeseen problems occur that require further adaptation of the policies. Moreover, the potential for resistance to the policies is high, because the more comprehensive the approach, the more vested interests are likely to be threatened. Third, there is a tendency to frame all problems in rationalistic policy terms while underestimating the political requirements for making the policies work. And fourth, the language of systemic reform can disguise fundamental disagreements, such as how much money will be required to make the reforms work.

Philadelphia provides a particularly apt example of all these disadvantages emerging during David Hornbeck's tenure. As Christman, Corcoran, Foley, and Luhm report in chapter 2, some aspects of the reforms were not clear. There was confusion about the new governance structures in Children Achieving. The division of authority and decision-making among officials at the streamlined central office, and between the central office and local schools, was unclear. In addition, many implementation problems occurred due to "reform overload" and sequencing of the reforms (the accountability system was put in place prior to the supports for teachers and principals). The political problems surrounding the reform were legion, such as loss of support from the state with a change in gubernatorial and legislative leadership, teachers' union opposition to the reforms, and withdrawal of business-community support. The resources required to fund the reforms, or even to maintain the school system and keep it out of insol-

TABLE 10.1

POSSIBLE IMPACT OF SYSTEMS REFORM ON IMPROVEMENT OF URBAN
PUBLIC-SCHOOL SYSTEMS

POTENTIAL ADVANTAGES

Focuses on multiple causes of school failure, not merely discrete symptoms, and on comprehensive responses.

Emphasizes improved coordination within the policy system.

POTENTIAL DISADVANTAGES

Is technically complex and not easily understood by the public, policymakers, or even teachers and administrators.

Significant implementation problems can occur due to unforeseen problems and resistance.

Problems tend to be framed in rationalistic policy terms, underestimating the political requirements for making the policies work.

The lack of clarity about key components of systemic reform and its requirements leads to political conflict.

ATTRIBUTES THAT INCREASE LIKELIHOOD OF SUCCESS

Effective alignment of previously disjointed policies.

Effective design of policies.

Contextually appropriate policies that build and sustain support.

Appropriate mix of accountability with capacity-building.

---

vency, became a major dispute. Yet these political requirements and problems surrounding a system's reform such as Children Achieving in Philadelphia tend to receive little attention from systems reformers. Even technical aspects of the reforms, such as the accountability system, lost credibility.

These political problems inherent in an ambitious program of systemic reform have been managed more effectively in Boston than in Philadelphia. Yee chronicles in chapter 5 how Mayor Menino runs political interference for Superintendent Payzant, which can provide him with more freedom to implement these policies. In chapter 4 Kirst and Bulkley raise the important question whether the relatively heavier focus on capacity-building in the Boston approach can maintain political support. At the same time, Boston's reforms have not been as ambitious as those undertaken by Hornbeck in Philadelphia.

While Cooper and Bloomfield are optimistic about strategic management in New York City, they *do* allude to many potential pitfalls. The creation of new borough-wide superintendents has left unclear how they relate to the 32 district offices that remain in place from the 1969 law and to the capacity of the community districts to carry out high school reforms. Also, there is a confusing three-tiered system of high schools with different controlling authorities and a focus on privatizing the management of low-performing schools. Indeed, the authors readily acknowledge that the logic uniting these evolving reforms is not immediately clear and offer a "Double-ACE" model to explain them. The reforms require balancing centralized authority, control, and enforcement to improve standards, while encouraging local autonomy, collaboration, and engagement. They rely, in other words, on skilled leadership, which will be vulnerable to a regulatory culture within the school system, incompetent board members and administrators, and other challenges. Again, these institutional and political constraints tend to operate outside the assumptions of systems reform strategists.

Integrated governance in Chicago also has not been without problems, as Wong and his colleagues make clear in chapter 7 in their analysis of high schools. In their view, the school system had not found an acceptable balance among sanctions, support, and professional discretion. Support to schools and the strategies for creating instructional improvements have been inadequate. Strategies for improving low-performing schools led to movements of faculty and students away from these schools, thus worsening matters in certain respects. The nature of their study focused on these lapses as implementation problems, but they acknowledge that the problems they found may be more fundamental flaws in the design of the policies themselves. Their chapter was completed before a change of leadership in the school system, which may carry important implications for how systems reform in Chicago will evolve.

All these cases underscore that systems reform is far from a panacea. When examined closely, systems reform is a rather fluid concept lending itself to many different policy designs likely to yield different consequences. Moreover, the varying institutional and political contexts of Chicago, Los Angeles, New York, and Philadelphia and other cities make it hard to predict what implementation problems will occur, but they are considerable. None of the cities presents a record of systems reform that has been sustained long enough for us to specify what essential elements will guarantee its success in improving student performance. It is possible, however, to lay out some general qualifications for this reform approach to work, as seen in table 10.1.

Systems reform requires aligning previously fragmented policies, which often means significant changes in the policy system itself; the appropriate policies must be designed so that they have the potential to be successful; policies must be sensitive to local contexts both in design and implementation; and the appropriate mix of capacity-building and accountability strategies must be put in place. All pressure with little support for new learning is likely to be no more effective than an approach that expects teachers and administrators to change behavior without asking them to be accountable for their performance.

STRONG MAYORAL ROLES IN EDUCATION REFORM

Chicago and Boston are two cities in which mayoral leadership has been strengthened. In all the cities, however, with the exception of Baltimore, mayors are attempting to assert greater influence over the public school systems in their city. In Washington, D.C., Anthony Williams now is able to appoint some school board members. Los Angeles's mayor at the time, Richard Riordan, sought greater accountability, firing of bad principals, and reconstitution of low-performing schools. He openly campaigned against the school board incumbents in the 1999 election, succeeded in installing four reform-slate candidates on the board, and forced out Superintendent Ruben Zacarias, whose pace of reform he viewed as too slow. In Philadelphia, a change to the city charter in 2000 at the time of the election of a new mayor, John Street, allowed him to appoint a new school board with terms of office identical to his own. Further, he appointed Debra Kahn, a former school board member, as his secretary of education. Although Street supported Superintendent David Hornbeck's reforms in the mayoral campaign, Hornbeck resigned only months after Street's election in protest over budget cutbacks imposed on the district by Governor Ridge.

New York's mayors, including Mayor Rudolph W. Giuliani, long have agitated for more formal control over school affairs, including selection of the board. Yet he had enough influence with the school board to force out School Chancellor Rudy Crew in 1999 after their close working relationship fell apart. They agreed on the need to end lifetime tenure for principals and ending social promotion. However, when Crew opposed some of Giuliani's cherished policy priorities such as school vouchers, he fell into disfavor with the mayor. A similar fate had befallen his predecessor, Ramon Cortines, who decided to resign when he lost Giuliani's support over how to cut the size of the school bureaucracy. Cortines had the temerity to refer to his feud with the mayor as "The Rudy and Ray Show." Subsequently, Chancellor Harold Levy, a former executive with CitiGroup, was hired by the Board of Education over the objections of Giuliani, who initially accused Levy of being too close to the teachers' union.

Perhaps because Boston's and Chicago's mayors have gained more formal control over their school systems than mayors in Los Angeles and New York, some of the political conflicts in other cities have been avoided under these new governance regimes. In Boston, as Gary Yee points out, mayoral control was preceded by several other important governance shifts. These included the replacement of a 13-member elected school committee with a seven-member committee initiated under Mayor Raymond Flynn, as well as consolidation of greater authority in the role of the superintendent. Since Thomas Menino became mayor in 1993, leadership of the city's school system has been relatively stable. While he forced out Lois Harrison-Jones as superintendent, being apparently impatient with the pace of her reforms and her unwillingness to fire principals, Menino has worked well with Thomas Payzant, who has been superintendent since 1995. Menino has staked his reputation and political future on reforming the quality of the school system and won a 1996 referendum by a 70 percent margin to create an appointed committee. Yet he has let Payzant, who is a member of his cabinet, implement a variety of reforms with relatively little micromanagement. This reflects a willingness to share control and to acquiesce to the professional judgments of an educator. As Yee points out, Menino has played a supporting role by garnering strong business support for Payzant's "Focus on Children" change strategy, raising money, helping to build and rehabilitate schools, and improving the coordination of city services related to the schools. At the same time, Menino's education-reform coalition has been able to secure the support of the Boston Teachers' Union.

Developments in Chicago, as discussed in the chapters by Shipps (chapter 6) and by Wong and colleagues (chapter 7), indicate that there are some common elements in Chicago and Boston. Kirst and Bulkley in chapter 4 point out that the reform coalitions are similar in both cities. These coalitions are broad-based, including business, labor, and a great deal of support from community organizations and racial–ethnic groups, although the latter have played somewhat marginal roles. Unlike Boston, Mayor Richard Daley had to turn to the Illinois State Legislature for additional authority. He used this authority to create a powerful, and relatively stable, political coalition in support of his school reforms. The mayor used his expanded powers to improve capital funding, balance the budget, and secure labor stability. Unlike Menino in Boston, however, Daley took a much more activist approach to reforming the school system. By appointing his former budget director Paul Vallas as superintendent rather than a professional educator, Daley played a hands-on role in shaping the reforms and their implementation. This new involvement of the Chicago mayor also introduced an element of stability in the leadership of the school system. Until Vallas's resignation in June 2001, there was no turnover in the position of the school system's chief executive officer.

At the same time, the management style Vallas brought from city hall was distinctly "top-down" in the demands it has made on teachers and administrators. While for decades centralized management was the hallmark of urban school administration, it has been out of fashion for a long time in these same circles due to new theories of management borrowed largely from the private sector. In Chicago, for example, there was an attempt to regionally decentralize the school system in 1966, followed by several subsequent waves of decentralizing reforms. At the same time, the political machine always found it in its self-interest to promote close control from city hall, even if covertly, as shown in Shipps's historical analysis of mayoral regimes in that city. Today, Richard Daley's embracing of recentralized control of the Chicago school system, while justified in terms of the mandate to fundamentally overhaul the school system, is really consistent with a long tradition of hierarchical authority exercised wherever possible by Chicago's mayors. Kirst and Bulkley argue that in Boston, Superintendent Payzant has focused more on capacity-building, and they raise the question whether this will work politically.

The contrast between the Boston and Chicago cases, therefore, highlights a question about the reassertion of mayoral influence over public schools. Does it signal a significant diminution of professional autonomy and a penchant for "command and control" approaches to management, both justified as a legitimate response to an educational crisis and institutional failure? In Boston, this has not occurred so dramatically, but Boston could be the exceptional case that proves the rule.

It is arguable which approach is more effective in raising student achievement, or, for that matter, if either approach makes any difference. It is really still an article of faith and hope that governance arrangements such as mayoral control can alter the educational performance of the school system. Both the Yee and Wong et al. chapters point to tentative evidence of improvements in student performance, but these are neither systematic nor sustained. Nor has the achievement gap between Whites and other students been closed or significantly narrowed.

Traditionally, in the history of urban schooling, concerns about the educational success of Black and Hispanic students as well as other minorities have been raised by advocacy groups with relatively similar agendas and constituencies. While some of these advocacy groups have city-wide, regional, and national ties, their base of support often is rooted in neighborhoods and community organizations. As school reform has become an imperative embraced by mayors, business leaders, and civic elites, these powerful groups have come to dominate the political coalitions created by mayors to defend their reform agendas. The language of productivity has supplanted the equity claims that normally are pressed by these advocacy groups. Thus, in both Boston and Chicago, many minority leaders and community groups complain of being marginalized under the current reform regimes, as the chapters by Shipps and by Wong et al. point out.

Again, just as is the case with the centralization/decentralization and professional control/political control debate, the link between the inclusion of these advocacy groups in the political coalition and its ultimate success in improving student achievement remains tenuous. Critics of the old equity agenda point to its palpable failure to reverse a pattern of institutional decline, and there was little evidence that the local school councils in Chicago were able to harness the necessary political support and resources. It is perhaps worth noting, on the other side of the argument, that the older mayoral coalitions in these two cities, long associated with political machines, were responsive to neighborhood interests, but largely by conferring discrete and narrow benefits on individuals (particularistic policies) rather than supporting universalistic policies that were likely to improve the life chances of entire groups. As Kirst and Bulkley point out, this tradition of patronage discredited the political control of schools and led to the Progressive Era reforms early in the twentieth century. Are the new urban mayors such as Daley and Menino more enlightened than their predecessors? Will the policies they support in education reform truly address the needs of all students? The mayoral tradition of control in Baltimore failed to reform that city's school system, even where a mayor of the new breed, Kurt Schmoke, made reform a high priority. As Cibulka points out in chapter 8, Schmoke's failure helped set the stage for the state of Maryland to sharply reduce mayoral control over the school system in 1997, ironically using precisely the arguments being employed in other cities to justify expanding mayoral control.

These facts remind us that mayoral control is only one element in a total reform strategy. It addresses the problem of political authority, and by implication institutional accountability for performance, but it is silent on the specific strategies that will bring about a transformation from high rates of educational failure to high rates of student success. In table 10.2 we attempt to summarize the main lessons drawn from these cases concerning the probable impact of expanding mayoral authority, recognizing that the small number of cases and the recency of these developments make our conclusions tentative.

One element determining the capacity of mayors to make needed changes in their city's school system will be how much control they exercise. Considerable variation exists among the cities in how much control mayors actually have to reform their city's school system. We argue, however, that mayoral control is not enough, unless mayors draw on the expertise of professional educators to assist them in providing leadership. Some mayors are recruiting nontraditional educators to lead their school systems. While this trend is not inherently problematic, it should be asked what expertise is available to create and implement educational policies grounded in knowledge of teaching and learning.

The strategy also assumes some stability among mayoral incumbents; frequent turnover is likely to have a major impact on whether school-reform strategies will be sustained. Similarly, a mayor must be committed to working on school reform over the long haul and not look for quick fixes that will turn around a school system in a couple of years. This long-term perspective has not been associated with elected leaders, who often place a premium on demonstrating outcomes within election cycles or within a timeframe that fits with the career ambitions of a politician.

The mayoral reform strategy also depends on civic commitment to school reform and a capacity of stakeholders to collaborate around the complex requirements for school reform if it is to be successful. Cities vary widely in the historic commitment that city elites have to making fiscal and human investments in their public school systems, and in the skills that these civic leaders bring to the school-reform discussion. While may-

TABLE 10.2

POSSIBLE IMPACT OF INCREASED MAYORAL AUTHORITY OVER URBAN
PUBLIC-SCHOOL SYSTEMS

POTENTIAL ADVANTAGES

Can build a city-wide coalition of stakeholders.

Can leverage other city services to assist schools.

Has hope of sustainability.

POTENTIAL DISADVANTAGES

Is an incomplete strategy, which is silent on strategic policies for improving student achievement.

Can reinforce top-down reform strategies dominated by elites, disempowering teachers, parents, and local communities.

Can politicize a wide range of educational issues.

ATTRIBUTES THAT INCREASE LIKELIHOOD OF SUCCESS

Strong professional leadership in tandem with sufficient mayoral control.

Mayoral leadership stability, sustained interest and leadership in school reform by the mayor.

Civic commitment to school reform and civic capacity, upon which mayoral leadership can build.

ors can harness resources and foster collaboration, they must work with the raw material that is available to them. They cannot work miracles alone, since they have finite political capital they can bring to the task of school renewal.

In short, any attempt to assess the potential efficacy of mayoral control is confounded by a whole list of "ifs." Some of these are additional strategic choices that mayors must make, but as indicated above, others have to do with their authority to make needed changes and with the civic capacity of their city.

EXTERNAL OVERSIGHT

Although accountability strategies all resort to the imposition of new policies from outside urban school systems, external oversight is a particular approach to externally imposed reforms. It is an intervention from a higher unit of governmental authority necessitated by a level of performance defined as inadequate by those authorities. Moreover, it carries explicit sanctions for failure to improve to some standard imposed by the intervening authority. Table 10.3 summarizes the potential advantages and disadvantages of external oversight as a reform strategy. Its primary ad-

TABLE 10.3

POTENTIAL ADVANTAGES AND DISADVANTAGES OF EXTERNAL OVERSIGHT

POTENTIAL ADVANTAGES

External intervention may be necessary to create institutional disequilibrium and change organizational culture.

Focus on incentives and sanctions can alter behavior.

Clear performance targets linked to consequences can alter behavior.

POTENTIAL DISADVANTAGES

May be based on incorrect or incomplete assumptions about what motivates teachers and/or administrators, or students.

Tends to be heavier on sanctions than rewards or support.

Tends to ignore institutional, social, and political contexts as forces shaping educators' behavior.

External intervention may be a weak motivator to change behavior where people have the capacity to exit.

External intervention may be resented or not accepted as necessary.

ATTRIBUTES THAT INCREASE LIKELIHOOD OF SUCCESS

Correct mix of sanctions and support.

Needs to be linked to other strategies for institutional renewal.

Requires clear performance targets for ending intervention.

External intervention must be accepted as legitimate in order to lead to lasting changes in organizational and individual behavior.

---

vantages are that in schools or school systems characterized by chronically poor performance, it may be necessary to destroy the equilibrium in the current organizational culture and replace it with new norms and values. Among these is a belief that all children can learn and that it is possible for a school to improve its performance. Only a strong external hand may be able to do this. Furthermore, it may be necessary to change the behavior of teachers and administrators by using extrinsic rewards or sanctions. The assumption that people change their behavior voluntarily without some pressure may be unrealistic. Also, part of the problem in low-performing schools may be the lack of clear goals, standards, and performance targets. External authorities may be in the best position to focus attention on improving performance.

Yet, by the same token, the assumptions underlying external intervention may be unduly simplistic. Does this approach to change really have a clear "theory" of motivation, and is that theory appropriate to the characteristics of both schoolteachers and administrators? External intervention assumes not only that people respond primarily to external stimuli, rather than to intrinsic sources of motivation, but also that regulatory requirements will be a more powerful shaper of behavior than other aspects of their work context. Yet in practice, professionals respond to a variety of "motivators" from actors other than an external authority. Moreover, too onerous a set of sanctions may invoke a stigma for working in a low-performing school, inducing those with the freedom to flee, seeking more desirable schools or school systems. External interventions also place faith in legal, regulatory approaches to changing individual and institutional behavior while underplaying the importance of institutional, social, and political contexts as forces shaping educators' behavior. These are powerful influences that are not easily neutralized or eliminated by an external change agent. One such contextual factor that becomes a constraint is the ability of teachers and administrators in some cities to exit from low-performing schools and school systems perceived as failing. Another disadvantage is that local school officials and stakeholders are likely to resent the external intervention or not accept it as legitimate.

As Cibulka explains, Washington, D.C.'s mayor, Tony Williams, ran into opposition from the city council and from Black voters when he tried to restructure the District's school board to give him more control. The council and many voters did not accept the legitimacy of a reduced citizen voice over the city's public schools, even though virtually everyone acknowledged a need to improve the quality of public education in the city. The same resentments have confronted state officials in Maryland over their intervention in the Baltimore City public schools. Initially, there was much denial that the dismal performance of the city schools was the fault of school officials. However, in the years since the partnership began, the school system has begun to accept responsibility for improving student achievement. Also, resentment of the state's new role as overseer (aka "partner") appears to have dissipated to a degree, particularly in view of improved elementary test scores, which permitted the state to compliment the newly constituted school board and new administrative regime for its improvements.

A continuing source of friction is the disputed adequacy of state funding for the city school system, which led to the partnership compromise in the first place. Developments in both Baltimore and the District of Columbia, therefore, illustrate the political obstacles an external change agent can face in gaining acceptance—not on the need for educational improvement *per se*, but on the thornier question of who shall have the authority to reverse the failure.

Cibulka and Mintrop discussed both these potential advantages and disadvantages in their chapters. The need for external intervention seemed clear in Baltimore when in 1997 the state of Maryland stepped in to create a "partnership" with the city school system in exchange for providing the cash-strapped school system with more state aid. The state aimed to create a new organizational culture focused on student performance rather than on an employment regime for adults. One aspect of this new governance arrangement was a reduction in mayoral authority. But it was far more than that. The school system's administrative system was altered dramatically, and new authorities were recruited to provide fresh leadership. The state did not attempt to provide a detailed blueprint for educational renewal within the partnership agreement itself. Rather, the agreement imposed rigorous planning and reporting requirements on the school system. The state was walking a careful line. It had neither the authority nor the knowledge of how to reverse the deplorable educational performance of the school system. Yet it hoped to create enough external levers to hold the school system accountable for improved performance. This points to the inherent limitation of external oversight as a strategy. Intervention itself cannot be a sufficient stratagem—it is only a means toward creating institutional capacity to adopt and implement other reforms. Results on the Maryland School Performance Assessments Program (MSPAP) suggest that the reforms have led to improvements at the elementary level, but overall performance remains low and no progress has occurred at middle and high school levels. External intervention, then, has been modestly successful. Yet the major external motivator has been money, and this remains a matter of perennial dispute between city officials and the state.

In Washington, D.C. the benefits of federal intervention have been still more oblique than in Baltimore. Federal officials sought to rescue the city from insolvency, thereby focusing on a broader set of issues than the poor performance of the school system. The financial control board's decision to reduce the power of the school board and replace it with a new structure proved to be controversial. District citizens interpreted the federal intervention as a reduction in their ability to control their public school system with an elected school board. The new board of trustees created by the financial control board eventually had a confrontation with the control board itself. As more authority was returned to Mayor Tony Williams, he complained about his lack of influence on the school system. However, his proposal to reform the board-selection process ended in a controversial and divisive compromise. Thus, federal intervention created at best a blurry set of improvements in school system governance. The educational performance of the school system has not improved, despite two very competent superintendents in recent years who have been committed to reform. Indeed, Arlene Ackerman resigned as superintendent complaining about the multiple reporting channels to different authorities and her lack of control over key functions such as personnel and procurement. Her lament listed the same pathologies that concern systems reformers: the fragmentation in the policy system and lack of authority to act effectively. In this respect, the external intervention by federal officials in the nation's capital has been an unqualified failure.

Mintrop's chapter (chapter 9) focuses on Maryland's policies for intervening in low-performing schools. Here we see how the particulars in the design of an external intervention plan are important. The overwhelming numbers of these schools that have been identified for improvement ("reconstitution-eligible" schools) have been in Baltimore, as have been all four schools placed under state or local reconstitution. However, Mintrop does not credit the policies with notable successes, although certainly some individual schools have improved. The findings suggest how difficult it is to design policies that improve teaching and thereby set the stage for raising student achievement. Teachers and principals do accept the needs for change, although many externalize blame for their schools' poor student performance. Mintrop argues that the motivational effect of the reconstitution policies on most teachers (with the exception of a few career teachers) is weak: "teachers' internal performance standards are not congruent with the external standards of the accountability agency." Indeed, the policies are perceived as more punitive than rewarding, although Maryland does have a separate school-performance reward program from which some reconstitution-eligible schools have benefited. Under such circumstances, when teachers have the option to exit, many do; the larger market context of teacher shortages tends to further weaken the motivational effect of the policies. On the other hand, principals have been motivated by the policies, because of potential sanctions (many principals' jobs have been "on the line") or because of potential rewards (career advancement for principals who raise test scores).

These same intricacies proved important in Chicago's policies for helping low-performing schools, according to Wong and colleagues. They conclude that such policies have been too heavy on the sanction side, with insufficient attention to helping schools improve their capacity. The external-partners concept was intended to do the latter, but has not been perceived as successful.

It is important to recognize that external-intervention plans can evolve in response to the lessons policy-makers derive as they implement a policy. Initially, when the reconstitution policies were designed in the early 1990s, Maryland state officials assumed that only a few schools would be so designated. The locus of failure was assumed to be the school and not the district. Eventually, it became clear that not all districts had equal capacity to help failing schools. The stark case was Baltimore City, which led in part to the decision to intervene with a partnership as an alternative to a state takeover.

State officials have tried to alter the reconstitution policies in other ways to make them more effective. For example, they have decreased regulatory and monitoring aspects of the policies to a degree and tried to increase the amount of support reaching the schools from state (and not merely local district officials). The longer the period of external intervention, the more the pressure builds on the external agent to prove that intervention is working—a dynamic that creates incentives for policy adjustments. Intervention has no legitimacy of its own; it must be justified with ultimate recourse to improved performance. Thus ironically the accountability shifts from exclusive attention on the failing schools or districts to the performance of the external agent itself. Yet, whatever objective indicators of performance are available, the way this performance is judged occurs within a political environment with no clear guidelines. External intervention, in other words, is not just a regulatory strategy whose effectiveness will be determined by the intricacies of its policy design. Rather, this reform strategy is unavoidably political.

Under what conditions, then, is external intervention as a change strategy most likely to succeed? We have extracted four attributes of such policies from the foregoing analyses. First, external intervention, just like systems reform change strategies, needs a mix of both sanctions and support—and a correct mix at that. All sanctions and no support brooks the danger of teacher, administrator, and community resistance, while a strategy based solely on support creates only capacity without incentives to change individual and organizational behavior. How to generate motivation to change that will lead to deep learning and sustained commitment, it turns out, is a complicated challenge. Second, external intervention is a relatively incomplete strategy. It quickly turns on strategies of institutional renewal, which are not only motivational but that require concrete strategies aimed at raising student achievement. How much should the external agent dictate the content of that intervention strategy, contrasted with merely setting in motion a *process* for renewal? Third, external-intervention strategies such as Maryland's policies for intervening in low-performing schools require clear performance targets for ending the external intervention. Being placed in perpetual purgatory is discouraging to local officials, and it may reduce the sense of efficacy required for teachers and administrators to commit their energies to school improvement. Yet setting too low a threshold for exiting from intervention may put the external agent in the position of endorsing largely symbolic and temporary improvements. Finally, there is the issue of legitimacy of external intervention. The evidence from the Baltimore City–state partnership and the federal and mayoral efforts to improve Washington, D.C.'s public school system suggest that external agents cannot rely merely on the *authority* to intervene as a means of legitimating their intervention. They must achieve local acquiescence of the need for the changes they seek and concurrence that the purported benefits of authoritative oversight exceed the perceived costs, such as loss of "face" and loss of citizen voice. Ultimately, these hurdles must be resolved, as we suggested above, within a political arena, and the legitimacy of the external intervention must be maintained over the time-span of the intervention.

CLOSING THOUGHTS

Not surprisingly, the preponderance of evidence from these case studies along with reports from a number of other American cities suggest that none of the three governance strategies is free from significant challenges. Alongside the advantages of each strategy is a parallel list of shortcomings. The success of each strategy is conditional; it depends on the presence of numerous factors that may or may not be present. Furthermore, the strategies are invariably incomplete. Their champions hail them as solutions, but these solutions beg for a clearer articulation of the problem(s) the solutions purportedly address. The need for more complete and comprehensive solutions is increasingly recognized. As Paul Hill (Hill and Celio 1998; Hill, Campbell, and Harvey 2000) argues, virtually all urban education reforms to date are weakened by inclusion of a "zone of wishful thinking"—that is, a sphere of actions or supports that is required for success but is not controlled by the reform.

Greater mayoral influence, systems reform, and external intervention are all solutions, but they tend to attack different aspects of the urban education problem and the causes that underlie it. The mayoral- and external-intervention strategies frame the accountability problem as the need to impose authoritative action from outside the educational system, in the first case through a lateral redistribution of authority within the city polity, and in the second case via a vertical intervention from a higher level of government at state or federal levels. Yet they leave many questions unanswered. The problems of low performance in the educational system and the concomitant strategies required to reverse student failure are not addressed directly in these two reform strategies. It is left to the mayor or external agent to articulate those educational and organizational reforms.

The accountability strategy of systems reform remedies the weaknesses of the other two approaches to a degree. Systems reform begins to deal with what must be reformed within the "black box" of the educational system. At the same time, systems reform relies very heavily on a design approach that sees the causes of institutional failure as being rooted in policy fragmentation and lack of coordination and information among policy actors. It also seeks to instill greater accountability for performance through incentives and possibly sanctions linked to performance. This rationalist paradigm begs the question of who will have the authority to transform urban educational systems from low-performing systems to high-performing ones. It is this authority problem that is attacked by the advocates of strong mayoral influence or external intervention. Moreover, the systems reform strategy suffers from a certain imprecise and inchoate character. The elements and boundaries of the educational system identified by systems reformers vary greatly, and the strategy is thus open to a wide variety of approaches. This flexibility is a potential strength, in that it can accommodate pluralist demands coming from a wide variety of interests who wish to attach their priorities to reform. Ironically, however, systems reforms often are as top-down as the other two accountability approaches. Their advocates see the problem as one of policy design in the foreground, while political requirements for systems reforms are viewed as necessary evils that can be relegated to the background. By the same token, the more that is dumped into the systems reform vessel, the more potential it has to implode from its overly ambitious expectations. The complexity of systems reforms makes it difficult to adopt as reformers plan, and even more likely to encounter significant implementation problems.

If the three accountability strategies discussed in this book are internally incomplete in their approach to accountability, they also represent only a fractional perspective on other requirements for urban education reform. None of the three accountability strategies deals very effectively with the issue of the *institutional capacity* of urban educational systems to improve or with the problem of *educational capacity*—the teaching and learning issues at the core of the difficulties. Accountability policies of the 1990s refocused educational reform away from capacity issues, which had often been framed within the logic of equalizing educational opportunity. Additional resources, new programs, and other efforts to improve the capacity of urban school systems came to be viewed as irrelevant to their productivity, or even counterproductive. Within the new productivity frame of reference, capacity came to be viewed as using more smartly what one has, sharpening one's focus, and increasing motivation and effort. To be sure, accountability approaches do not altogether eschew the need for program enhancements and additional resources. Generally, mayors or external agents make the provision of additional resources conditional on urban education officials instituting other changes. Within limits, this bargaining approach to capacity-building can be defended. In addition, systems reformers in particular have given some credence to capacity-building, in their emphasis on professional development.

Yet, the limits of this approach to capacity-building from within the accountability framework are now becoming apparent. As urban school systems work to improve their performance, how much can be expected when most (although not all) have significantly less revenue per pupil than suburban counterparts, even when the needs of urban schools are greater? School-finance experts and the courts continue to refine the concept of educational adequacy, which may provide a framework to address more effectively, if never totally resolve, this policy debate.

Another aspect of institutional capacity dramatically underestimated in the accountability perspective is what Stone and colleagues call "civic capacity" (Stone, Henig, Jones, and Pierannunzi 2001; see also, Hill, Campbell, and Harvey 2000). Civic capacity, simply stated, is about "various sectors of the community coming together to address a major problem" (Stone, Henig, Jones, and Pierannunzi 2001, 4), in this case, education. Civic capacity may involve mayoral leadership, according to those authors, but it is both broader and more complicated. It requires collective action leading to a substantial civic coalition. The racial dimensions of urban education issues greatly complicate school-reform efforts in cities (Henig, Hula, Orr, and Pedescleaux 1999). From this perspective, attempts to alter the institution through new authorities or new policy alignments are at best incomplete, and in some cases counterproductive. While this is not the place to discuss all of the evidence surrounding the civic-capacity perspective and its potential as a reform strategy to reverse the decline of urban education, we do believe that conscious efforts to increase civic capacity need to be a component of urban education-reform strategies.

Voucher proponents and those in favor of introducing more parental choice and market mechanisms take a very different approach to capacity-building. They take the logic of accountability one-step farther than systems reforms, increased mayoral influence, or external intervention. All three rest on the assumption that urban education systems can be reformed by strengthening bureaucratic and political authority. By contrast, most of those who favor vouchers, charter schools, and other market approaches seek to reduce such authority and place it in the hands of parents, even by-passing or reducing the role of school boards. The impulse from which these proposals spring, while rooted in the rhetoric of accountability, is to loosen and even break up the education system in order to increase its capacity for improving student performance. Such experiments already are underway in a limited number of cities, such as Milwaukee.

Clearly, the current governance strategies relying on accountability mechanisms are in a race against time. Impatience with the performance of urban school systems continues to mount. If the current generation of accountability reforms proves disappointing, as some of the evidence in this book suggests, the next wave of policy reform (already occurring in some cities) may call for radical solutions such as dismantling the remnants of the "one best system" upon which urban educational enterprises have been erected for the last century (Tyack 1974). Alternatively, more experiments with existing institutional arrangements may occur. For example, market reforms may be infused within current accountability strategies as appendages to mayoral influence, systems reform, or external oversight. These hybrids of bureaucratic and market systems would make the current institutional framework for urban schooling more complex and perhaps less coherent. Yet so far, accountability strategies have not led to significant and sustained urban education renewal. The search continues for the right combination of policies and political strategies to make that renaissance in urban education possible.

NOTE

1. There are a number of reasons why multiple strategies are employed. First, reform policies may reflect compromises among different actors and interest groups that desire different reform approaches. And second, reliance on a particular strategy may become discredited, leading policy-makers to turn to other approaches. Past policies are rarely discarded altogether; instead, new reforms are grafted onto previous ones.

references

Allison, G. T. (1971). *The essence of decision.* Boston: Little, Brown.

Anand, G. (1996, January 18). Menino pledges better schools. *Boston Globe,* p. 25.

Anderson, J. (1997, June 18). Getting better by design: Transforming districts to support high-performance schools. Commentary. *Education Week 16*(no. 38): 34, 48.

Anderson, V. (1998). Teacher raises trail those of principals, administrators. *Catalyst 10*(1): 22.

Ascher, C., K. Ikeda, and N. Fruchter. (1997). *Schools on notice—a policy study of New York State's 1996–1997: Schools under registration review process.* New York: New York State Department of Education.

Ashton, P., and R. Webb. (1986). *Making a difference: Teachers' sense of efficacy and student achievement.* New York: Longman.

Associated Black Charities. (1992). *A study of the management of the Baltimore City Public Schools.* Baltimore: Associate Black Charities.

Aucoin, D. (1991, December 25). Aide won't act as shadow chief of schools, Flynn says. *Boston Globe.*

———. (1992, October 10). School panel chief slams top aide. *Boston Globe.*

Avenoso, K. (1996, January 19). Mayor's school plan called costly. *Boston Globe.*

Beinart, P. (1997, June 30). The pride of the cities: The new breed of Progressive mayors. *New Republic,* pp. 16–25.

Benning, V. (1994, June 23). Era of hope seen in hub schools pact. *Boston Globe.*

Biddle, F. (1991, June 19). House votes to have mayor appoint school board. *Boston Globe.*

Blum, J., and M. Cottman. (2000, June 28). School referendum splits voters; board makeup hinges on uncounted ballots. *Washington Post,* p. A1.

Boston Globe. (1982, July 1). Political past haunts schools in Boston (Spotlight section).

———. (1991, June 27). Toward school stability, p. 12.

———. (1994, December 19). A school system on the verge (editorial), p. 18.

———. (1996a, October 28). The election/Massachusetts, p. B5.

———. (1996b, November 1). At last: Schools that mean business (editorial), p. 26.

Boston Municipal Research Bureau. (1996). *Bureau briefs, BB96–2, BB96–3, BB96–4*. Boston: Boston Municipal Research Bureau.

Boston Plan for Excellence. (1999). *21st-century school grants*. Boston: Boston Plan for Excellence in the Public Schools.

Boston Public Schools. (1993). *School profiles, 1992–1993*. Boston: Boston Public Schools.

———. (1996a). *Focus on children, A comprehensive reform plan for the Boston Public Schools*. Boston: Boston Public Schools.

———. (1996b). *School profiles, 1995–1996*. Boston: Boston Public Schools.

———. (2000). *Facts and figures: The Boston Public Schools at a glance*. <http://boston.k12.ma.us/bps/bpsglance.asp>.

Bowie, L., and E. Niedowski. (2001, May 18). Improving test scores hailed as turnaround. *Baltimore Sun*, pp.1A, 8A.

Boyarsky, B. (1997, October 16). Riordan storms an educational Bastille. *Los Angeles Times*, p. B1.

Boyd, W. L. (1988). The balance of control and autonomy in school reform, in *The education reform movement of the 1980s: Perspectives and cases*. Berkeley, CA: McCutchen.

———. (2000, September). The "R's of school reform" and the politics of reforming or replacing public schools. *Journal of Educational Change 1*(3): 225–52.

Boyd, W. L., C. T. Kerchner (eds.). (1988). *The politics of excellence and choice in education*. New York: Falmer Press.

Bryk, A. S., J. Q. Easton, D. Kerbow, S. G. Rollow, and P. A. Sebring. (1993). *A view from the elementary schools*. Chicago: Consortium on Chicago School Research.

Bush, G. W. (2000). *No child left behind*. Report available at: <http://www.ed.gov/offices/OESE/esea/nclb/titlepage.html>.

Byrne, J. (1992). *My Chicago*. New York: W. W. Norton.

Catalyst. (1998, November). Board keeps test data under wraps, pp. 25–27.

———. (2000a). Remediation and probation guidelines for attendance centers <www.catalyst–chicago.org>.

———. (2000b). High school accountability strategies 1996–2000: A scorecard <www.catalyst–chicago.org>.

Century, J. (1998). *A citizen's guide to the Philadelphia school budget*. Philadelphia: Greater Philadelphia First.

Chicago Public Schools. (1997). *School probation information packet*. Chicago: Office of Accountability.

———. (2000a, June 29). *Clinton looks in on what's working in Chicago schools* <www.CPS.k-12.il.us>.

———. (2000b). *Intervention status (02–P36–C)* <www.CPS.k-12.il.us>.

———. (2000c). *Lists of schools on academic probation (FY1999–2000)* <www.CPS.k-12.il.us>.

Chicago United. (1981). *Special taskforce on education: Chicago school system*. Chicago: author.

Chow, C. (1992, November 16). Consalvo quits hub school post. *Boston Globe*.

Chubb, J. E., and T. M. Moe. (1990). *Politics, markets, and America's schools*. Washington, DC: Brookings Institution.

Cibulka, J. G. (1996). The reform and survival of American public schools: An institutional perspective, in R. L. Crowson, W. L. Boyd, and H. B. Mawhinney (eds.), *The politics of education and the new institutionalism: Reinventing the American school.* Washington, DC: Falmer Press.

———. (1997). Two eras of urban schooling: The decline of the old order and the emergence of new organizational forms. *Education and Urban Society 29,* pp. 317–41.

———. (2003). The city–state partnership to reform Baltimore's public schools, in L. Cuban and M. Usdan (eds.), *Powerful reforms with shallow roots.* New York: Teachers College Press.

Ciotti, P. (1998, March 16). Money and school performance: Lessons from the Kansas City desegregation experiment. *Cato Policy Analysis 298* <http://www.cato.org/pubs/pas/pa-298.html>.

Civic Committee of the Commercial Club of Chicago. (1995). Special committee of school funding meeting notes. Unpublished document.

Clavel, P., and W. Wiewel (eds.). (1991). *Harold Washington and the neighborhoods: Progressive city government in Chicago, 1983–1987.* New Brunswick, NJ: Rutgers University Press.

Clune, W. (1987). Institutional choice as a theoretical framework for research on educational policy. *Educational Evaluation and Policy Analysis 9*(2): 117–32.

Cohen, A., and E. Taylor. (2000). *American pharaoh: Mayor Richard M. Daley.* Boston: Little, Brown.

Cohen, M. (1983, December 18). Report on city schools challenges new regime. *Boston Globe.*

Colvin, R. L., and L. Sahagun. (1999, August 14). Riordan in discussions about next schools chief. *Los Angeles Times.*

Committee on Effective School Governance. (1999). *Los Angeles unified school district governance: Our future at risk.* Los Angeles: author.

Conley, S., and A. Odden. (1995). Linking teacher compensation to teacher career development. *Educational Evaluation and Policy Analysis 17,* pp. 219–37.

Cooper, K. (1982, August 15). A school chief who enjoys a good fight. *Boston Globe* (Focus section), p. 3.

Counts, G. (1928). *School and society in Chicago.* New York: Harcourt Brace.

Critical Friends. (1997, October). *Status report on Boston's public schools after two years of reform.* Boston: author.

Cronin, J. M. (1973). *The control of urban schools.* New York: Free Press.

Cuban, L. (1976). *Urban school chiefs under fire.* Chicago: University of Chicago Press.

Cuban, L., and M. Usdan. (2003). *Powerful reforms with shallow roots: Getting good schools in six cities.* New York: Teachers College Press.

Daley, R. M. (1997, June 5). *Speech to the National Press Club* (video recording). Washington, DC: CSPAN-2.

David, J. L. (1990). Restructuring in progress: Lessons from pioneering districts, in R. Elmore and Associates (eds.), *Restructuring schools: The next generation of educational reform* (pp. 209–50). San Francisco: Jossey-Bass.

David, S. M., and P. Kantor. (1979). Political theory and transformations in budgetary arenas: The case of New York City, in D. R. Marshall (ed.), *Urban policymaking* (pp. 183–220). Beverly Hills, CA: Sage.

Dentler, R., and M. Scott. (1981). *Schools on trial: An inside account of the Boston desegregation case.* Cambridge, MA: Abt Books.

DiMaggio, P., and W. Powell. (1983). The iron cage revisited: Institutional isomorphism and collective rationality in organizational fields. *American Sociological Review 48*, pp. 147–60.

Dooley, E. (1994). *The culture of possibility: The story of the Boston Plan for Excellence in the public schools.* Boston: Boston Plan for Excellence in the Public Schools.

Duffrin, E. (1998). Middle grades math stuck in basic skills. *Catalyst 10*(1): 1–8.

Easton, D. (1965). *A systems analysis of political life.* New York: Wiley.

Easton, J. Q., et al. (1991). *Charting reform: The teachers' turn.* Chicago: Consortium on Chicago School Research.

Eisinger, P. (1997). Cities in the new federal order: Effects of devolution. *LaFollette Policy Report 8*(1): 1–7.

Elmore, R. F. (1993). School decentralization: Who gains? Who loses? in J. Hannaway and M. Carnoy (eds.), *Decentralization and school improvement: Can we fulfill the promise?* (pp. 33–54). San Francisco: Jossey-Bass.

Elmore, R. F., C. Abelmann, and S. Fuhrman. (1996). The new accountability in state education reform: From process to performance, in H. Ladd (ed.), *Holding schools accountable: Performance-based reform in education* (pp. 65–98). Washington, DC: Brookings Institution.

Farnham, W. D. (1963). The weakened spring of government: A study of nineteenth-century American history. *American Historical Review 68*, pp. 662–80.

Feeney, M. (1999, September 18). Boston desegregation judge is dead at 79. *Boston Globe.*

Finn, C., Jr., and M. J. Petrilli. (1999). *Reforming the schools from city hall: 10 ways mayors can revitalize public education.* New York: Manhattan Institute.

Firestone, W., D. Magrowicz, and J. Fairman. (1997). Rethink high stakes: External obligation in assessment policy. Paper presented at the annual conference of the American Educational Research Association, Chicago.

Firestone, W., and J. Pennel. (1993). Teacher commitment, working conditions, and differential incentive policies. *Review of Educational Research 63*(4): 489–525.

Flake, F. (1998, February 6). Vouchers: A hope for poor kids. *New York Post*, p. A4.

Fuhrman, S. (1994). *Challenges in systemic education reform.* Washington, DC: Office of Educational Research and Improvement.

———. (ed.). (2001). *From the capitol to the classroom: Standards-based reform in the states. One hundredth yearbook of the National Society for the Study of Education*, part II. Chicago: University of Chicago Press.

Fuhrman, S. H., and R. F. Elmore. (1993). Understanding local control in the wake of state education reform. *Educational Evaluation and Policy Analysis 12*(1): 82–96.

Gewertz, C. (2000, April 26). A hard lesson for Kansas City's troubled schools. *Education Week 19*(33): 1, 20–21.

Goldberg, C. (1999, July 15). Busing's day end: Boston drops race in pupil placement. *New York Times* <www.nytimes.com/library/national/busing–edu.html>.

Goldberg, M. F. (1995). An interview with mayor Rudolph Giuliani: Education in New York City. *Phi Delta Kappan*, pp. 317–20.

Golden, D., and D. Lowery. (1982, September 27). Boston and the postwar racial strain—blacks and whites in Boston: 1945–1982. *Boston Globe.*

Goldstein, J., M. Kelemen, and W. S. Koski. (1998, April). Reconstitution in theory and practice: The experience of San Francisco. Paper presented at the annual conference of the American Educational Research Association, San Diego.

Granger, B., and L. Granger. (1980). *Fighting Jane: Mayor Jane Byrne and the Chicago machine.* New York: Dial Press.

Green, P. M. (1991, June). Chicago's 1991 mayoral elections: Richard M. Daley wins second term. *Illinois Issues,* pp. 17–20.

Grimshaw, W. J. (1979). *Union rule in the schools: Big city politics in transformation.* Toronto, ON: Lexington Books.

Grunwald, M. (1998). The myth of the super mayor. *American Prospect 40,* pp. 20–28.

Guskey, T. (ed.). (1994). *High-stakes performance assessment: Perspectives on Kentucky's reform.* Thousand Oaks, CA: Corwin Press.

Hannaway, J., and M. Carnoy. (1993). *Decentralization and school improvement: Can we fulfill the promise?* San Francisco: Jossey-Bass.

Hanushek, E., et al. (1994). *Making schools work: Improving performance and controlling costs.* Washington, DC: Brookings Institution.

Hardy, T. (1998, November 7). Chicago school reforms receive A's. *Los Angeles Daily News,* p. 1.

Harris, C. W. (1995). *Congress and the governance of the nation's capitol: The conflict of federal and local interests.* Washington, DC: Georgetown University Press.

Hart, J. (1995a, January 19). Harrison-Jones see lack of respect for role. *Boston Globe.*

———. (1995b, March 9). Mayor names panel to find school chief. *Boston Globe.*

———. (1995c, June 30). Harrison-Jones ends rocky 4–year tenure. *Boston Globe.*

———. (1995d, July 24). Group seeks school resignations. *Boston Globe.*

Hart, J., and A. Walker. (1994, December 22). Activists defend school chief. *Boston Globe.*

Hayes, G. (1999). Inaugural address.

Hefland, D. (2002, August 30). Test scores rise; goals still unmet. *Los Angeles Times,* p. A1.

Hendrie, C. (1996, November 13). By 2–1 ratio, Boston retains appointed board. *Education Week.*

Henig, J. R., R. C. Hula, M. Orr, and D. S. Pedescleaux. (1999). *The color of school reform: Race, politics, and the challenge of urban education.* Princeton, NJ: Princeton University Press.

Hentschke, G. C. (1997). Beyond competing school reforms: A redefinition of *public* in public schooling. *Education and Urban Society 29*(4): 474–89.

Hernandez, P. (1986, September 14). Boston school situation seen improving. *Boston Globe.*

Herrick, M. (1971). *Chicago schools: A social and political history.* Beverly Hills, CA: Sage.

Hess, F. M. (1999). *Spinning wheels: The politics of urban school reform.* Washington, DC: Brookings Institution.

Hess, G. A., Jr. (1991). *School restructuring: Chicago style.* Newbury Park, CA: Corwin Press.

Heubert, J. P., and R. M. Hauser. (1999). *High stakes: Testing for tracking, promotion, and graduation.* Washington, DC: National Academy Press.

Hill, P. T. (1992). Making governance change happen. Unpublished paper.

Hill, P. T., C. Campbell, and J. Harvey. (2000). *It takes a city: Getting serious about urban school reform.* Washington, DC: Brookings Institution.

Hill, P. T., and M. B. Celio. (1998). *Fixing urban schools.* Washington, DC: Brookings Institution.

Hill, P. T., G. Foster, and T. Gendler. (1990). *High Schools with character.* Santa Monica, CA: RAND.

Howe, P. (1989, November 11). Flynn school plan heads for compromise. *Boston Globe.*

Hunter, R. C. (1997). The mayor versus the school superintendent: Political incursions into metropolitan school politics. *Education and Urban Society 29*(2): 217–32.

Jackson, D. (1999, September). Garrity is gone, but his foes live on in ignorance. *Boston Globe.*

Jaffe, H. S., and T. Sherwood. (1994). *Dream city: Race, power, and the decline of Washington, D.C.* New York: Simon & Schuster.

Jarrett, V. (1991, November 12). Why Blacks nixed Daley's school bill. *Chicago Sun-Times,* op ed.

Johnson, S. (1990). *Teachers at work: Achieving success in our schools.* New York: HarperCollins.

Joint House and Senate Chicago Board of Education Investigation Committee. (1981, January 31). *The Chicago Board of Education's 1979 financial crisis and its implications on other Illinois school districts.* Springfield: 81st Illinois General Assembly.

Jones, H. (1997, April 15). At last stars are in alignment for school reform in Boston. *Boston Globe.*

———. (1998, July 26). What is "reform" with so little effect? *Boston Globe.*

Kass, J. (1995, June 30). Daley names school team: Now comes the difficult part: turning everything around. *Chicago Tribune.*

Kaufman, H. (1956, December). Emerging conflicts in the doctrine of public administration. *American Political Science Review,* pp. 1057–73.

Kelley, C., and J. Protsik. (1997). Risk and reward: Perspectives on the implementation of Kentucky's school-based performance award program. *Educational Administration Quarterly 33*(4): 474–505.

Kirp. D. (1982). *Just schools: The idea of racial equality in American education.* Berkeley: University of California Press.

Kirst, M., and M. McLaughlin. (1990). Rethinking children's policy, in L. Cunningham (ed.), *Educational leadership and changing contexts.* Chicago: University of Chicago Press.

Knott, J. H., and G. J. Miller. (1987). *Reforming bureaucracy: The politics of institutional choice.* Englewood Cliffs, NJ: Prentice-Hall.

Komesar, N. K. (1994). *Imperfect alternatives.* Chicago: University of Chicago Press.

Kozol, J. (1991). *Savage inequalities: Children in America's schools.* New York: Crown.

Kyle, C. L., and E. R. Kantowitz. (1992). *Kids first–Primero Los Niños: Chicago School Reform in the 1980's.* Springfield: Illinois Issues.

Lauglo, J., and M. McLean. (1985). *The control of education: International perspectives on the centralization/decentralization debate.* Portsmouth, NH: Heineman Educational Books.

Lawler, E. (1973). *Motivation in work organizations*. San Francisco: Jossey-Bass.

Lawrence, C. (1998, October 31). Delegates approve teachers contract. *Chicago Sun-Times*, p. 16.

LeCompte, M., and A. Dworkin. (1991). *Giving up on school: Student dropouts and teacher burnouts*. Thousand Oaks, CA: Corwin Press.

Lenz, L. (1988, April 29). School summit wants outsiders kept out. *Chicago Sun-Times*, p. 16.

Light, P. C. (1997). *The tides of reform: Making government work, 1945–1995*. New Haven, CT: Yale University Press.

Lindblom, C. E. (1959). The science of muddling through. *Public Administration Review 19*(2): 79–88.

Locke, E. (1968). Toward a theory of task motivation and incentives. *Organizational Behavior and Human Performance 3*, pp. 157–89.

Lortie, D. (1975). *Schoolteacher—a sociological study*. Chicago: University of Chicago Press.

Los Angeles Times. (1999, March 14). School board candidates interviews, p. M3.

———. (2000, June 7). A bad fit for LAUSD. Editorial, p. B10.

Lukas, J. (1986). *Common ground*. New York: Vintage Books.

Malen, B. (1999). On rewards, punishments and possibilities: Teacher compensation as an instrument for education reform. *Journal of Personnel Evaluation in Education 12*(4): 387–94.

March, J. G., and J. P. Olsen. (1989). *Rediscovering institutions*. New York: Free Press.

Marchi, J. J. (1991). *Governing for results: Decentralization with accountability*. Albany: Temporary State Commission on New York City School Governance.

Martinez, M. (1997, October 20). Schools still slow to fire inept teachers. *Chicago Tribune*, p. 11.

Maryland State Department of Education. (1989). *The report of the Governor's Commission on School Performance*. Annapolis: Office of the Governor.

———. (1997). *Criteria for reconstitution*. Baltimore: author.

Massell, D. (1998, July 25). State strategies for building local capacity: Addressing the needs of standards-based reform. *CPRE Policy Brief*.

Matsui, B. (1998). *Impact of UCLA's Advanced Management Program (AMP) training on LEARN cohort IV schools*. Claremont, CA: Claremont Graduate University.

Mazzoni, T. L. (1991). Analyzing state school policymaking: An arena model. *Education Evaluation and Policy Analysis 13*(2): II 5–138.

McKersie, W. S. (1996). Reforming Chicago's public schools: Philanthropic persistence, 1987–1993, in K. K. Wong (ed.), *Advances in educational policy*, vol. 2 (pp. 141–57). Greenwich, CT: JAI Press.

McLaughlin, M. W. (1991). Learning from experience: Lessons from policy implementation, in A. Odden (ed.), *Education policy implementation* (pp. 185–95). Albany: State University of New York Press.

Menefee-Libey, D., B. Diehl, K. Lipsitz, and N. Rahimtoola. (1997). The historic separation of schools from city politics. *Education and Urban Society 29*(4): 453–73.

Menefee-Libey, D., and D. Shipps. (1997). The new politics of decentralization. Paper presented at the annual conference of the American Educational Research Association, Chicago.

Meyer, J. W., and B. Rowan. (1978). The structure of educational organizations, in J. W. Meyer (ed.), *Environments and Organizations*. San Francisco: Jossey-Bass.

Meyer, J. W., W. R. Scott, and D. Strang. (1987). Centralization, fragmentation, and school district complexity. *Administrative Science Quarterly 32*(1): 186–201.

Meyer, J. W., W. R. Scott, D. Strang, and A. Creighton. (1985). *Bureaucratization without centralization: Changes in the organizational system of American public education, 1940–1980* (report no. 85-A11). Stanford, CA: Institute for Research on Education Finance and Governance, Stanford University.

Meyerson, H. (1998, March). Why liberalism fled the city. *American Prospect*, pp. 46–55.

MGT of America. (1995, January 12). *A report on the monitoring and evaluating implementation of management study recommendations in Baltimore City Public Schools*. Baltimore: author.

Mirel, J. (1993). School reform, Chicago style: Educational innovation in a changing urban context, 1976–1991. *Urban Education 28*(2): 116–49.

Mohrman, A., S. Mohrman, and A. Odden. (1996). Aligning teacher compensation with systemic school reform: Skill-based pay and group-based performance rewards. *Educational Evaluation and Policy Analysis 18*(1): 51–71.

Mohrman, S., E. Lawler, and A. Mohrman. (1992). Applying employee involvement in schools. *Education Evaluation and Policy Analysis 14*(4): 347–60.

Montgomery, L. (2002, April 6). Montgomery's all-or-nothing win in Annapolis. *Washington Post*, pp. B1–B6.

Mooney, B. (1995, December 11). Mayor gets wakeup call on school committee. *Boston Globe*.

Moore, D. (1990). Voice and choice in Chicago, in W. H. Clune and J. Witte (eds.), *Choice and control in American education*, vol. 2 (pp. 153–98). Bristol, PA: Falmer Press.

———. (2000). *Chicago's grade-retention program fails to help retained students*. Chicago: Designs for Change.

Moore, M. (1988). What sort of ideas become public ideas? in R. B. Reich, *The power of public ideas*. Boston: Harvard University Press.

Moore, S., and D. Hefland. (2002, November 7). School bonds set state record. *Los Angeles Times*, p. B1.

National Commission on Excellence in Education. (1983). *A nation at risk: The imperative for educational reform, a report to the Secretary of Education* (226006 ed.). Washington, DC: U.S. Department of Education.

Newton, J. (1997, October 16). Mayors are called best hope to reform troubled schools. *Los Angeles Times*.

O'Connell, M. (1991). *School reform Chicago style: How citizens organized to change public policy*. Chicago: Center for Neighborhood Technology.

O'Day, J., M. E. Goertz, and R. E. Floden. (1995, December). Building capacity for education reform. *CPRE Policy Brief*.

O'Day, J., and M. Smith. (1993). Systemic reform and educational opportunity, in S. Fuhrman (ed.), *Designing coherent education policy: Improving the system* (pp. 250–312). San Francisco: Jossey-Bass.

Odden, A., and S. Conley. (1992). *Restructuring teacher compensation*. San Francisco: Jossey-Bass.

Office of the Press Secretary. (1998, January 27). *The state of the union speech by the president*. Washington, DC: The White House.

Orfield, G., et al. (1996). *Dismantling desegregation: The quiet reversal of* Brown v. Board of Education. New York: New Press.

Ornstein, A. C. (1989). Centralization and decentralization of large public school systems. *Urban Education 24*, pp. 233–35.

Orr, M. (1999). *Black social capital: The politics of school reform in Baltimore, 1986–1998.* Lawrence: University Press of Kansas.

Osborne, D., and T. Gaebler. (1992). *Reinventing government: How the entrepreneurial spirit is transforming the public sector from schoolhouse to statehouse, city hall to the Pentagon.* Reading, MA: Addison-Wesley.

PACE. (1995). *Conditions of education in California 1994–95.* Berkeley: Policy Analysis for California Education.

Perl, P., and D. Wilgoren. (1997, May 11). Basic training. *Washington Post Magazine*, pp. 79–89.

Peterson, P. E. (1981). *City limits.* Chicago: University of Chicago Press.

Peterson, P. E., B. Rabe, and K. Wong. (1981). The maturation of redistributive programs, in A. Odden (ed.), *Education policy implementation* (pp. 65–80). Albany: State University of New York Press.

Petrosko, J. M. (1996). Assessment and accountability, in J. Lindle, J. Petrosko, and R. Pankratz (eds.), *1996 review of research on the Kentucky Education Reform Act* (pp. 3–51). Frankfort: Kentucky Institute for Education Research.

Philadelphia Inquirer. (1994, October 23). A district in distress, pp. G1–G8.

Pierre, R. E. (2000, November 16). School picks calculated to provide needed skills. *Washington Post*, p. B7.

Pitkin H. F. (1967). *The concept of representation.* Berkeley: University of California Press.

Plank, D., and W. Boyd. (1994). Antipolitics, education, and institutional choice: The flight from democracy. *American Educational Research Journal 31*(2): 263–81.

Portner, J. (1999, January 20). Massive failure rates on new tests dazzle Virginia. *Education Week on the Web.*

Portz, J. (1996). Problem definitions and policy agendas: Shaping the educational agenda in Boston. *Policy Studies Journal 24*(3): 371–86.

———. (1997). *External actors and the Boston Public Schools: The courts, the business community, and the mayor.* Washington, DC: Woodrow Wilson International Center for Scholars, occasional paper on comparative urban studies no. 12.

———. (In press). Urban regimes and public education: Corporatists and political paths to supporting education reform. *Urban Education.*

Price, H. (1997, February 14). "No Excuses" era of urban school reform. Speech delivered to the Urban League.

Rakove, M. L. (1982). Jane Byrne and the new Chicago politics, in S. K. Gove and L. H. Masotti (eds.), *After Daley: Chicago politics in transition.* Chicago: University of Illinois Press.

Rakowsky, J. (1993, March 15). Flynn, school board trade-off war of words. *Boston Globe*, p. 15.

———. (1998, May 7). Education efforts make Menino a guest of honor at mayors event. *Boston Globe*, p. B9.

Ravitch, D. (1974). *The great school wars: New York City, 1805–1973.* New York: Basic Books.

————. *The troubled crusade: American education, 1945–1980.* New York: Basic Books.

Rezendes, M. (1992, November 20). Consalvo renews criticism of school superintendent. *Boston Globe.*

Rezendes, M., and S. Marantz. (1990, December 6). Council ok's end to school board plan. *Boston Globe.*

Ribadeneira, D. (1989a, October 16). Education and politics clash on the school board. *Boston Globe,* p. 21.

————. (1989b, November 3). Supporters of appointed school board defend plan. *Boston Globe,* p. 77.

————. (1989c, November 5). Flynn's referendum on school committee a clear test of his popularity. *Boston Globe,* p. 45.

————. (1990a, February 14). School committee ousts Supt. Wilson. *Boston Globe,* p. 1.

————. (1990b, March 19). Revamp school panel, says Wilson. *Boston Globe,* p. 13.

————. (1990c, September 28). Lawmakers scuttle bid to overhaul Boston schools. *Boston Globe,* p. 21.

————. (1991, December 12). Politics cast shadow as school panel exits. *Boston Globe,* p. 58.

Rich, W. C. (1996). *Black mayors and school politics.* New York: Garland Publishing.

Riley, R. (1997). *Fourth annual state of American education address: Putting standards of excellence in action.* Speech delivered at the Carter Center, Atlanta.

Robinson, L. (1992, October 8). Harrison-Jones assails attacks as unprofessional, unwarranted. *Boston Globe.*

Roderick, M., A. S. Bryk, B. A. Jacob, J. Q. Easton, and E. Allensworth. (1999). *Ending social promotion.* Chicago: Consortium on Chicago School Research.

Romer, P. (1989). *Human capital and growth: Theory and evidence.* Cambridge, MA: National Bureau of Economic Research.

Rossi, R., and F. Speilman. (1997, June 5). Daley backs board: Mayor opposes "sham" graduation for 8th graders. *Chicago Sun-Times,* p. 10.

Rowan, B., F. S. Chiang, and R. L. Miller. (1997). Using research on employees' performance to study the effect of teachers on student performance. *Sociology of Education 70*(4): 256–84.

Ryan, S., A. S. Bryk, K. P. Williams, K. Hall, and S. Luppescu. (1997). *Charting reform: LSCs—local leadership at work.* Chicago: Consortium on Chicago School Research.

Sahagun, L. (1999, April 4). Few Angelenos give school board good grades. *Los Angeles Times.*

Sahagun, L., and K. Sauerwein. (2000, June 16). L.A. unified appoints 11 leaders for subdistricts. *Los Angeles Times,* p. B1.

Sanchez, R. (1990, August 22). District schools will test the mettle of next mayor. *Washington Post,* p. 31.

Sandham, J. (2000, August 2). Reporter's notebook. *Education Week on the Web.*

Schneider, H., and D. E. Wise. (1995, March 1). Control board may exclude D.C. officials; plan would give 5 members authority over city's affairs. *Washington Post,* p. A1.

School District of Philadelphia. (1995). *Children Achieving action design.* Philadelphia: School District of Philadelphia.

Schrag, P. (1967). *Village school downtown: Boston schools, Boston politics.* Boston: Beacon Press.

Sebring, P. A., and A. S. Bryk. (2000). School leadership and the bottom line in Chicago. *Phi Delta Kappan 81*(6): 440–43.

Sebring, P.A., et al. (1995). *Charting reform: Chicago teachers take stock.* Chicago: Consortium on Chicago School Research.

Sege, I. (1985, June 28). Parting words from Spillane. *Boston Globe.*

Sengupta, S. (1997, June 27). Chancellor Crew rejects a board's pick for top post: Uses new power to veto Queens superintendent. *New York Times,* pp. B1, B6.

SFA (School Finance Authority). (1993). Schedule of board appointments. Unpublished document.

Shamir, B. (1991). Meaning, self, and motivation in organizations. *Organization Studies 12*(3): 405–24.

Sharpe, L. J. (ed.). (1979). *Decentralist trends in Western democracies.* Newbury Park, CA: Sage.

Shatzkin, K., and M. Bowler. (1995, October 21). Maryland fires a salvo in school dispute: Amprey accused of mismanagement; reorganization sought. *Baltimore Sun,* p. 1A.

Shipps, D. (1995). Big business and school reform: The case of Chicago, 1988. Unpublished dissertation, Stanford University.

———. (1997, fall). The invisible hand: Big business and Chicago school reform. *Teachers College Record 99*(1): 73–116.

———. (1998). Corporate involvement in school reform, in C. Stone (ed.), *Changing urban education.* Lawrence: University Press of Kansas.

Shipps, D., J. Kahne, and M. Smylie. (1999, September). The politics of urban school reform: Legitimacy, city growth and school improvement in Chicago. *Education Policy 13*(4): 518–45.

Shipps, D., K. Sconzert, and H. Swyers. (1999). *The Chicago Annenberg Challenge: The first three years.* Chicago: Consortium on Chicago School Research.

Shirley, D. (1997). *Community organizing for urban school reform.* Austin: University of Texas Press.

Smith, D. (1999a, July 27). Roos quits as head of school reform group. *Los Angeles Times,* p. A1.

———. (1999b, October 13). L.A. School Board limits Zacarias' role. *Los Angeles Times,* p. A1.

Smith, D., and L. Sahagun. (1999, April 11). Issues may be scarce, but passion and politics aren't. *Los Angeles Times.*

Smith, J. B., B. Smith, and A. S. Bryk. (1998). *Setting the pace: Opportunities to learn in Chicago's elementary schools.* Chicago: Consortium on Chicago School Research.

Smith, M. E., and J. O'Day. (1991). Systemic school reform, in S. H. Fuhrman and B. Malen (eds.), *The politics of curriculum and testing* (pp. 233–67). New York: Falmer Press.

Spring, J. (1994). *The American school: 1642–1993.* New York: McGraw-Hill.

Stone, C. N. (1989). *Regime politics: Governing Atlanta, 1946–1988.* Lawrence: University Press of Kansas.

———. (1993). Urban regimes and the capacity to govern: A political economy approach. *Journal of Urban Affairs 15*(1): 1–28.

Stone, C. N., J. R. Henig, B. D. Jones, and C. Pierannunzi. (2001). *Building civic capacity: The politics of reforming urban schools.* Lawrence: University Press of Kansas.

Strauss, V. (2001, September 25). School budget deficit in D.C. causes firings, reorganization. *Washington Post*, p. B1.

Sullivan, J. (1990, December 10). School committee rejects job cuts. *Boston Globe.*

Szanton, P. L. (1986). *Baltimore 2000: A choice of futures.* Baltimore: Morris Goldseker Foundation.

Thompson, J., and E. Siegel. (1996, November 27). City, state sign deal for schools. *Baltimore Sun*, p. 1A.

Traitel, D. (1990, March 9). Payzant vows to change way blacks taught. *San Diego Tribune.*

Tyack, D. B. (1974). *The one best system: A history of American urban education.* Cambridge, MA: Harvard University Press.

———. (1990). Restructuring in historical perspective: Tinkering toward utopia. *Teachers College Record 92*, pp. 170–91.

———. (1993). School governance in the United States: Historical puzzles and anomalies, in J. Hannaway and M. Carnoy (eds.), *Decentralization and school improvement: Can we fulfill the promise?* (pp. 1–32). San Francisco: Jossey-Bass.

Tyack, D., and L. Cuban. (1995). *Tinkering toward utopia: A century of public school reform.* Cambridge, MA: Harvard University Press.

Tyack, D., and E. Hansot. (1982). *Managers of virtue: Public school leadership in America, 1820–1980.* New York: Basic Books.

U.S. Conference of Mayors. (1994). *The federal budget and the cities.* Washington, DC: USCM.

Useem, B. (1999). *Perspectives on Philadelphia's teacher shortage: Evidence from five studies of prospective and new teachers.* Philadelphia: Philadelphia Education Fund.

Vogel, N. (2000, July 26). TV ads escalate in campaign over school vouchers. *Los Angeles Times.*

Walberg, H. J., M. J. Bakalis, J. L. Bast, and S. Baer. (1988). *We can rescue our children.* Chicago: Heartland Institute.

Walker, A. (1995, July 2). Menino's basic vision is of a city that works. *Boston Globe*, p. 1.

Washington Post. District ally on Hill tells Clinton to prepare for intervention in city, p. B6.

Weick, K. (1976). Education organizations as loosely coupled systems. *Administrative Science Quarterly 21*, pp. 1–19.

Weiner, B. (1986). *An attributional theory of motivation and emotion.* New York: Springer Publishing.

Weissman, D. (1997). Can middle-class kids be lured back? *Catalyst 9*(3): 1–6.

———. (1998). Everyone wins, some win more. *Catalyst 10*(3): 1–9.

Wen, P. (1989, April 9). School cautious on school plan. *Boston Globe.*

Wen, P., and S. Marantz. (1988, September 21). Some see politics driving Flynn's move toward schools. *Boston Globe.*

Wilgoren, J. (2000, October 9). Young blacks turn to school vouchers as civil rights issue. *New York Times.*

Wilgoren, J., and R. O'Reilly. (1994, April 10). Scoring of school tests found to be inaccurate. *Los Angeles Times*, p. A1.

Wirt, F., and M. Kirst. (1972). *Political and social foundations of education*. Berkeley, CA: McCutchan Publishing.

———. (1997). *The political dynamics of American education*. Berkeley, CA: McCutchan Publishing.

Wise, D. E., and H. Schneider. (1995, April 18). Clinton signs D.C. control board; in upbeat ceremony, president envisions "a city that works." *Washington Post*, p. A1.

Wohlstetter, P. (1995). Getting school-based management right: What works and what doesn't. *Phi Delta Kappan 77*(1): 22–25.

Wong, K. K. (1999, September). Mayors and schools. Paper presented at the annual meeting of the American Political Science Association, Atlanta.

———. (2001). Integrated governance in Chicago and Birmingham (UK), in M. C. Wang and H. J. Walberg (eds.), *School choice or best systems: What improves education?* (pp. 161–212). Mahwah, NJ: Lawrence Erlbaum Associates.

Wong, K. K., and D. Anagnostopoulos. (1998, January/March). Can integrated governance restructure teaching? Lessons learned from two low-performing Chicago high schools. *Educational Policy 12*(1–2): 31–47.

Wong, K. K., R. Dreeben, L. E. Lynn, Jr., and G. I. Sunderman. (2000). Education policy: Integrated governance as a reform strategy in schools. *International Journal of Economic Development 2*(2): 218–55.

Wong, K. K., and P. Jain. (1999, November). Newspapers as policy actors in urban school systems: The Chicago story. *Urban Affairs Review 35*(2): 210–46.

Wong, K. K., and F. Sheh. (2001). Does school-district takeover work? Assessing the effectiveness of city and state takeover as a school-reform strategy. Paper presented at the annual meeting of the American Political Science Association, San Francisco.

index

about the editors and contributors

DOROTHEA ANAGNOSTOPOULOS is assistant professor in teacher education at Michigan State University. Her research interests include high school reform, student learning, and teacher development. She earned her doctorate degree at the University of Chicago.

DAVID C. BLOOMFIELD is associate professor of educational administration and policy and chair of the Department of Educational Administration at Brooklyn College. He is the former general counsel to the New York City Board of Education.

WILLIAM LOWE BOYD is Batschelet Chair Professor of Educational Administration and professor-in-charge of graduate programs in educational administration at The Pennsylvania State University. He has been a visiting scholar at seven universities abroad and has served as president of the Politics of Education Association and as an officer of the American Educational Research Association.

KATRINA E. BULKLEY is an assistant professor of educational policy at the Rutgers University Graduate School of Education. Her work focuses on educational policy, politics, governance, and policy implementation, with a focus on charter schools. She has worked on projects for the Consortium for Policy Research in Education and the Center for Education Policy Analysis.

JOLLEY BRUCE CHRISTMAN is the principal of Research for Action, a Philadelphia-based nonprofit organization engaged in educational research and reform.

JAMES G. CIBULKA is dean of the College of Education and professor of educational administration and education policy and evaluation at the University of Kentucky. He is past president of the Politics of Education Association. His research interests include urban education and education policy and politics.

BRUCE S. COOPER is professor and vice-chair, Division of Administration, Policy and Urban Education at Fordham University's Graduate School of Education.

TOM CORCORAN is the co-director of the Consortium for Policy Research in Education at the University of Pennsylvania and the principal investigator of the Children Achieving evaluation.

ROBERT DREEBEN is professor emeritus in education at the University of Chicago. A former chair of the Department of Education at the University of Chicago, he specializes in the sociology of education and instructional organization.

ELLEN FOLEY is a senior researcher at the Annenberg Institute for School Reform at Brown University.

CHARLES TAYLOR KERCHNER is the Hollis P. Allen Professor of Education at The Claremont Graduate University. He is a specialist in educational organizations, educational policy, and teachers' unions.

MICHAEL W. KIRST is professor of education at the Stanford University School of Education. He is also a senior researcher for the Consortium for Policy Research in Education.

THERESA LUHM is a research associate at the Consortium for Policy Research in Education at the University of Pennsylvania.

LAURENCE LYNN holds an endowed professorship in the Harris School of Public Policy Studies and the School of Social-Service Administration at the University of Chicago. His research areas include public management and leadership.

DAVID MENEFEE-LIBEY is associate professor of politics at Pomona College. His current research focuses on reform politics and the conditions of K–12 education in the Los Angeles region.

HEINRICH MINTROP is assistant professor at the University of California, Los Angeles. He is interested in the study of school accountability and democracy in a cross-national perspective.

STACEY RUTLEDGE is a doctoral candidate in education at the University of Chicago. Her dissertation focuses on school leadership and organizational response to district-wide standards and sanctions.

DOROTHY SHIPPS is assistant professor of education, Teachers College, Columbia University. She researches the contribution of civic actors to the politics of urban school reform, for which she was awarded one of 12 national Carnegie Scholar awards in 2000–2001.

KENNETH K. WONG is professor of public policy and education and political science and associate director of the Peabody Center for Education Policy at Vanderbilt University. His most recent book is *Funding Public Schools: Politics and Policy*. His areas of research include urban school politics and federal program implementation.

GARY YEE is associate professor of education and chair of the Education Department at Holy Names College, Oakland, California. His interests include research on the urban superintendency. He is also executive director of the Oakland Education Cabinet, located at Mills College.